The Altar and the City
A Reading of Vergil's *Aeneid*

The Altar and the City
A Reading of Vergil's *Aeneid*

Mario A. Di Cesare

1974

COLUMBIA UNIVERSITY PRESS

New York and London

The Stanwood Cockey Lodge Foundation has generously provided funds to assist in the publication of this work.

Library of Congress Cataloging in Publication Data

Di Cesare, Mario A
    The altar and the city; a reading of Vergil's Aeneid.

    Bibliography: p. [257]–262
    1. Vergilius Maro, Publius. Aeneis.   2. Vergilius
Maro, Publius—Criticism, Textual.   I. Title.
PA6825.D47   873'.01   74-3436
ISBN 0-231-03830-5
ISBN 0-231-03831-3 (pbk.)

For
Carol Lee

CONJUGI · AMANTI · DILECTAE

There is in love a sweetnesse readie penn'd:
Copie out onely that, and save expense.

George Herbert

PREFACE

This book is, simply, a reading of Vergil's *Aeneid*.

In writing it—an ongoing process over the past fifteen years—I am attempting to illuminate some of the poetry, to expound and examine some of the meanings that have evolved for me, and to suggest some possibilities. I am not trying to say the last word, because I do not believe it can be said; you cannot constrict the meanings of a truly great work. The practicing critic usually discovers not that he has achieved a final meaning but that his understanding has been enlarged so that he can probe further and understand more.

An inexhaustible work, the *Aeneid* ultimately eludes criticism just as it finally resists scholarship. That is why a study like this one—or any one—must be called "A Reading." It is *one* reading, not the only one. And it is a *reading.* That is to say, it tries to confront the poem. Too much Vergil criticism and scholarship has been eccentric; it has remained on the periphery, away from the poem itself. Since Viktor Pöschl, criticism has tended to be somewhat more relevant and substantive—witness particularly the work of Brooks Otis or Michael Putnam. Otis understands Vergil's style and has some brilliant insights into individual scenes, characters, or passages. Nonetheless, he begins with certainty of the end, with basic (but unfounded) assumptions about the poet's intention and, thus, the poem's meaning. Such assumptions inhibit proper criticism. Putnam, for all the ingenuity that distracts the reader, is surely right in his emphasis on the poetry itself.

Like most books, this one is a compromise. The original aim was a study of the Vergilian epic tradition. I entertained the naïve view that the massive scholarship and criticism on the *Aeneid* would surely provide clarity about both the meaning of that poem and the nature of Vergilian epic. But my attempts to get beyond the position developed in *Vida's Christiad and Vergilian Epic* (Columbia University Press, 1964) were stymied. The more I tried to understand the epic nature of Vergil's poem, the more I found it necessary to study the poem itself closely. What had been the point of departure became my subject.

During the year 1963–64, on a Guggenheim Fellowship, I wrote a complete first draft, a running critical discussion which also attempted to deal with every important scholar and critic up to that time. This book is essentially that one. It has been delayed by the large expansion in higher education during the 1960s, for in the years since, I have served as Master of a college and chairman of two different departments, among other administrative duties. But the earlier version was burdened with polemic, for one important aim was to demonstrate the right way to read the poem, the requirement of careful attention to the literary text. Thanks to Otis, Putnam, and others, the need for such polemic seems sharply reduced now; hence, I have discarded much of the apparatus that encumbered the earlier version, so that what remains seems almost embarrassingly free from such traditional supports as numerous and complex footnotes, commentary upon commentary, and an arcanely selected bibliography. Such apparatus sometimes looks like the sea of commentary that surrounded Renaissance texts of Vergil, though surely the reader must find modern scholarly apparatus rarely as useful or as entertaining.

My central principle has been critical reading of the poem as a whole poem, attending that is to the poem itself. Not to Vergil's times or his friends or his relationship to Maecenas and Augustus; nor to the strands of legend or history leading to and from the poem; nor even to the venerable art of *Quellenforschung.* These matters are interesting and worthy, and they concern me, but not in this book. Nor have I been concerned with Vergil's "intention." I must confess that I do not know what Vergil's intention was, or even if he had one in the sense in which that term is commonly understood. The thought of this intelligent, sensitive, reflective poet, at the height of his powers and in the maturity of his later years, subscribing to a limited political program as the basis of his epic—surely, that is artificial and mind-boggling. It is also degrading. Dress it up as one will, apologize for it in whatever way one will, the fact remains that to believe that Vergil clearly and persistently "intended" to glorify Rome and Augustus is to degrade the poet. And, certainly, preconceptions about the intention obscure the poem itself. The critic must, rather, approach the poem and attempt to learn from it—from structure, action, image, rhythm, character, episode, words—what may approximate meaning.

Other distractions from the poem itself include the tales about incompleteness, the fragments of biographical hearsay, the various educated guesses about the genesis and composition of the poem and about the order of the books, the history of Rome as we know it, and other matters devolving out of historical hindsight. Such external problems can be avoided by determination and good sense. But there are also problems that might be called internal to the poem— such as one's knowledge of the action, the digressions and the inconsistencies, the voice of the author. These can be more serious. To manage them, the reader must keep his critical faculties alert. The problem of knowledge, of distinguishing our knowledge from Aeneas's, is complicated by the prophecies and by the common critical practice of superimposing historical hindsight on the action. Of a different kind, the so-called inconsistencies and digressions are dangerous temptations away from honest reading of the poem—as tempting and as dangerous as the habit of referring rhythmic phenomena to that serviceable lady, Metri Gratia.

Since my study aims at both a general view or interpretation and a running commentary, the book is simply organized. I begin at the beginning and continue to the end. For fairly obvious reasons, I have treated Books I and IV together in the first chapter and Books III and V together in chapter 3. Because the text itself is primary, I have quoted Vergil's poem fairly liberally. Some of my commentary on the poetry is highly compressed, some of it simply suggestive. Good criticism should stimulate the reader to go further himself; critical argument should never substitute for the poem. Every perspective that criticism offers should open new perspectives. It follows that, in discussing images, motifs, word patterns, structures, rhythms, I do not consider my views to be either comprehensive or exclusive. They attempt to be approximations to the poem. I have not hesitated to offer some conjectures or speculate about undercurrents or imaginative patterns, or even to risk overstating a case.

The context in which this book is written is both broad and eclectic, both ancient and modern. I have consulted commentators from Servius and Macrobius to Heyne and Conington. The substrata of this study include readings in the medieval and Renaissance poets and critics—including Dante, Petrarch, Poliziano, Vida, Douglas, Spenser, Tasso, Milton, and Dryden; other Humanists like Salutati, Angelo Decembrio, and Landino; and modern students of these like Georg Voigt, Remigio Sabbadini, and Vladimir Zabughin. Of the modern editors and commentators, besides Heyne and Conington, I have consulted Henry, Page, Mackail, and Sabbadini; the commentaries on individual books by R. G. Austin (I, II, IV), R. D. Williams (III, V), Buscaroli and Pease (IV), Norden and Fletcher (VI), Fowler (VII, VIII, XII), and Maguiness (XII). All have been helpful in so many ways that I hesitate to single any out. Nonetheless, I must note that the commentaries on II and IV by R. G. Austin have been, for me, the most rewarding—rich and precise in information, revealing in many details, and remarkably sensitive to the poetry. It would be an endless task to catalogue more specific debts, whether agreements or quarrels (themselves a form of debt). In the massive library of modern Vergilian studies, I have profited especially from the work of Sainte-Beuve, Sellar, Mambelli, Norden, Heinze, Rand, Mackail, Guillemin, Duckworth, Knight, Bowra, Knox, Paratore, Pöschl, Perret, Büchner, Otis, Putnam, and Quinn. To attempt to document either my agreement or disagreement would encumber this book pointlessly. Commentary on commentary can, in fact, become ludicrous. This book is long enough without more running arguments, endless and boring documentation, and other expressions of the pedantic compulsion to be thorough.

The basic text I have used is the Oxford Classical Text edited by Frederick Hirtzel (1900). Where it seemed necessary, I have emended Hirtzel's readings, following the more recent text of R. A. B. Mynors (1969). All Latin passages are translated or at least paraphrased. In a few cases, I have quoted the translation of W. F. Jackson Knight or of C. Day Lewis; usually, I have made my own rendering, with liberal help from other translations. Since this book is written not only for the scholar but for anyone interested in Vergil's great poem, I have thought it useful to make the text more accessible even to those whose Latin has become rusty.

It is pleasant to acknowledge at least some of the debts incurred over the years.

The John Simon Guggenheim Memorial Foundation provided a free year in 1963–64 and the Research Foundation of the State University of New York supported me during three summers between 1962 and 1966. To both these modern patrons of classical studies, I express my thanks.

Once again, the Stanwood Cockey Lodge Foundation has provided a generous subsidy toward the costs of publication. I am profoundly grateful to the Foundation for this continued assistance. I am grateful as well to the Foundation of the State University of New York at Binghamton, which has also helped meet publication costs.

More than a quarter-century ago, Father Matthew Jacoby insisted in his warm but firm way that we read Vergil precisely and carefully; at Columbia, Gilbert Highet and the late Moses Hadas gave generous tutelage and encouraged my critical views even while challenging them vigorously. More recently, friends, colleagues, and students have listened patiently and responded, sometimes with hard questions; I can name only a few here. Helpful in various ways have been Aliki Halls, Jonis Bobbitt, Irene Fandel, Susan Nelson, Carol Horsburgh, John Radigan, Donald Blake, and James Holoka. At various stages, Zoya Pavlovskis, Seymour Pitcher, and John Weld have read the manuscript and commented helpfully. Saul Levin and R. G. Austin criticized the work in searching detail, forcing me to reconsider many points and to modify some. All have helped generously in the common pursuit.

I am indebted to Penguin Books for permission to quote from W. F. Jackson Knight's translation of the *Aeneid* (Penguin Classics, 1956; copyright © the Estate of W. F. Jackson Knight, 1956); to Doubleday and Co. for permission to quote from C. Day Lewis's translation of the *Aeneid;* and to Holt, Rinehart and Winston for permission to quote from H. R. Huse's translation of Dante's *Divine*

Comedy. Portions of chapters 5 and 7 appeared, in germinal form, in *"Paradise Lost* and Epic Tradition," *Milton Studies,* I (1969), 31–50; an early version of some parts of the book was used for *A Critical Study-Guide to Vergil's Aeneid,* published by Educational Research Associates and Littlefield-Adams (1968); part of chapter 6 appeared as *"Aeneid* IX: The Failure of Strategy," *Rivista di Studi Classici,* XX (1972), 411–22.

Harpur College   MARIO A. DI CESARE
State University of New York at Binghamton
September, 1973

CONTENTS

ONE   *Carthage: Search for the City*   1

TWO   *Troy: Fall of the City*   38

THREE   *The Wanderer*   61

FOUR   *Hades: Journey Through the Wood*   94

FIVE   *Italy*   123

SIX   *War in Italy*   140

SEVEN   Pius Aeneas *and the Wages of War*   172

EIGHT   *Aeneas and Turnus*   198

        Notes   241

        Bibliography   257

        Index of Passages from Aeneid   263

        General Index   272

The Altar and the City
A Reading of Vergil's *Aeneid*

CHAPTER ONE

CARTHAGE: SEARCH FOR THE CITY

The search for the city adumbrated in the opening lines of the *Aeneid* is a controlling metaphor of Books I–IV and, in important ways, of the entire poem. The early commentators on the *Aeneid* observed that the dynamic of the poem is a spiritual movement from Troy to Carthage to Rome. Perceptive as this may be, such allegorical schemata are not equal to the *Aeneid.* The individual cities are larger than allegory—they contribute to the great metaphor of the city. Carthage turns out to be merely a shadow of the city. While Rome is announced as the object of the search, *Troiae,* central by position and force in the first line, distills a state of mind and of feeling: it comes from, indeed *is,* the past. Its smoldering ashes pervade Aeneas's known world. Priam's headless trunk forever encumbers its shores and any other shores that Aeneas touches during his quest.

Two conditions resound in the opening lines. Though *fato profugus,* Aeneas is destined to found a city—*conderet urbem.* But *fato profugus* is syntactically and metrically ambiguous. It means both driven (or exiled) by Fate and also destined, by Fate, for Italy:

Italiam fato/profugus/Lavinaque....

Moreover, "exile" is not quite adequate for *profugus.* Our times have provided us with a more complex figure—the Displaced Person. Thus, another reading of the opening phrases: this particular DP has been displaced because *Fatum* (whatever it may mean) has directed him toward his true homeland. Ultimately, this land must be Rome, defined by its high walls, but also, more importantly, by the soul-searing labor that is the price of those walls:

> tantae molis erat Romanam condere gentem.   (I.33)

But we must put by historical hindsight. In terms of the developing metaphor, Augustus's Rome lies far beyond the bounds of the poem. What Aeneas feels is the want of *a* city, *any* city. His outcry, as he observes the labors of the *Tyrii ... coloni,* is not for a lineage, a race, or an empire; it is for *moenia,* walls which define without limiting the city:

> 'o fortunati, quorum iam moenia surgunt!'   (I.437)

"Oh fortunate people, whose walls are already rising!"

The force of this outcry can be measured in the fact that Aeneas stays so long at Carthage, as if that city can serve him as *his* city.[1] We know that it cannot, just as Troy itself could not, and as other cities, replicas of Troy, could not. It will, indeed, be the tragedy of the queen of Carthage that she gives too compassionate an ear to Aeneas's tale of Troy and, finding herself and her city in that tale, grasps comfort in mistaken hope. Infatuated with the glories of Troy, she grossly misvalues the man she takes to herself and confuses his past with her future. In the end, the death of Dido is the symbolic consummation of Carthage itself—it goes up in smoke.

    The opening lines suggested all this and much more:

> Arma virumque cano, Troiae qui primus ab oris
> Italiam fato profugus Lavinaque venit
> litora—multum ille et terris iactatus et alto
> vi superum, saevae memorem Iunonis ob iram,
> multa quoque et bello passus, dum conderet urbem
> inferretque deos Latio—genus unde Latinum
> Albanique patres atque altae moenia Romae.
>   Musa, mihi causas memora, quo numine laeso
> quidve dolens regina deum tot volvere casus
> insignem pietate virum, tot adire labores
> impulerit. tantaene animis caelestibus irae?   (I.1–11)

I sing of arms and the man who first from the shores of Troy, displaced
by Fate, came to Italy and to the Lavinian shores—a man harassed
much on both land and sea by the power of the gods, because of the
brooding anger of savage Juno; in war too he suffered greatly until he
could establish a city and bring his gods to Latium—whence would
come the Latin race and the Alban fathers and the lofty walls of Rome.

Tell me, Muse, the causes: what injury was done to her godhead? What
grievance did the queen of the gods have, to drive a man so renowned for
piety through so many trials, force him to endure so many hardships? Can
divine spirits have such terrible wrath?

The lines emphasize divine power and divine wrath as well as the
quest of Aeneas. The power and wrath of both Juno and the other
gods are the whole burden of the last four lines, as everyone knows,
but they are quite central also to the first seven lines. Indeed, divine
power and wrath are the pivot of those lines. Line 4, central to the
first seven, dominates the passage and diminishes the imperial grandeur of line 7. Line 4 provides a resonant ambiguity to the opening
words, *Arma virumque,* setting them against each other in a counterpoint that will turn out to be deeply troubling. The counterpoint is
developed in the striking parallels between lines around line 4—
for example, *Arma / Albanique patres,* and *Troiae / Romae,* in
lines 1 and 7; *Italiam / Latio,* and *Lavina / Latinum,* in lines 2
and 6; *litora / urbem,* and *multum / multa,* in lines 3 and 5. Thus
the lines suggest other aspects of Fate by which Aeneas is made the
displaced seeker for a city; the same Fate which has lined up Troy
and Italy as the poles of action and has provided for the *genus Latinum* and the *Albani patres* is at the root of his troubles. Thus too
the shock in line 11 derives as much from the subtle manipulation
and architectural construction of lines 1–7 as from its own skeptical tone. In both line 4 and line 11, Vergil is talking primarily of
Juno (*ira* becomes almost a tag for her), but the generality in each
line (*vi superum / animis*) enlarges the scope considerably.

These angers inform the following passage. The *ira* of Juno resounds in lines 25 and 57, and is echoed by Venus in her indictment
(*"unius ob iram,"* 1.251). Though the triple injury done to Juno by
Troy (25 f.) is important, it is presented in a elliptical, parenthetical
passage. Far more to the point is her feeling for her ancient city

(12 f.), that city which is *Italiam contra* ("opposite Italy") both geo-graphically and politically. Juno's abiding *dolores* feed on her sense of fading power, because, foster her favored city as she would, it was des-tined not to be the center of glory and empire: *sic volvere Parcas* (22).

Given this sharp sense of the furious goddess and her turbulent, frus-trated anger, the texture formed by *iactatus, saevae, dolens, casus,* and *labores* (from the opening eleven lines) is rewoven in lines 23–32 to become context for the memorable statement, "tantae molis erat Romanam condere gentem" (33), which Jackson Knight translates, "Such was the cost in heavy toil of beginning the life of Rome." Scholarly erudition merely inflates the obvious grandeur; as Knight perceived clearly, the line also verges on despair. It crystallizes lines 29–32, in which we have a momentary glimpse of the objects of Juno's fury and their state: they are the survivors of the Greeks and cruel Achilles, driven across the whole ocean, kept far from Latium, driven by the fates and wandering for years round all the seas:

> iactatos aequore toto
> Troas, reliquias Danaum atque immitis Achilli,
> arcebat longe Latio, multosque per annos
> errabant acti fatis maria omnia circum.   (I.29–32)

Completing the prologue, then, lines 12–33 move from Carthage and its goddess to the condition of the present Trojans–future Ro-mans. In the next passage, we return to Juno herself, in a vague psy-cho-geographical setting, with Sicily and the Trojan ships at the pe-riphery. At Aeolia (50 f.), the mountain symbolizes the latent forces of disorder in nature and the universe—disorder parallel to that in gods (*tantaene animis* ...) and in men (Ajax, for instance). Juno's ad-dress to Aeolus bristles with savagery; the sudden sweetness of tone when she promises seven nymphs does not deceive the keeper of the winds. *"Fas est,"* he says (77). His assent and his obsequious tone are protective coloration, disavowal of responsibility, and appeal to her stature and power to protect him. Hoping to make the best of a bad bargain, he must trust in her ancient power.

In this context of infuriated divinity and disordered universe, Aeneas is the human figure, and the contrast between human Aeneas and his divine antagonist is telling. Her brooding anger is furious, cold-blooded, monumental, yet a parody of the heroic. But as the storm strikes, Aeneas's *pietas* cries out, almost by instinct:

> 'o terque quaterque beati,
> quis ante ora patrum Troiae sub moenibus altis
> contigit oppetere! o Danaum fortissime gentis
> Tydide! mene Iliacis occumbere campis
> non potuisse tuaque animam hanc effundere dextra,
> saevus ubi Aeacidae telo iacet Hector, ubi ingens
> Sarpedon, ubi tot Simois correpta sub undis
> scuta virum galeasque et fortia corpora volvit?'   (I.94–101)

"Oh, thrice and four times blessed were you who had the good fortune to fall before your fathers' eyes beneath the lofty walls of Troy! O Diomede, the bravest of the Greeks, why could not I have fallen on the battlefields of Ilium and poured out this life upon your sword—on those fields where fierce Hector lies, slain by Achilles' lance, where mighty Sarpedon lies, where Simois rolls so many shields and helmets and valiant heroes together beneath its stream?"

In heroic manner, Aeneas fears death without burial and without glory. He turns immediately to those at the emotional center of his world, his heroic friends Hector and Sarpedon, and cries out about the injustice that they died with glory, at home, while he wanders *maria omnia circum.* These heroic feelings are instinctive; *patria* and *patres* evoke the glory of homeland and battlefield, the only glory that has so far made any sense.

On shore, after the storm, deeper traits of this human figure appear. With notable strength, he rallies the Trojans. Masking his concern for the missing, he professes confidence and maintains stern and self-less control over his own frustration and loneliness. He calls his men *socii,* declaring their comradeship in suffering—they had faced many evils together ("neque enim ignari sumus ante malorum," I.198)—though none of them can replace the friends who fell at Troy. Even so, his address to them is remarkable:

> 'forsan et haec olim meminisse iuvabit.
> per varios casus, per tot discrimina rerum
> tendimus in Latium, sedes ubi fata quietas
> ostendunt; illic fas regna resurgere Troiae.'   (I.203–6)

"Someday perhaps it will be pleasant to remember even these hardships. Through all manner of trials, through many dangers, we make our way to Latium, where the fates show us peaceful homes; there the kingdom of Troy may have the right to rise again."

Aeneas's willed conviction strikingly contrasts with the elusiveness of that ultimate goal. He is not being willfully vague here; he doesn't really know any more than this. Many commentators have struggled with the extent of Aeneas's knowledge; Conington, for instance, offers the following (*ad* 1.205):

Heyne inquires how Aeneas came to know the name of Latium, when elsewhere he exhibits so much ignorance about his destination, and answers that he must have been told it by Anchises in the shades,—meaning probably by Helenus in Epirus, as Aeneas does not visit the shades till afterwards. But the proportions of Aeneas's knowledge and ignorance at various times even Virg. himself would probably have found it difficult to adjust (compare e.g. his knowledge of Italy from Creusa 2.781 with his ignorance afterwards, 3.100 foll.), so that we need hardly invent an explanation where the poet most likely had none.

Later, Conington observes on line 554:

Ilioneus has not previously mentioned Latium, while he has spoken of Italy . . . as an unknown country; but Virg.'s love of variety leads him to neglect these minutiae. So Dido talks of "Saturnia arva" below v. 569.

But all this genteel fuss confuses any real issue. Such criticism presumes a certain linear development in the action. What in fact is portentously obvious in the text is the elusive nature of Aeneas's knowledge. The important point is that Aeneas does *not* know, that his statement (like that of Ilioneus) is not knowledge but faith, not certainty but hope.

The reader must not impose his own "knowledge" on Aeneas. Aeneas is a DP searching for a city. He is searching also for identity —identity as a man and as a warrior and leader. Offspring of Venus, object of Juno's wrath, he is more responsible than either. His view of the gods seems sober and realistic. Because he is human, like Job or Antigone or the pilgrim Dante or Milton's Adam, he has but limited insight into the divine plan. He is trying to do what he thinks he must, but that effort strains both his humanity and his religious convictions. Often, his religious convictions must subsist without emotional support.

There is more involved. Aeneas's search for city and home is often preempted into his "mission," or at least manipulated for it. But such preempting is accomplished by Fate or its agents—Jupiter, Venus —not by Aeneas. In Vergil's poem, Aeneas acts mainly in human, heroic, moral, and spiritual terms; the political and historical "levels" of the poem are imposed by fate and the gods. So too what is called, for want of a better term, the "cosmic level"—the level on which we as readers can perceive the striving for order and universal harmony; perhaps the level on which the idealized Rome can be seen to exist.

Throughout the storm and the landing on the beach at Carthage, it is Aeneas's humanity which is central. His compassion for his men is a measure of that humanity. In the first episodes, he himself receives little compassion. He begs his mother Venus for some human contact:

> 'cur dextrae iungere dextram
> non datur ac veras audire et reddere voces?'   (1.408–9)

"Why can I not take your hand in mine, or hear you and speak to you frankly?"

But she disappears, unconcernedly returning to Paphos. The goddess displays neither personal nor even generic concern for Aeneas himself. Only Dido seems generous. Her compassion toward Aeneas's men is large, and Aeneas largely acknowledges it, for his Trojans are the pitiful survivors of the Greeks, exhausted by hardships on land and sea: "reliquias Danaum, terraeque marisque/ omnibus exhaustos iam casibus" (1.598–99). For her goodness, Aeneas warmly invokes appropriate reward:

> 'di tibi, si qua pios respectant numina, si quid
> usquam iustitiae est et mens sibi conscia recti,
> praemia digna ferant....
>   . . . .

in freta dum fluvii current, dum montibus umbrae
lustrabunt convexa, polus dum sidera pascet,
semper honos nomenque tuum laudesque manebunt,
quae me cumque vocant terrae.'   (1.603–10)

"May the gods—if there are any deities who look after the good, if
there is anywhere any justice at all or any mind aware of the right—
may they give you worthy reward. . . . As long as rivers shall course to
the sea and the shadows shall cross the mountain ridges and heaven afford
pasture to the stars, your honor, your name, your praises shall endure,
whatever lands may summon me."

A little formal, a little stiff, nonetheless these lines convey the humanity of Aeneas responding warmly to the compassionate humanity
of Dido. The skepticism in the first few lines glances—with
reason—only at the gods. In the later lines, there is bitter (though
unwitting) irony, for the stay at Carthage will add to the tragic burden of his journey.

It is clear that the city-image suggested contains both more and
less than most commentary indicates. The polarity of Troy-Rome is
obvious but facile; we should accredit it only to the extent that the
poem forces us to. Although Troy is surely there, it is not historic but
mythic, the Troy created by Vergil. A fortiori Rome. The historical
Rome was part of the datum with which Vergil worked. It allowed
him less leeway; since much of its history was known, he could not always invent episodes to fit his design. But he could and did select according to that design, and he could provide the historical material
with relevance and function within that larger design.

Though the development of the city-image begins in the first line
—Troy, its shores, Aeneas's memory of the symbolic headless trunk
of Priam—and includes the "Vrbs antiqua" favored by Juno (12),
its meaning is elusive in the opening lines. The first simile of the
poem, however, calls attention to this image. Neptune, calming the
angry waves of the storm, is compared to a statesman calming the
angry mob:

ac veluti magno in populo cum saepe coorta est
seditio saevitque animis ignobile vulgus;

iamque faces et saxa volant, furor arma ministrat;
tum, pietate gravem ac meritis si forte virum quem
conspexere, silent arrectisque auribus astant;
ille regit dictis animos et pectora mulcet.   (I.148–53)

Thus, it often happens, when riot begins in a large crowd, and the vulgar
mob begins to seethe; and soon torches and stones go flying: their rage
supplies weapons—then if they should happen to see some man whose
goodness and character command their respect, they fall silent and stand
attentively; by his words he can control their passions and calm their spirits.

The first extended simile in the poem, this is unusual in its urban details, in the possible contemporaneous historical allusion, and in the
fact that it is non-Homeric. The inversion is startling to the reader
who expects the Homeric conventions. In making its immediate
point—Neptune's strength—the simile reflects the wild disorder
of nature. That disorder was symbolized in the passage describing the
cave of the winds, in the tensions and stresses of meter and texture;
but the disorder was more widespread, as Vergil's specific choice of
words indicates: *saevit ... faces ... furor,* words that reflect the earlier
descriptions of Juno's state of mind and feeling, and that are themselves
later reflected in various contexts.

The focus then shifts to the strong man whose very presence quells
the inchoate sedition: *ille regit.* The suggested theme of order runs
through the poem. Here, it implies both the salvation of the city, by
the presence and control of the noble man who calms the mob and
changes its direction, and also the continuing problems of the city.
The man here is defined as *pietate gravem ac meritis;* as it happens,
this is Neptune, *genitor.* But from what we know of Vergil's use of
imagery and symbol, we cannot consider Neptune discretely from the
god who helps raze Troy: in II.608–12, he is businesslike and un-
emotional in his task, with the buoyancy and appearance of contained
power that Pöschl discerns here.[2]

The simile conveys conflict on three levels—the natural, the celestial, and the human and civil. These latter two are important in
considering the next large image of the city in Book I, the historic
city foretold by Jove (223–304). The episode begins with a highly

rhetorical speech by Venus. Upset by Juno's persecution of the Trojans, *tristior* and weeping, Venus is surprising and perhaps disturbing
to any who think Vergil wanted simply to elevate frivolous Aphrodite. This thesis we need not trouble ourselves about. The poem shows
her cheerful, carefree, stormy, power-hungry, unmaternal, irresponsi-
ble, and shrewd. Here, she may seem sober and stuffy, compared to
venomous Juno; but enough spite lurks under the neat clauses to
dramatize her pose.

Venus employs her arts skillfully. The opening tears suggest how
shrewd she is and how well she understands the stakes in her power
struggle with Juno. Her ringing statement in lines 234–37, breath-
lessly periodic, allows the sad question to resound: "Why, my father,
did you change your mind?" ("quae te, genitor, sententia vertit?"
237). The contrast between Antenor and Aeneas (247–52) prepares for the full-toned, indignant climax: "hic pietatis honos? sic nos
in sceptra reponis?" ("Is *this* the reward for our piety? Do you *thus*
restore us to power?" 253). The first half of this line balances
250–52, and the second half balances 247–49, Antenor and his
success. There are two other questions, one quite crucial, echoing the
fall of Troy and the hope of future good (238–41): "quem das
finem, rex magne, laborum?" ("Oh great ruler, what rest will you
grant them from their toils?" 241). This question Jupiter does not answer directly.

Jupiter's prophecy is grand and strong, resounding with future
greatness. It falls into two parts: a general statement, 257–60, followed by distinct prophecy regarding Aeneas, 261–66; then thirty
lines on *tuorum,* that is, Venus's future descendants from Ascanius on.
"Fate" resounds through the first six lines (*fatur* 256, *fata* 258, *fabor*
261, and *fatorum arcana* 262; the echo in *fatigat,* 280, is instructive).
Texture clarifies meaning: Destiny, Jupiter says, is clear and unchang-
ing for Aeneas and the Trojans. But when he reveals in detail the *fatorum arcana,* he talks of a future lying beyond the limits of the
poem. What end will there be to labors? None, in this poem; for the
lines about Aeneas refer only to great war and then to the third *ae-
stas.* There is a gap; Aeneas will, presumably, die in winter quarters,
his three years of service to the future appropriately completed. The
next lines foretell Ascanius's rule of 30 years, then a kingdom of 300

years, until Romulus and the founding of Rome which will endure
not 3, not 30, not 300 years, but forever. The progression is imposing,
and the climax resounds splendidly:

> 'his ego nec metas rerum nec tempora pono:
> imperium sine fine dedi.'   (I.278–79)

"To these men, I set no limits either of time or of space. I have granted
them a kingdom without end."

In Jupiter's mind Venus is interested less in Aeneas and his troubles
than in the future of the Trojan race. The suggested city is actually a
dynasty; Aeneas is to be merely an instrument, the first figure in the
3–30–300–infinity progression. In the divine economy, his importance depends on his usefulness.

Vergil brackets the divine dialogue with two glimpses of *pius
Aeneas*. In the first (220), Aeneas worries about his missing Trojans;
in the second (305), Aeneas sets out at first light to explore the ter-
rain. Seeking a city, he remains the harassed leader of the Trojan
remnant; meanwhile, Jupiter and Venus envision dynasties and
power. The contrast is striking. Although Aeneas is a man with a mission, a man who bears the future on his shoulders, a man destined to
found the great city of Rome—all of this future, destiny, mission is
not something immediately before him, informing his every deed,
consciously or even unconsciously providing him immediate motivation. The outlines of the future city are very dim indeed; for Aeneas,
they are often a mirage.

What Aeneas *feels* is the city of his past. *Imperium sine fine* will
not do as a center of gravity for this poem; more massive, more immediate is the experienced Troy. Juno defines it in her scornful line,
"Ilium in Italiam portans victosque penatis" ("He is bringing Troy
and the vanquished Penates to Italy," I.68).

At Carthage, the history of Dido recounted to Aeneas by the disguised Venus (335 f.) is followed immediately by the ecphrasis on the
portals of the Carthaginian temple (441 f.). The ironies of the situation are numerous, ironies both immediate and eventual, beginning
with the love-goddess's disguise as a huntress, devotee of chaste
Diana. The Carthaginian temple, Vergil emphasizes, is dedicated to

Juno, prime mover not only of Aeneas's abiding troubles but quite
distinctly of the Trojan fall these panels celebrate. Further, the fate of
Troy bears heavily on the enterprise of Aeneas, and, for a time, even
more heavily on Dido and her city.

Seeing the panels, Aeneas cries out to Achates,

> 'quae regio in terris nostri non plena laboris?
> en Priamus.'   (1.460–61)

"What region on earth is not replete with our suffering? Look—
Priam!"

En Priamus evokes the haunting figure of Priam, symbolic of Troy:
the trunk on the shore. In the context of this image, their labors
transcend fame: the Fall of Troy, like the Fall of Adam, impinges on
all history and all reality.

The ecphrasis is organized in eight sections or panels: [3]

1. (467) The Greeks in flight, presumably from Hector
2. (468) The Trojans in flight from Achilles
3. (469–73) Diomedes' slaughter of Rhesus and theft of the
   horses
4. (474–78) Achilles' slaughter of Troilus
5. (479–82) The Trojan women at the temple; Pallas's denial of
   their prayers
6. (483–87) Priam begging for Hector's body
7. (488) Aeneas in the front line
8. (489–93) Memnon; Penthesilea leading the Amazons

If these scenes are chronological, they span the gap between the cause
of the war vividly apprehended by Juno (the judgment of Paris and
the scorning of her beauty—"iudicium Paridis spretaeque iniuria
formae," 1.27) and the action of Troy's last hours detailed in Book 11.
The scenes give some substance to the image of Troy that obsesses
Aeneas. The formal development of the panels, controlled by the
pairing and balancing of passages, moves from the general contest
(1–2) to the erosion of the Trojan forces (3–4) and their aware-

ness of defeat epitomized in the two supplication scenes (5–6). The last scenes are epilogue: they show the war being carried on by Aeneas and by Memnon and Penthesilea.

For Aeneas, these vivid and vividly remembered episodes are points on the circumference of Troy; they are not quite of the essence. What remains is the heroism that brought the Trojans fame—a heroism rooted in mortality. Aeneas weeps as he looks; his tears recall the tears of other heroes looking back on the past, like Odysseus hearing Demodocus's song. But these tears are also the water of life for Aeneas:

> animum pictura pascit inani
> multa gemens, largoque umectat flumine vultum.   (1.464–65)

He nourished his spirit on the lifeless portrayal, sighing deeply, while tears bathed his face.

The striking image—*pictura pascit inani*—is evoked again later by other images in parallel contexts that show Dido hopelessly in love with Aeneas, his Troy, and his past:

> infelix Dido longumque bibebat amorem,
> multa super Priamo rogitans, super Hectore multa;
> nunc quibus Aurorae venisset filius armis,
> nunc quales Diomedis equi, nunc quantus Achilles.
> 'immo age et a prima dic, hospes, origine nobis....'
>
> (1.749–53)

Unhappy Dido drank deep of her love, asking again and again about Priam and about Hector; now asking what armor the son of Aurora had when he came, now about the quality of Diomedes' horses or the stature of Achilles. "But come, dear guest, tell us, from the very beginning. . . ."

Later that night:

> At regina gravi iamdudum saucia cura
> vulnus alit venis et caeco carpitur igni.   (IV.1–2)

But now the queen, suffering long the pangs of love, nourished the wound in her veins and is consumed by the hidden fire.

And:

> est mollis flamma medullas
> interea et tacitum vivit sub pectore vulnus.
> uritur infelix Dido totaque vagatur
> urbe furens.   (IV.66–69)

The flame meanwhile eats into the soft marrow and the wound lives silently in her breast. Unhappy Dido is aflame and wanders at large through the city in anguish.

Dido is both feeding her wound with her lifeblood and being consumed by the blind fire. As James Henry observed, *vulnus* and *igni* (IV.1–2) obviously refer to the end of Book I and are *the* wound and *the* fire, fixed most distinctly by Venus's command to her son Amor: "occultum inspires ignem fallasque veneno" ("Breathe into her the hidden fire and deceive her with poison," I.688).

One meaning of these images is plain enough. Aeneas is nourished by dead Troy, and Dido, in love with Aeneas, is in love with his past, with what gave him unsubstantial life; and this love consumes her. The motif of the hunt gives these images ominous dimensions. Venus as huntress (the garb may not be unrealistic, but in a mythological context it is certainly startling) foreshadows both Dido's relationship to Hecate in Book IV and Aeneas's role as hunter.[4] In presenting Venus as huntress, Vergil evokes the Artemis-Phaedra-Aphrodite complex from *Hippolytus*. Rather than verbal echoes, there are broad effects which suggest this. Venus's treatment of Dido, both via Amor and in her conspiracy with Juno, recalls Aphrodite's attack on Phaedra. Dido's unduly prolonged widowhood, like Hippolytus's unduly prolonged virginity, exposes her to an enormous and inextricable involvement which cannot lead to any wholesome satisfaction. Dido is condemned and destroyed by her obsession with a man divinely marked for *other* things.

The Amazon Penthesilea, *bellatrix ... virgo* (493), is juxtaposed with *regina ... forma pulcherrima Dido* (496). The image of huntress continues in the simile that follows:

> qualis in Eurotae ripis aut per iuga Cynthi
> exercet Diana choros, quam mille secutae

> hinc atque hinc glomerantur Oreades; illa pharetram
> fert umero gradiensque deas supereminet omnis
> (Latonae tacitum pertemptant gaudia pectus)....   (I.498–502)

Just as on the banks of Eurotas or over the ridges of Cynthus, Diana leads the dance, with a thousand Oreads following her on this side and on that; bearing her quiver on her shoulder, she excels all the goddesses as she walks; joy thrills the silent heart of Latona. . . .

This simile is paralleled in IV.143–49, which compares Aeneas to Apollo.[5] In Book IV, the hunt provides the setting for the union of Dido and Aeneas in the cave, but Aeneas unknowingly has already brought down his prey—the *pastor nescius* of IV.69–73. Dido's dreams testify to his disastrous effect; in them, he becomes a hunter who pursues her remorselessly, then abandons her (465 f.).

Even more substantive images of the Trojan past are the gifts that Aeneas brings, "munera ... Iliacis erepta ruinis,"

> pallam signis auroque rigentem
> et circumtextum croceo velamen acantho,
> ornatus Argivae Helenae, quos illa Mycenis,
> Pergama cum peteret inconcessosque hymenaeos,
> extulerat, matris Ledae mirabile donum;
> praeterea sceptrum....   (I.648–53)

a gown stiff with gold brocade and a veil woven all around with yellow acanthus leaves—the adornments once of Argive Helen, which she had brought with her from Mycenae when she sought Troy and the forbidden marriage, the marvellous gift of her mother, Leda. Besides, a sceptre. . . .

The Carthaginians wonder at these gifts and at the blazing countenance of Amor-Iulus—*flagrantis dei vultus* (I.710)—but Dido (*pesti devota futurae*, 712) finds in them both objects of passion:

> ardescitque tuendo
> Phoenissa et pariter puero donisque movetur.

And gazing, Phoenician Dido glows with ardor and is excited by the boy and the gifts alike.

In this larger context, verisimilitude—that is, justifying Dido's knowledge of Aeneas's history—is a minor function of the panels on the Carthaginian temple. The important thing is the symbolic past of Troy. In the formal lines in which Dido first addresses Aeneas, the emphases are clear:

> 'tune ille Aeneas quem Dardanio Anchisae
> alma Venus Phrygii genuit Simoentis ad undam?'   (1.617–18)

What Dido *knows* is the past of this hero Aeneas, the offspring of Dardanian Anchises, whom the loving Venus bore by the waters of Simois in Phrygia. The story of Teucer supports this particular view of the past; later on when Aeneas protests the Destiny imposed, Dido cannot believe him, not because of her blind rage but because of her total obsession with the past.

In many ways, Dido and Aeneas are like each other. The similarities are sometimes suggested indirectly by the poet, as in the paired similes of Diana the huntress and Apollo the hunter, or in the juxtaposition of Aeneas and Penthesilea, figure of Dido, in the last panels of the ecphrasis. There is also the similarity in situation. Both were warned in dreams to flee, Dido by her husband, Aeneas by Hector. Both are in flight from treachery, Dido from the city usurped by her brother, Pygmalion; Aeneas from the city destroyed by the gods. Both have lost loved ones to the destroyers: Aeneas has lost his wife Creusa to the gods; Dido, her husband Sychaeus to her brother. Each is a displaced person and a respected and noble leader of displaced persons, and each is trying to build a lasting city. Each bears responsibility well. Each has the dubious benefit of a watchful goddess, presumably protecting the interests of each. Each is noble, attractive, and lonely.

The first reference to Dido, *fati nescia* (1.299), almost casual, is highly charged. *Fati* contains both Aeneas's special destiny and her own doom. The phrase might well also apply to Aeneas, as Book IV instructs us. In any event, the two tragically share the illusion that they can build a lasting city at Carthage.

Dido is brought into the narrative directly by Venus; shortly thereafter, Aeneas first sees her. Venus described her to him as *"dux femina facti"* (364); the woman he sees walks like a goddess (501); [6] and he pays sincere tribute to her goodness, as the one who alone took pity: *"sola infandos Troiae miserata labores"* (597).

But Venus is preparing Dido's destruction. The suppliant of Jove and the mother-guide sheds all pretense here. She is the intriguer and the embodiment of passion. Her view of Juno and Carthage gives her away—she thinks in terms of serpents (*Tyrios bilinguis,* 661) and of fire (*urit atrox Juno,* 662); she dispatches Amor to carry out the fiery siege (673 f.).[7] Venus relishes every detail of the erotic intrigue. As Amor goes out,

> ...Venus Ascanio placidam per membra quietem
> inrigat, et fotum gremio dea tollit in altos
> Idaliae lucos, ubi mollis amaracus illum
> floribus et dulci aspirans complectitur umbra.   (1.691–94)

Venus poured peaceful sleep on the limbs of Ascanius, and caressing him on her breast, the goddess carried him off to the high Idalian groves, where soft marjoram wraps him about in flowers and sweet, fragrant shade.

The lines are brilliantly effective. The gentle sleep, like rain, suffuses Ascanius; movement, meter, and sound release the tension mounting in the preceding passage of fiery passion and erotic terror. But not the sense of foreboding—*fotum gremio dea tollit* preludes Dido's fondling of the love-god: *gremio fovet inscia Dido* (718). Combining *fotum gremio* and *fati nescia Dido* (1.299), this conveys the sharp passion and delusion, and concentrates the terror of Dido's love. While Amor carries out his sexual assault on Dido, all around her there is general hilarity; the banquet is a great success. The song of Iopas presents a vision of peace and order, of unalterable law and cosmic harmony.

The final episode of Book I is mistakenly considered a conventional banquet scene and a setting for the recapitulation books that follow. Dido's love demands knowledge; her detailed request reflects what she knows well already—the scenes engraved on the temple doors. But now she wants Aeneas's story, a point highlighted in Aeneas's own words, *"si tantus amor casus cognoscere nostros ..."* (II.10). By *tantus amor* Aeneas seems to mean, literally, Dido's affection for the Trojans and for Troy; the reader also sees Amor on her lap. But the *amor* is linked directly with the *supremum laborem,* the final heroic

hour of Troy (11); that grand story becomes central to Dido's spiritual heritage, and prefigures her own fall.

In this context, the opening of Book II get full value:

> Conticuere omnes intentique ora tenebant.

In the midst of the feasting, the line suggest shock. It is very late, the
revelry has become unrestrained; but Dido calls on Aeneas to tell the
tragic story and tell it in full: *"a prima origine"*(I.753). Everyone falls
silent—because of the great hero, but also because of the excitement shown by the queen. So they fall silent, and stare—at Aeneas
or at Dido? Both, for unless we would detach Books II and III from I
and IV, we must recognize that the setting provides embarrassed interest to the Tyrians.

This setting for the tale of Troy is an important element in the
telling itself; the powers assaulting Dido are not so different from the
powers at work in II and III, and the frame of the past is precisely the
frame that Vergil appropriates to Dido herself. At the end of III,
Aeneas is, momentarily at least, blessed with release, freed from his
burden. He falls silent and comes to rest. But not Dido. Book IV
opens *At regina gravi,* in a formula that will mark important stages of
Dido's tragedy.[8] The last phrase of the opening paragraph emphasizes
the contrast more markedly: "nec placidam membris dat cura quietem" ("her desire gave her limbs no peaceful sleep," IV.5). This echoes
I.691, *Venus Ascanio placidam per membra quietem....* But
IV.1–5 bristles with echoes of the Venus episode, and the restlessness of these echoes persists until Iris cuts the lock.

The structure of Book IV bears out this observation.

1–89: Dido's passion; Dido and Anna; the sacrifice; *furor*
90–172: the plot; the hunt; the storm; the cave
173–218: Fama; Iarbas's prayer

. . . .

219–95: Jupiter and Mercury; Aeneas's resolve to go
296–392: Dido's plea; Aeneas's defense; Dido's fury
  [331–61, Aeneas's defense, is the center of Book IV]
393–449: Aeneas's return to the ships; Anna and Aeneas

. . . .

450–553: Dido's longing for death; preparations
554–631: Mercury: Trojans depart; Dido's fury
632–93: Dido's suicide; mourning; Dido's death
694–705: Juno sends Iris

The book falls into three major sections: Dido's passion and the brief marriage; the decision to leave and Dido's attempts to win back Aeneas; the departure and Dido's suicide. Dido's confidante, Anna, figures consistently in each section; around her, everything else changes in the rise and fall of action and passion. Dido's tormented ravings before she finally forsakes her vow, in the first section, and her rages in her final madness, ending in suicide, correspond with each other. Aeneas's defense, with its key words and phrases, occurs at the very center of the book.

The careful design of Book IV is well known and needs no further elaboration. This subtle symmetry maintains in equipoise conflicting themes and motifs, particularly one major motif that pervades the whole of Book IV—that of the primitive, the elemental, the chthonic.[9] So brilliantly does the poet control sound, rhythm, imagery, and texture that primitive elements are easily missed. They are very emphatically present, crowding the story of Dido from beginning to end and investing it with terrible beauty and harsh significance. The motif had its prelude in the erotic passage discussed earlier, where Venus's character is amply manifest; as it works in Book IV, the motif expresses and embodies several major themes, especially the destructive nature of the gods' ancient powers and the profound continuing conflict between passion and reason, chaos and order, the primitive and the civilized.

Symbolic of this motif is the god Mercury, messenger of Jupiter, spanning life and death as Atlas spans earth and heaven. He is both the winged god (*talaria*, 239 f.) and the god of the underworld (*virgam*, 242 f.). *Dat somnos adimitque*—he brings sleep and takes it away. As Austin remarks, "Death is . . . the twin-brother of sleep." Mercury need pay no heed to Dido, have no particular part in her affairs. It suffices that this figure from the older chthonic order of gods embody doom.

Both Juno and Venus display stark, elemental power in Book IV. Though they assume grand airs and maneuver shrewdly, the points they score off each other are scored in isolation, dislocated from the reality at hand. For Dido herself (or any other individual), they have only brutal disregard. Neither cares much about the outcome of this adventure; in the manner of chthonic gods, each stretches her divine powers to a narrow end. Venus finds her pleasure in the stratagem, in Dido's violent passion, and in the deception of Juno, rather than in her success in protecting Aeneas. She never answers Juno's taunt:

> 'habes, tota quod mente petisti:
> ardet amans Dido traxitque per ossa furorem.' (IV.100–1)

"You have gotten what you set your whole heart on: Dido is burning with love, she has drawn the furious passion deep into her bones."

Juno herself, while noting that Dido is *miserrima,* proposes only an impossible solution. The harsh favors Dido receives from the goddess of her city must lead from cave to pyre.

It is Juno who presides over storm and cave and who turns *culpa* into *coniugium* (172). *Pronuba* there, patroness of marriage, she is significantly called *Saturnia* on her first appearance in Book IV (92) and *omnipotens* on her last (693).

The hunt begins in excited splendor; however, the joy of the hunt, its color and gaiety, belong only to Ascanius, unattuned to the world of his elders. The quarry is taken in the cave, whither *pronuba Iuno* guides Dido and Aeneas:

> speluncam Dido dux et Troianus eandem
> deveniunt. (IV.165–66)

The primitive character of this episode belies its tact. What seems a formal ceremony is highly explosive. The witnesses are the primal elements—primeval Earth, Air, Fire, and Water; chanting the wedding song, the mountain Nymphs are also crying out in horror: *ulularunt* (168). The lines that follow express terror, climaxing in the contrast of *coniugium vocat* and *nomine culpam* surrounding *prae-texit* (both the word and the line structure itself suggest the cave):

> ille dies primus leti primusque malorum
> causa fuit; neque enim specie famave movetur

nec iam furtivum Dido meditatur amorem;
coniugium vocat, hoc praetexit nomine culpam.   (IV.169–72)

That day was the beginning of doom and the first cause of evils: Dido
cared nothing for appearance or reputation, was no longer concerned
about keeping her love secret; she called it marriage, with this word she
covered her shame.

The effect of this depends partly on the primitive symbolism of the
"ceremony," partly on Vergil's careful preparation earlier.

At the beginning of Book IV, Dido's oath (24–29) is a "solemn
and awful prayer" heavy with the darkness of the underworld and lit
with the imagery of fire.[10] Her sacrifice to the deities associated with
marriage echoes this oath while mocking it; this ritual invocation depends on the notion of expiatory sacrifice to reconcile the gods to a
sin not yet committed. She sacrifices to Ceres, Apollo, Bacchus, and
particularly Juno (as most concerned with the *curae* of marriage).[11]
The narrator exclaims, "quid vota furentem,/ quid delubra iuvant?"
(IV.65–66); *furentem* reflects the impact of Venus and Amor on
Dido.

In the verbal texture, one notes the predominance of *fatum* or
words echoing it and the darkness in which Aeneas and Dido are
caught.[12] In one simile (69–73), Aeneas is compared to a *pastor*
who has wounded a deer, but unknowingly: *nescius: illa fuga* ...
(72). All reality seems to cease; Dido wanders about in the dark,
sleepless, caught in a moment of time; "illum absens absentem au-
ditque videtque" (83).[13] And the work on the city itself has come to a
standstill, as shown in the subtle image of *pendet:*

Iliacosque iterum demens audire labores
exposcit pendetque iterum narrantis ab ore.   (IV.78–79)

In her obsession Dido insists on hearing again the Trojan labors, and she
hangs on his words as again he tells the story.

Dido wants only to remain in past Troy, in the words which re-create
it, but all around her in Carthage, activity ceases:

                    pendent opera interrupta minaeque
murorum ingentes aequataque machina caelo.   (IV.88–89)

The picture, as Austin remarks, "is of a crane high up, towering to the sky, its burden left in mid-air because no one is now there to work it."

These images of suspension contribute to the primitive quality: the movement of civilization has been paralyzed. Even geography is relevant; as Anna insists (40 f.), Carthage is hemmed in by the Gaetulians, the barbaric Numidians, and the fierce Barcans, by the quicksands of the Syrtes and the parched desert. Anna's pragmatic view is accurate. After the cave scene, grotesque Fama wings through Libya. This Fama has troubled some readers, perhaps because they expected some sort of sophisticated melodrama. But the realism here is rightly grotesque. Fama is monstrous, born of Earth (*ira inritata deorum,* 178), primitive sister to the Olympophobic giants Coeus and Enceladus. As it happens, this monster comes to Iarbas, also a primitive figure: Iarbas is the son of Hammon, the Libyan god, by the ravished Garamantian nymph. Iarbas has a vast array of temples, characterized as *immania*—the word implies cruelty or horror. His prayer to Jupiter is bitter and scornful, reflecting his primitive mind. In Jupiter, he sees mainly thunder, lightning, and terror. His diatribe against Aeneas displays barbaric contempt for civilization. When Jupiter responds by sending Mercury, Vergil calls him *Omnipotens,* echoing and underlining the scornful word of Iarbas.

In her practical way, Anna hoped to calm Dido's fears about taking Aeneas, but the political expediency which she proposed loses all point. As Aeneas, prodded by Mercury, prepares to leave, reality becomes nightmare for Dido. Waking and sleeping, she hears ghostly murmurs from the shrine of Sychaeus, accompanied by the cries of the owl (460 f.). Throughout this passage, her nightmarish condition is expressed in resonant echoes:[14]

fatis 450	*effata* 456
relinquat 452	*relinqui* 466
visum 456	*visa* 461
voces 460	*vocantis* 460
sola 462	*sola* 467
voces 463	*voces* 463
longas 463	*longam* 467
semper 466	*semper* 467

Husband and owl, one a dream visitor, the other an image of isolation, return in a recurrent fantasy in which she is hunted down by
Aeneas and abandoned in a wasteland:

> agit ipse furentem
> in somnis ferus Aeneas, semperque relinqui
> sola sibi, semper longam incomitata videtur
> ire viam et Tyrios deserta quaerere terra.   (IV.465–68)

In her dreams, Aeneas himself pursued her ruthlessly, driving her wild;
and she saw herself left alone, forever alone, companionless, traveling end-
lessly down a long road, through a deserted land, in search of her Tyrians.

These desolate visitations are quite different from earlier ones, such as
the *imago* of her husband (I. 353 f.) urging her to flee bloody Pygmalion.[15] In the incantatory reduplications and the remorseless rhythms,
these visitations are almost tangible. The unusual simile that follows,
of Pentheus and Orestes hounded by Furies, climaxes this tight, rich
passage:

> Eumenidum veluti demens videt agmina Pentheus
> et solem geminum et duplicis se ostendere Thebas,
> aut Agamemnonius scaenis agitatus Orestes
> armatam facibus matrem et serpentibus atris
> cum fugit ultricesque sedent in limine Dirae.   (IV.469–73)

Just so does the raving Pentheus see an army of Furies advancing and two
suns in the sky and a twofold Thebes revealed; or on the stage, Orestes,
the son of Agamemnon, pursued, as he runs from his mother armed with
torches and black snakes, and the avenging Furies wait at the door.

The double sun and the double Thebes seen by Pentheus and the
torch and serpent-laden mother seen by Orestes illustrate their de-
mented hallucinations. But the simile goes further. The lines are enclosed by Furies in their ancient chthonic horror—inexorable
agents of blood, grim executors of primitive law and primitive instinct. Even the stage setting (which some editors have found distaste-
ful) contributes to the duplication by presenting myth in stasis; like
the structure of Book IV, the stage setting controls the primitive elements. The dominant motif of the simile is search and pursuit, coun-

terpointing the pursuit and search of Dido's nightmare; in the simile both search and pursuit are as disembodied and as desolate as in the nightmare. What the simile, indeed, makes frighteningly vivid is the character of Dido's wasteland: it is a wasteland of primitive terror.

Dido's last words to Aeneas quiver with a rage expressed in harsh primitive terms. Her definition of his parentage is less insult than an attempt to place him:

> 'duris genuit te cautibus horrens
> Caucasus Hyrcanaeque admorunt ubera tigres.'   (IV.366–67)

"Harsh Caucasus begot you on his flinty rocks, and Hyrcanian tigers nursed you."

This is, of course, a figure wrought by Dido herself; the images reveal Dido's feelings. She goes on to speak of him in an impersonal way, in the third person, for the next dozen lines. It is not so much as if "Aeneas were not with her, she is alone with her thoughts as she goes over what he has said" (Austin); rather, she has for the moment put him at a distance so that she can, albeit with violence, define the reasons for and the meaning of the primitive images which she has evoked. When she again addresses him directly, the hissing violent lines culminate in a threat that she will haunt him like a Fury and take some sort of vengeance on him:

> 'sequar atris ignibus absens
> et, cum frigida mors anima seduxerit artus,
> omnibus umbra locis adero. dabis, improbe, poenas.
> audiam et haec manis veniet mihi fama sub imos.'   (IV.384–87)

"From far off, I will hound you with dark fires and, when chill death has separated spirit from limbs, as a spectre I will be present wherever you are. You will be punished, you wretch. The news of your punishment will reach me, I will hear it, even down among the deepest shades."

This final image of a Fury returns to the opening statement and to her subsequent madness, nightmares, and sorcery. Dido faints and is carried off to her *marmoreo ... thalamo*—that sepulchral chamber—and never leaves the palace again.

Even before this speech, "death" becomes a refrain in the texture of the poetry. Mackail pointed out the word *moritura* in lines 308, 415, 519, and 604, a "single bell-stroke" tolling at significant intervals. It is worth adding (without exploring here the contextual refinements) how that bell-stroke echoes throughout the whole text from line 308 to line 696. In Dido's speeches: *moritura* 308, *moribundam* 323, *morte* 375, *frigida mors* 385, *morte* 436, *morere* 547, *moritura* 604, *morientis* 610, *moriemur* 659, *moriamur* 660, *mortis* 662 (her last word). Other occurrences, directly or indirectly referring to Dido: *mortalia* 412, *moritura* 415, *mortem orat* 450, *decrevit mori* 475, *morte Sychaei* 502, *moritura* 519, *certa mori* 564, *morte* 644, *morientem* 674, *moriens* 678, *morte* 696.

For Dido, death is almost a physical entity. She expresses her memory of Sychaeus in terms of "ashes," but with a more specific meaning than the word *cinis* usually has. Her crime she sees as

'non servata fides cineri promissa Sychaeo.' (IV.552)

"the vow sworn to the ashes of Sychaeus has not been kept."

Misunderstanding Aeneas's statement about his father's shade—
"me patris Anchisae ... turbida terret imago" (351, 353)—she speaks of it distinctly in terms of the ashes of the dead:

'nec patris Anchisae cineres manisve revelli:' (IV.427)

"I never disturbed the ashes or the spirit of father Anchises."

Dido feels strongly the physical presence of the dead. For her, death and dreams are closely linked to the chthonic.[16]

Dido's rage when she learns of Aeneas's plans to leave is expressed primitively:

saevit inops animi totamque incensa per urbem
bacchatur, qualis commotis excita sacris
Thyias, ubi audito stimulant trieterica Baccho
orgia nocturnusque vocat clamore Cithaeron. (IV.300-3)

Helpless, she raged and ran feverishly about the city, like some Bacchante wild with frenzy as the emblems of Bacchus are shaken and the cry of his name is heard, when the triennial orgies arouse her and Mount Cithaeron summons her with cries in the night.[17]

The magic rite to which Dido has recourse (474 f.) is functional to the whole. Her invocations of the powers of darkness during the rite and in her last moments are terrifying, particularly those which serve as context for the curses she calls down on Aeneas and the Trojans. She evokes the shocking figure of Thyestes:

> 'non ipsum absumere ferro
> Ascanium patriisque epulandum ponere mensis?'   (IV.601–2)

"Why did I not slaughter Ascanius and serve him up, a banquet for his father's table?'

The harsh power and terrible beauty of this monologue reach a shrill climax in the curses. Dido calls on the blazing sun and on Hecate, on *conscia Iuno* and the avenging Furies—"Dirae ultrices et di morientis Elissae" (610)—to afflict Aeneas, that *infandum caput,* with war and exile, with the loss of Ascanius and the death of his friends, with a harsh peace in victory and bitter ashes in conquest. Dido remembers Aeneas's own image of Priam:

> 'sed cadat ante diem mediaque inhumatus harena.'   (IV.620)

"May he fall before his time and lie unburied on the strand."

The famous call for an avenger (625–29) projects in powerful and ringing lines not just the historical conflict between Carthage and Rome but, more importantly, the sense of universal conflict that must inevitably work itself out in the self-destruction of civil war. The curses have their strongest impact when we recognize that they are part of the whole demonic pattern. They are followed quickly by her suicide, an act of worship to the chthonic deities. At the end, *Iuno omnipotens* sends Iris to release Dido from her agony.[18]

I have tried to illuminate the poetry of Dido's tragedy while pre-
scinding from the questions of love and guilt, on which I agree generally with Austin's penetrating commentary. The tale of Dido provides
the major portion of "Carthage." The primitive and chthonic elements, generally ignored by commentators, invest the story with
much of its incredible power. Further, these elements point to the
major reason why the interlude is for Aeneas almost a disaster. In his
symbolic return to the depths of his past, Aeneas has virtually abandoned himself to that past, to its premises and its fundamental will,
and to its inevitable destruction. Paradoxically, however, this very ex-
tremity saves him—from himself, cliché though this is. A look at
the interrelationships between Aeneas, Dido, and the city may help to
clarify this point.

Dido's last words and thoughts are of Aeneas:

> 'hauriat hunc oculis ignem crudelis ab alto
> Dardanus et nostrae secum ferat omina mortis.'   (IV.661–62)

"May the heartless Dardanian, far out at sea, drink deep of the sight of
this fire and carry with him the evil omen of my death."

Words and images recall her first address to him:

> 'tune ille Aeneas quem Dardanio Anchisae
> alma Venus Phrygii genuit Simoentis ad undam?'   (I.617–18)

"Are you really Aeneas, whom the loving Venus bore to Dardanian Anchises by the waters of Simois in Phrygia?"

The span of life and death, suggested in the contrasts of water and
fire, of the birth at the riverbank (historicity does not matter; Dido's
feeling does) and of the fiery omen of death: this is part of Dido's
feeling. Consciously or not, she has it just right. The important point
is that her very last line (662), enclosed by *Dardanus* and *mortis,* focuses on the figure who deals death in order to live, the Aeneas who
is specifically Dardanian Aeneas, destined to return to *Italiam ...
matrem* whence his ancestor Dardanus came. As effective a word as

moritura, and thematically more significant, *Dardanus* [19] inexorably marks her last moments:

> 'Dardaniique rogum capitis permittere flammae.'
>   . . . .
> conscendit furibunda rogos ensemque recludit
> Dardanium....
>   . . . .
> 'felix, heu nimium felix, si litora tantum
> numquam Dardaniae tetigissent nostra carinae.'   (IV.640, 646 f., 657 f.)

"Commit to the flames the funeral pyre of that Dardanian. . . ." Frenzied, she climbed up the pyre and unsheathed the Dardanian sword. . . . "Happy, alas too happy, if only the Dardanian ships had never touched my shores."

The emphasis on the word *Dardanian* is too pointed to miss. It epitomizes Aeneas's future, while the funeral pyre holds the past which Dido took to herself. That past is symbolized in the *Iliacas vestes* (648) which were the *ornatus* of Helen, the *dulces exuviae* (651), and the Dardanian sword, Aeneas's gift to Dido (*munus,* 647). Though it is Aeneas's destiny which destroys her, she dies embracing, not rejecting, the past, her love still overpowering.

The implicit parallelism between the fall of Dido and the fall of Troy may be drawn out a bit further. Though Dido is enthralled by the *Troius heros,* she herself could be for him no more enduring than Troy itself. Both she and Troy are out of date; the loss of each is part of Aeneas's Dardanian destiny. Dido's welcoming of Aeneas recalls the Wooden Horse; blinded by "favorable" gods, Dido receives Aeneas just as Troy took in the Horse. In Book IV, as in Book II, the gods are important, but they act on a level distinct from the emotional action. In both, the gods are the destructive energizers, *Iuppiter ... ipse* in II, here *Iuno omnipotens* (IV.693): Dido is never more nor less than a pawn for Juno.

Dido's city suffered during the winter of her sin. She saw, but for a time she did not care, until Aeneas was preparing to leave. Her people become disenchanted. By her act, she has left herself and her city naked to their enemies—thus the recurrent cry of *deserta* and *capta*

in her plea to Aeneas (323–30). Even shallow Anna, who thought
she knew her sister, sees for a moment the appalling catastrophe:

> 'exstinxti te meque, soror, populumque patresque
> Sidonios urbemque tuam.'   (IV.682–83)

"You have destroyed yourself and me, sister, and the people and the nobles of Sidon, and your city."

As Austin points out, the whole fabric of the city-state is suggested
in these words. That is the point of the rich and ironic echo, in

> 'urbem praeclaram statui, mea moenia vidi,'   (IV.655)

"I founded a noble city, I saw my walls rise."

of Dido's earlier statement to the Trojans, "urbem quam statuo, vestra
est" (I.573).

Dido may not, perhaps, have a cataclysmic vision, yet a cataclysm
is what Vergil's simile at her death implies.[20] As the people realize
what has happened,

> it clamor ad alta
> atria: concussam bacchatur Fama per urbem.
> lamentis gemituque et femineo ululatu
> tecta fremunt, resonat magnis plangoribus aether,
> non aliter quam si immissis ruat hostibus omnis
> Karthago aut antiqua Tyros, flammaeque furentes
> culmina perque hominum volvantur perque deorum.   (IV.665–71)

The cry rose to the roof of the palace; then Fama ran mad through the
stricken city. The buildings shook with laments and groans and the wail-
ing of women; the heaven resounded with the terrible cries. It was as if
enemy troops had broken through and all Carthage were falling, or ancient Tyre, while the blazing flames were rolling through the dwellings of
men and of gods.

The short simile resounds with Troy's tragedy and Dido's. But the
point of the simile is more than the extent or pitch of outcry and
shock. This city is not merely Carthage, this is *antiqua Tyros,* the archetypal city that Dido symbolizes, now being shattered. The histori-

cal allusion is apt: the death of love destroys both cities, centuries apart. But overriding the historical aspect, the rich evocation calls up Aeneas's own past city, with its maternal aspect, real and false. Real, in the sense that the fallen Troy of Book II remains the city of Aeneas and his remnant; yet false, for that elusive land of Dardanus is their true homeland. Most impressive of all is the collapse, in the fury of flame, of the whole fabric of order and community—the fabric so carefully woven in the early description of Carthage.

Aeneas's search for the city faltered badly at Carthage. It would be naïve to see the Dido episode as an unfortunate escapade modeled on Odysseus's supposedly free-spirited affairs. Shipwrecked by Juno on the shores of her ancient city, Aeneas is vulnerable. He slips into unreflecting passivity. The end of Book III itself suggested as much; having told of Troy and of his wanderings, climaxing in the death of Anchises, he falls silent:

> Sic pater Aeneas ...,
>
> . . . .
>
> conticuit tandem factoque hic fine quievit.   (III.716, 718)

The slow final line trails off into rest and peace. It is the rest and peace sought at the beginning of Book II—*"suadentque cadentia sidera somnos"*—but it is also the quiet of moral and emotional fatigue, like that in Aeneas's *"cessi"* at the end of that book, when he finally turned from Troy.

The emphasis on his "fatherhood" which frames the story of Books II and III is no idle repetition. Throughout, *pater* and *genitor* are generally identified with Anchises, or with Jupiter; Anchises dead, Aeneas must now become the figure of authority and leadership. Instead, at Carthage, he searches for quiet; there is a distinct slackening in his dedication. The echo of this *quievit* in Dido's inability to find *quies* ("nec placidam membris dat cura quietem," IV.5) lingers through the emotional and moral tempests of Book IV.

Aeneas's sense of desertion at the death of his father (which briefly preceded the storm of Book I) is part of this slackening:

> 'hic me, pater optime, fessum
> deseris.'   (III.710–11)

This weary sense of desertion contrasts sharply with Dido's passion at the beginning of Book IV. Aeneas submits, partly because Dido is strong and dominating, partly because her city seems to answer to the object of his search. Put it another way: Aeneas does not, cannot, and perhaps cannot be expected to "understand his destiny," to have a clear apprehension of his goal. He is taken in; in one sense, indeed, the interlude at Carthage is for Aeneas a mistake made in all good faith, an error arising honestly from the complexity of his position (and the weakness of human flesh and spirit), that helps to illuminate for the reader how complex that position is.

Mercury, symbol of life and death, comes twice to Aeneas, by day and by night. Neither symbol is quite separate from the other: we cannot allegorize and say that Mercury brings life to Aeneas, death to Dido. At the first visitation of Mercury, the condition of Aeneas is death-in-life.

> ut primum alatis tetigit magalia plantis,
> Aenean fundantem arces ac tecta novantem
> conspicit. atque illi stellatus iaspide fulva
> ensis erat Tyrioque ardebat murice laena
> demissa ex umeris, dives quae munera Dido
> fecerat, et tenui telas discreverat auro.   (IV.259–64)

As soon as he alighted on his winged feet among the huts, he saw Aeneas working on the foundations of the towers and building new homes. He had a sword studded with yellow jasper; the cloak draped on his shoulders blazed with Tyrian purple, which wealthy Dido had made for him as a gift, interweaving the fabric with threads of gold.

Commentators have had difficulty with the description of Aeneas here; Mackail considers lines 261–64 "a rather infelicitous parenthesis." On the other hand, Austin suggests that "the lines are a glimpse, seldom seen, of Vergil's hero as a happy man." He says also, "The work is being continued by Aeneas in a happy partnership, now that she has won him—a subtle point. Yet it is an Aeneas with a jewelled sword and purple cloak, a Tyrian Aeneas, dressed out in magnificence by Dido, not a grave and sober man of destiny." At first sight, Aeneas may seem happy. He is working, he is royal, he is secure, he does not have to make real decisions. But later details banish this impression.

Vergil could have had Aeneas in any number of places, doing any number of things, for this encounter. When Mercury comes, Aeneas is laying the foundations for the citadels and renewing the buildings. That is, he is absorbed in playing at building a city. The text says nothing of workmen, whether Trojan or Tyrian; Aeneas's outfit is strikingly inept. Shortly, we learn that the Tyrians are *infensi* with Dido, and presumably with Aeneas as well. In line 295, the Trojans are *laeti*—delighted to get moving again. Restless, discontented with their leader's role of silk-costumed engineer, they highlight Aeneas's condition. If he is actually at work, he is building the wrong city. In any event, his "work" is a bizarre parody of his proper role, a desperate clutching at the illusion of happiness. Mercury's sharp words dispel the illusion:

> 'tu nunc Karthaginis altae
> fundamenta locas pulchramque uxorius urbem
> exstruis?'   (IV.265–67)

"Now are you laying foundations for a grand Carthage and building a beautiful city for the sake of a woman?"

The important aspect of Aeneas's ready obedience to Mercury is not his lack of individuality or independence but rather the clear implication that he was ready for Mercury's order, that his self-delusion could be carried on no longer. It is the moment of truth. Aeneas's defense, at the very heart of Book IV, reveals what Mercury forced him to see. It is a subtle speech, powerfully understated, with rich implications.[21] The speech shows why Aeneas can again be called *pius* (393). It reveals the difficult situation Aeneas is in and the complexities we must take into account. He was quite vague about what he would do, and how to do it. Apparently, Aeneas intended to get all ready and bid Dido farewell at the last possible moment. Forced to speak now, he says *pauca,* not only because he cannot let his emotions get away from him, but because he is confused; in the course of his struggles with duty and feelings, he is attempting to clarify things to himself. The truths he utters virtually escape from him.

'pro re pauca loquar. neque ego hanc abscondere furto
speravi (ne finge) fugam, nec coniugis umquam
praetendi taedas.'   (IV.337–39)

"On this matter, briefly: I did not intend to hide my departure by any
deceit—do not imagine that; nor have I ever pretended to be your husband."

The words are quite legalistic, as if this is the only way he can control
them. He does try to deny his own part in the affair, to assert his lack
of guile. But Aeneas's "view" is not the operative factor here; rather,
it is the necessity that he defend himself against Dido's charges.

Aeneas's claims that he had no intention of sneaking off and that
he never considered their relationship a marriage are at least ques-
tionable. He had in fact submitted to her and become *uxorius,* and he
had ordered furtive preparations. But what keeps intruding on the attempt to justify himself is the stern power of the gods which will not
be put off. He asserts that his true feelings direct him neither to Carthage nor to Italy:

'me si fata meis paterentur ducere vitam
auspiciis et sponte mea componere curas,
urbem Troianam primum dulcisque meorum
reliquias colerem, Priami tecta alta manerent,
et recidiva manu posuissem Pergama victis.'   (IV.340–44)

"If fate allowed me to lead my life as I wished and to solve my problems
in my own way, I would be tending the city of Troy first and the remnants of my loved ones. The lofty palace of Priam would stand and I
would have restored Troy's citadel to her conquered sons."

As Austin observes, the whole passage is qualified by *victis:* "Aeneas
can never forget the pitiful lines of refugees of Troy . . . , and all his
promised destiny can make no atonement for the bitter past." *Meis
auspiciis* and *sponte mea* (and *non sponte* which ends the speech) are
counterpointed by fate, which pervades and dominates the speech:
fando, fata, fas, fatalibus. Aeneas's argument is not persuasive because
the counteremotion is distinctly present, as he cries out that he feels
deeply the desire to establish a city for his own people. But the prox-

imity of fate clarifies meaning for Aeneas himself. *Fatum* is the force
that defines his whole enterprise; it is that damnable will of the gods
to which he must submit. The pressure of the gods comes through in
the terrifying nightly visitations of his father's shade ("me patris Anchisae ...,/admonet in somnis et turbida terret imago," 351 f.), in the
felt duty toward his son ("me puer Ascanius ...," 354), and finally
in the revelation of Mercury's descent.

He concludes:

> 'desine meque tuis incendere teque querelis;
> Italiam non sponte sequor.'   (iv.360–61)

"Stop arousing both me and yourself with your reproaches; I do not journey to Italy willingly."

These lines verge on despair, even while they sum up the speech. The
temptation to trade off Anchises, Ascanius, Italy, all of it, for Dido,
must be strong. Aeneas is emotionally besieged by what he has said
and by the reasons he has been giving, both to Dido and to himself.
He has less feeling here for family, race, future, and destiny than he
has cold terror at the divine commands, the ultimate *timor Domini,*
the divine chill that cannot let him off. In Book vi, the cost to
Aeneas is underlined in his tearful words to Dido, in the pain-
wracked feeling behind his whole futile speech to her:

> 'funeris heu tibi causa fui? per sidera iuro,
> per superos et si qua fides tellure sub ima est,
> invitus, regina, tuo de litore cessi.'   (vi.458–60)

"Alas! was it death I brought you? I swear by the stars, by the powers
above, by whatever truth there is beneath the earth, it was not by my own
will, O queen, that I left your land."

After his defense speech, in fact, Aeneas has said no more to Dido till
this meeting in Hades; his very last words to her are:

> 'quem fugis? extremum fato quod te adloquor hoc est.'   (vi.466)

"Why do you fly from me? This is the last word I am allowed by fate to
speak to you."

Servius explains *fato* by pointing out that, since Aeneas's place in the afterlife will be different from Dido's, it is fated that he never speak to her again. But this explanation is farfetched. Clearly, the word is used emotionally, from Aeneas's deep and troubled sense of the import of *fatum* in his life. The word carries the burden of his relationship to Dido, a relationship foredoomed by *fatum*.

When Aeneas leaves Dido's palace and goes to the ships, he is again *pius Aeneas,* as Vergil emphasizes in a celebrated passage:

> At pius Aeneas, quamquam lenire dolentem
> solando cupit et dictis avertere curas,
> multa gemens magnoque animum labefactus amore
> iussa tamen divum exsequitur classemque revisit.   (iv.393–96)

But the good Aeneas, although he longed to soothe her in her grief and to dispel her misery with gentle words, sighing deeply, his spirit shaken by the strength of his love—even so, he obeyed the gods' commands and returned to his fleet.

Rhythm and movement, while releasing the tension, show that the regained stature brings no joy to Aeneas. So too does the following simile of the ants (402–7), prudent, disciplined, orderly, their labor soberly divided and carried out without feeling. The sense of restraint conveys Aeneas's state, as, drained of all feeling, he does what he must. When Anna comes, he is unmoved: *fata obstant* (440). The tears flow—Anna's, Aeneas's, and Dido's—but Aeneas stands firm:

> ac velut annoso validam cum robore quercum
> Alpini Boreae nunc hinc nunc flatibus illinc
> eruere inter se certant; it stridor, et altae
> consternunt terram concusso stipite frondes;
> ipsa haeret scopulis et quantum vertice ad auras
> aetherias, tantum radice in Tartara tendit.   (iv.441–46)

As when a stout oak tree, hardened by the years when northern winds from the Alps assaulted it this way and that, vying among themselves to tear it from the ground—the trunk creaks, the lofty branches strew the earth as the wind whistles. Still the tree stands firm among the rocks, for its roots push as far down toward Tartarus as its head towers toward the heavens.

Often an illustration of physical conflict, this simile suggests the dimensions of Aeneas's emotional and spiritual struggle. The oak is appropriate both in its natural features and its usual connection with Jupiter, god of power. Details and rhythm belie the apparent immobility; the last two lines (which Page thought exaggerated and unnatural) enrich meaning: the life-death polarity of *auras aetherias* and *Tartara* reminds us of the difference between Aeneas and the gods. Unlike them, he cannot afford to be moved, and unlike them, he cannot help being deeply hurt and wounded.

The epilogue to the Carthaginian episode is v.1–7:

> Interea medium Aeneas iam classe tenebat
> certus iter fluctusque atros Aquilone secabat
> moenia respiciens, quae iam infelicis Elissae
> conlucent flammis. quae tantum accenderit ignem
> causa latet; duri magno sed amore dolores
> polluto, notumque furens quid femina possit,
> triste per augurium Teucrorum pectora ducunt.

Meanwhile Aeneas held his fleet right on its course through the deep sea, cutting through waves black with the north wind. He looked back at the city-walls, which blazed with unhappy Dido's fire. The cause of that great fire was obscure; but, aware what bitter sorrow comes from a great love that is dishonored, and what a furious woman is capable of, the Trojans felt it an unhappy omen.

Here Aeneas *tenebat / certus iter,* but context shows that this does not mean "confident." The fires rising above the walls of the city are an unhappy omen, though the Trojans can only guess what the fires mean. Their knowledge of a *furens … femina* is largely derived from Mercury, who hinted dark things to Aeneas. The cause of the fires is hidden, as hidden as was the whole progress of the goddesses' pressures on hapless Dido; as hidden too, until revealed to Aeneas, as the root cause of Troy's own fires; as hidden as the wound and the flame consuming Dido during banquet and tale; and, perhaps, as hidden as the banked fires of Aeneas himself. The familiar phrases emphasize that this is a break.[22] Thematically, the break is necessary: it clarifies *certus* and *iter*—Aeneas must not look back. His obligation is not to Troy or Carthage but to Dardanus and his city. The point is not that Aeneas's inability to discover the cause of the fire argues dullness or want of imagination; the point is rather that, whatever he knows, he cannot afford to think about it. Dido's last words return: *hauriat ... Dardanus* [i.e., Aeneas] ... *omina mortis.* He is drinking deep. As later events in Book V show, the misery and unhappiness he hides are very strong.

Though the Carthage episode began in mutual need and compassion, at its core was the conflict between reason and passion, between the primitive and the civilized. This conflict reflects obliquely a major polarity of the poem, between arms and the man, between violence and humanity. Apollonius of Rhodes' mixture of melodrama and romance, in a thin epic shell, survives only in traces here; while the Carthage episode approaches melodrama or tragedy, it remains part of the epic construction.

In some respects, Aeneas comes off badly in his departure. But that is beside the point. Vergil is far less "romantic" than many of his critics. In Hades, Dido does not let Aeneas explain; he wants a crumb of comfort, some meager recognition of the price extorted by the gods. But he gets nothing, so harsh a purity does his mission entail. He must put it all by, into an irrevocable past.

The pastness of the Dido episode is enlarged upon in story, imagery, and motifs. It is suggested in the pathetic futility of his posture when Mercury first comes upon him. It is embodied in the smoke rising from Carthage, the climactic image of the city destroyed recalling his last sight of Troy. The billows of smoke cap his unhappy insights into the exigencies of his destiny and comment finally on his notion of rebuilding Troy. That notion was not merely a point scored in debate with Dido, it was a poignantly true and impossible outcry, as true and impossible as the first outcry, the abiding sadness that he had not died at Troy.

The importance of Troy in Aeneas's spiritual life may be seen in his own tale of the Fall of Troy.

CHAPTER TWO

TROY: FALL OF THE CITY

Aeneas's tale to Dido is *infandum,* the renewal of *unspeakable* grief and horror (so that he weeps furtively and turns away to look out into the night, 6–9). Dante felt keenly the force of the word and its context when he twice echoed the beginning of *Aeneid* II. The latter example is Ugolino beginning his story:

> "Tu vuo' ch' io rinnovelli
> Disperato dolor ch 'l cor mi preme
> Già pur pensando, pria ch' io ne favelli."   (*Inf.* XXXIII.4–6)

"You wish me to renew that desperate grief, the very thought of which wrings my heart even before I speak of it." [1]

The unspeakable, *infandum,* is that which must be said. Clearly Aeneas has not told this tale of Troy before; nor will he ever tell it again, not like this. Just as clearly, however, that desperate memory has never been far from him. The Night of Troy, with its strange lights and shadows, the friendly silences of the moon and the crashes of fire—that Night casts its long, uncertain shadow over the whole life of Aeneas and his whole enterprise. It qualifies and circumscribes many episodes of the poem, including the Italian half. If it seems to be history, it can be so only in the sense in which Stephen Dedalus defined it, "a nightmare from which I am trying to awake," with "God. . . . A shout in the street." [2] For the event is ahistorical to Aeneas; it is massively mythic, archetypal.

The general ordering of events in the tale is simply but brilliantly conceived. The action falls into four large sections:

13–267   Laocoon, Sinon, the Wooden Horse
268–401 Hector, and the counterattack (ending with the Greeks climbing back into the Horse)
402–558 Priam and the collapse of Troy
559–804 Anchises and the flight from Troy

The internal balance of the two middle sections is clear enough; interestingly, that balance (on the story level) pivots on the Trojans' disguise. The first and last sections are also balanced in many ways, particularly by the unusual revelations of the gods' will and the gods' power.

The details of the narrative do not need repetition. The story is told, in C. M. Bowra's brilliant phrase, from the viewpoint of the defeated. From the very beginning, we are aware of Greek trickery. The patterns of words surrounding the Horse, itself an awesome monument to that perilous trickery, bring this out. It was made *divina Palladis arte* (15); Thymoetes urges that it be brought in, moved perhaps by treachery (*dolo*, 34), but others are suspicious of *Danaum insidias* (36), particularly Laocoon (*dolis*, 44). Sinon is well versed in guile —*versare dolos* (62), *dolis instructus et arte Pelasga* (152)—and can carry out *Danaum insidias* (65). Thus, when he has finished relating Sinon's story, Aeneas comments—

> 'Talibus *insidiis* periurique *arte* Sinonis
> credita res, captique *dolis*....'   (II.195–96)

"Taken in by such stratagems, by the craft of perjured Sinon, and by his treachery, we believed . . . "

—combining the three damning terms that mark the first half of Book II.[3]

The patterning of words is quite important: the association of *arte* first with Pallas, then with the Greeks in general (*Pelasga*, 152), then specifically with Sinon (195) just before the appearance of the snakes sent obviously by Pallas. These words remind us that the war at hand is only too real. The impression is strengthened by omission: *fortis*, a

common word in the poem, is used only once in Book II, when
Aeneas calls the Trojans *"fortissima frustra/ pectora"* ("hearts
which are so brave in vain," 348). *Virtus,* similarly common, occurs
only twice in Book II, and like *fortis* is distinctly circumscribed:[4] in
one instance, it is submerged by the sense of helpless defeat:

> 'quondam etiam victis redit in praecordia virtus
> victoresque cadunt Danai.'   (II.367–68)

"Sometimes our courage revived, even though we were beaten, and the
conquering Greeks fell."

In the other, the usage is highly ambivalent; Coroebus cries,

> ' "dolus an virtus, quis in hoste requirat?" '   (390)

" 'Treachery or courage—where the enemy is concerned, who would
care?' "

The traits appropriate to heroic encounters can hardly apply here.
   The central symbol in the first part of the book is the Wooden
Horse, and the structure of this section is based on deception. But, as
the structure shows, this deception is strange and noteworthy:

   13–39   The Horse and the Greeks
      40–56   Laocoon
         57–198   Sinon and his tale
      199–233   Laocoon
   234–67   The Horse and the Greeks

Sinon's tale falls into three parts: an introduction developing the
enmity of Ulysses; his condemnation as a human sacrifice; and the expiatory offering of the Horse to Pallas. The central place given
human sacrifice may be highly significant; for, while the actual details are obviously false, there is no reason to doubt that the story is a
clever mixture of truth and falsehood. Similarly, we need not doubt
that the Horse was intended, in part at least, as expiatory offering.
The crucial point is the *possibility* of truth in Sinon's deception. This

is important for the plot and for the larger element of fate and divine power.

Sinon's tale is a tissue of truths and falsehoods woven around Ulysses, the arch-deceiver. The complex deception exfoliates into a large, disturbing rhythm of illusion. The nightmare of Troy could hardly stand a serious test for verisimilitude. It demands a willing suspension of disbelief and entry into areas beyond the natural. Thus reality is dislocated not so much by Sinon's tale as by its whole context; the dislocation remains significant in the later domestic scenes.

This dislocation, with its symbol in the Wooden Horse for Pallas, is highlighted in the verbal texture of the first one-third of Book II. A sense of doom pervades this section. Little happens, though there is much talk, by Laocoon, Priam, and Sinon. But the foreboding is sounded in the numerous derivations from *fa* -, the root of *fatum*. From the *infandum* of the narrator (3) to *fata* in Sinon's last line (196), words like *fas, fatale, fando,* and *fatur* interweave in a complex texture with the patterns of *ars, dolus,* and *insidiae* already noted. Developed here in unspeakable speech, the doom is then acted out in the next passage, the Laocoon episode.

Laocoon saw the danger most clearly. His arguments reveal his character and his patriotic heroism, as well as his feelings toward the Greeks:

> ' "aut hoc inclusi ligno occultantur Achivi,
> aut haec in nostros fabricata est machina muros,
> inspectura domos venturaque desuper urbi,
> aut aliquis latet error; equo ne credite, Teucri.
> quidquid id est, timeo Danaos et dona ferentis." '   (II.45—49)

" 'Either there are Greeks enclosed and hiding in this piece of wood; or it is an engine built to do harm to our walls—looking into our houses and threatening the city from its height; or there is some other trick concealed here. Trojans, do not trust that horse. Whatever it is, I fear the Greeks, even when they bear gifts.' "

It takes more than Sinon's art to keep the Trojans from seeing the logic and the sense in Laocoon's arguments. It would be so easy to have a look inside; indeed, Laocoon's spear crashing into the Horse's flank cleared the way. But they do not; and the fall of Laocoon and his failure are, in some ways, an epitome of this whole book. Laocoon shows strength and an unmitigating sense of conflict. He rejects as patently absurd the notion that the Greeks have gone, precisely because he is a warrior and a hero. But his heroism is rendered completely futile, like the spear shivering in the Horse's flank. Sinon's Greek-Palladian art leads the Trojans from wild hostility to interest and curiosity, and then sympathy, and finally complete credence. But it is not this that dooms Laocoon or the Trojans themselves. The *mens laeva* of the Trojans is a microcosm of the *fata deum* (54). The great irony, after all, is that Sinon wins them over by appeal to their *religio* and their *pietas divis* (154 f., 162 f.).

The relentless march of lines 199–227 makes inexorable the brutal, slow death of Laocoon. The whole passage is sculptural in its sharpness of detail and in the subtle symmetry of action and sound. In the simile (223 f.), the horrible bellowing of the wounded sacrificial bull emphasizes the fact that Laocoon was just then beginning a ritual act:

> 'sollemnis taurum ingentem mactabat ad aras.'   (II.202)

"He was solemnly sacrificing an enormous bull at the altar."

The details heighten the central horror: his death, accomplished during solemn sacrifice, is itself a violation of the sacrifice.

The most effective element is the sound, voicing the unspeakable. Here are the snakes, gliding over the water:

> 'pectora quorum inter fluctus arrecta iubaeque
> sanguineae superant undas; pars cetera pontum
> pone legit sinuatque immensa volumine terga.
> fit sonitus spumante salo; iamque arva tenebant
> ardentisque oculos suffecti sanguine et igni
> sibila lambebant linguis vibrantibus ora.'   (II.206–11)

"Their breasts rose erect above the sea foam and their blood-red crests towered over the waves; the rest slithered over the water, their backs arched in enormous coils. The sea foam crashed and roared. And now they reached the land, their blazing eyes tinged with blood and fire, and they licked their hissing mouths with shimmering tongues."

In the death, these sounds are mixed with the bellowing of the bull:

> 'ille simul manibus tendit divellere nodos
> perfusus sanie vittas atroque veneno,
> clamores simul horrendos ad sidera tollit:
> qualis mugitus, fugit cum saucius aram
> taurus et incertam excussit cervice securim.'   (II.220–24)

"At the same time, his hands tried to wrech the knots apart; his priestly headband was covered with blood and black venom; and all the time he shrieked horribly to the heavens, like the bellowing of a bull which is running, wounded, from the sacrificial altar, as it shakes off its neck the badly aimed axe."

These sounds, giving substance to the echoing *fatum,* embody the significance of Sinon's tale. They are heard again in the following lines:

> 'tum vero tremefacta novus per pectora cunctis
> insinuat pavor, et scelus expendisse merentem
> Laocoonta ferunt, sacrum qui cuspide robur
> laeserit et tergo sceleratam intorserit hastam.
> ducendum ad sedes simulacrum....'   (II.228–32)

"Then utter panic slipped into every fear-stricken heart; they agreed that Laocoon deserved to suffer for his crime—a man who had desecrated the sacred wood with his blade, who had twisted that accursed spear in its side. 'Lead the holy thing to the shrine. . . .'"

They spill over into the next passage, which describes the introduction of the Horse into Troy. The sensation of sound continues through the day and then into the night, with only that brief silence as the Greek fleet returns while Sinon opens the Horse:

> 'a Tenedo tacitae per amica silentia lunae
> litora nota petens....'   (II.255–56)

" [It came] from Tenedos, seeking the well-known shores, through the favorable silence of the hidden moon."

Grotesquely numinous, the sounds of the Laocoon death-passage are a comment on *fatum* and the fall of Troy.

As he narrates the tale, Aeneas is seeing again and reliving the whole experience. The art of Vergil is most subtle here. Aeneas's exclamations, which punctuate the narrative at several points, transcend conventional expressions of grief or anger; they arise from and hover about the center of his concern, the mystery-laden loss of his city. He participated in that by both action and inaction, and his own uncertainty lingers to trouble him. At the crucial moment when the Horse is brought into the city and the magic circle protecting Troy is broken, Aeneas's narrative reflects besetting puzzlement, puzzlement that indicates guilt as well as loss:

> 'dividimus muros et moenia pandimus urbis.
> accingunt omnes operi pedibusque rotarum
> subiciunt lapsus, et stuppea vincula collo
> intendunt: scandit fatalis machina muros
> feta armis. pueri circum innuptaeque puellae
> sacra canunt funemque manu contingere gaudent:
> illa subit mediaeque minans inlabitur urbi.
> o patria, o divum domus Ilium et incluta bello
> moenia Dardanidum!'   (II.234–42)

"We cut through the walls and lay bare the defenses of the city. All gird themselves for the task, placing rollers beneath the horse's hooves and tying lines of hemp around its neck. That fateful engine, pregnant with soldiery, mounts our walls. Boys and unwed girls sing hymns around it, happily touching the rope. The brute thing climbs on, then slides to rest, menacing, in the middle of the city. O fatherland, O Ilium, home of our gods, O Dardan walls so famous in war!"

He tells his hearers, without needing to, how he helped to throw open Troy, but then immediately the scene becomes again the object of painful observation.

Images of circles predominate as the *fated* and *fatal* Horse is brought in, pregnant with soldiery and escorted by virgins in a ritual celebrating the barren rape of Troy. The Horse, threatening and unwieldy, towers over the city as does the citadel of Pallas. In this rich context, the exclamation of Aeneas is essentially a vision of destruction and its elusive import.

The imagery of vision becomes important at this stage in the narrative. Laocoon was destroyed by serpents, an offering to Pallas; the serpents come to rest at her feet. Laocoon had seen too clearly as he plunged down from the citadel, *ardens* (41)—the word is echoed in the *ardentis oculos* (210) of the serpents. The other Trojans were blind: *improvida pectora* (200), *caeci furore* (244); the hopeless struggle of the *portarum vigiles* (266), the watchers of the gates, is described by Panthus: *"caeco Marte resistunt"* (335).[5]

But Panthus, the priest of Apollo, can be no more effective in his counsels than Cassandra, victim of Apollo, doomed not to be believed. Panthus sees clearly; his first words present apocalyptically the shape of things:

> ' "venit summa dies et ineluctabile tempus
> Dardaniae. fuimus Troes, fuit Ilium et ingens
> gloria Teucrorum; ferus omnia Iuppiter Argos
> transtulit." '   (II.324–27)

" 'The final day has come, the fatal hour for our Dardan land. We Trojans are no more; Ilium is no more, and the splendid glory of the Trojans. Savage Jupiter has given over everything to Argos.' "

Ferus Iuppiter powerfully conveys the traditional departure of the gods from a doomed city and their participation in its doom. Panthus dies shortly, unprotected by his holy state:

> 'nec te tua plurima, Panthu,
> labentem pietas nec Apollinis infula texit.'   (II.429–30)

"And you, Panthus—not all your holiness nor the headband of Apollo could save you from death."

The figure of Panthus symbolically parallels the figure of Hector, who comes in a dream vision to Aeneas (268 f.). The sight surprises Aeneas—the visible outline so pitifully repulsive and so different from that lingering image of Hector to which Aeneas instinctively turns. Aeneas's words are strikingly confused. He addresses Hector as if the fight is still going on; as if he has been expecting the dead hero to return and resume his place in the conflict; and yet as if remembering (naturally enough) the washed figure, cleansed of wounds and disfigurement and prepared for burial. Psychologically and symbolically, the mangled appearance of Hector is appropriate. It is what Aeneas would most readily recall, both as hero and as friend to Hector, and it suggests the present state of Troy, both as Aeneas knows it and as it actually is.

But Hector's words brush this aside:

> ' "heu fuge, nate dea, teque his" ait "eripe flammis.
> hostis habet muros; ruit alto a culmine Troia.
> sat patriae Priamoque datum: si Pergama dextra
> defendi possent, etiam hac defensa fuissent.
> sacra suosque tibi commendat Troia penatis;
> hos cape fatorum comites, his moenia quaere
> magna, pererrato statues quae denique ponto." '   (II.289–95)

"'Goddess-born, oh, flee, and save yourself from these flames,' he said. 'The enemy has captured the walls; Troy is falling from its height. You have given enough to Priam and your country. If Troy could have been saved at all, this right arm would have saved her. Troy entrusts to you her holy things and her home-gods: take them as the companions of your destiny, seek out the great city-walls which, at long last, you will establish for them when your sea journey is over.' "

The heroic age is dead, now is the time for other deeds. This massacre is the epitaph; go and found a new city. The Hector of wounds speaks these words: "Save yourself from the death of the old world." In Book IV, visitations of the future will prod Aeneas again toward the new world; the irony clearly is that, even as he narrates all this to Dido, Dido belongs spiritually to this old world, and that Aeneas ought to understand this, but doesn't.

The *aeternum ignem* Hector entrusts to Aeneas is unlike the fire Hector had cast on the Greek ships (276) or the flames now engulfing Troy. It symbolizes continuity and points to the new world that must replace the old. But Aeneas understands neither Hector's words nor his full action. Like Dido, he still—even at Carthage—sees

the destruction of Troy as another episode in the heroic life, more disastrous than most such episodes, but one whose effects could be repaired. The fact that Dido is inflamed by the very traits of *honos* and
virtus that link Aeneas to Troy is qualified by Aeneas's own continuing attachment to old Troy. The bare command to leave and the en-
joinder to save the Penates merely have the effect of keeping Aeneas
there. Psychologically, nothing could be so calculated to spur Aeneas
on to a last stand in defense of Priam and *patria* than Hector's words.
The grandeur and scope of Hector's prophetic counsel cannot compete
with the demands of the heroic instinct.

Aeneas climbs onto the roof and sees nothing, but he hears the
sounds of fiery destruction:

> 'in segetem veluti cum flamma furentibus Austris
> incidit, aut rapidus montano flumine torrens
> sternit agros, sternit sata laeta boumque labores
> praecipitisque trahit silvas: stupet inscius alto
> accipiens sonitum saxi de vertice pastor.'   (II.304–8)

"As when a fire, fanned by the wild south winds, sweeps through a cornfield, or a swift torrent sweeps across the fields from a mountain stream,
destroying the healthy crops, products of oxen's labors, and dragging
clumps of trees headlong; the shepherd, high up on a rock, is bewildered
by the noise he hears and not aware what it means."

The sounds lead to sight of a kind:

> 'tum vero manifesta fides, Danaumque patescunt
> insidiae.'   (II.309–10)

"Now the truth was manifest and the treachery of the Greeks was plain to
behold."

But this manifestation confirms neither the command nor the prophecy of Hector. The terrible force on Aeneas of *insidiae* here is conveyed by the prosody; the last word of its sentence, rushing to a close,
it is the first word of a new hexameter. It focuses Aeneas's reaction, a
reaction that does not seem different seven years later as he tells
about it. The imagery in the simile carries forward the suggestions

evoked earlier and reshapes them slightly; thus the *pastor* is ironically *inscius* of the import of the noise; *flamma* suggests the *flammis* that Hector urged Aeneas to escape; the flood may well suggest the *pontus* which Aeneas must cope with. In context, one meaning of this simile is prophetic, but it is a meaning Aeneas is hardly prepared to cope with.

Apprehending only the horror, Aeneas's full response is *arma:*

> 'arma amens capio; nec sat rationis in armis,
> sed glomerare manum bello et concurrere in arcem
> cum sociis ardent animi; furor iraque mentem
> praecipitat pulchrumque mori succurrit in armis.'   (II.314–17)

"My arms I madly snatch up, though there was no sense in taking up arms—except that my spirit was burning to rally some men for war and run up to the citadel with them. Fury and rage drive me headlong; my only thought was that it is glorious to die in battle."

The sentence is carefully wrought, its three balanced clauses focused and framed by the war cry of heroic enterprise: *arma ... armis.* But that response is fraught with the madness instinct in heroism, and with *ira,* a trait associated with Juno in the first book. Later, Turnus will waken from another dream in ways similar, and react much like this:

> arma amens fremit, arma toro tectisque requirit:
> saevit amor ferri et scelerata insania belli,
> ira super.   (VII.460–62)

Arms he roars for madly, arms he seeks by his bed and all through the house. Lust for steel rages in him, the accursed madness of war, and anger besides.

Panthus, carrying the *sacra* and leading his grandson, presents yet again Hector's command and underlines the immediacy of doom, but Aeneas plunges on, conscious only of absolute despair and driven by the *tristis Erinys.*

> ' "una salus victis nullam sperare salutem." '   (II.354)

" 'For the conquered, there is only one hope—and that is not to hope.' "

This clear call for death seems the only possible response to the Greek conquest. Aeneas leads the Trojans headlong into the charnel house; the night itself—"nox atra cava circumvolat umbra" (360) [6]— is and signifies death: "ubique pavor et plurima mortis imago" (369).

The disguise they adopt, urged by Coroebus, Cassandra's beloved, reflects their condition. They do drive some Greeks back to the ships, others to the Horse, as if to belie Hector's words. But the action, neither strategic nor heroic, is illusory: *"dolus an virtus...."* In the darkness, illusion distorts reality further; their ruse collapses when, trying to save Cassandra from Greek hands, they are attacked both by the Greeks in force and by their own countrymen. In the massacre, Coroebus goes down at the altar of Pallas (425).

The desperate ruse—an act of deception more ephemeral and irrelevant than the Greek deception (which it imitates: *"arma dabunt ipsi,"* 391)—is the last attempt to fight back. This phase is over; Aeneas, with Pelias and Iphitus—one old, one slowed by a wound —now witnesses the actual crumbling of Troy. There is a parody of resistance in the tower episode, an act more like self-destruction. The following lines present the palace of Priam being laid open.

Aeneas again becomes an observer; in effect, there is no more fighting. The Greeks are in charge—"immissi Danai et late loca milite complent" (495): the simile that follows compares the invaders to a raging river in flood and its devastation of fields and herds (*"evicit gurgite moles,"* 497). The occupation extends into the very heart of Priam's palace, marked by altar and laurel tree. Here is also the dynastic and imperial center of old Troy, represented by the promise of posterity in the numerous bridal chambers and by the pillars rich with spoils:

'quinquaginta illi thalami, spes ampla nepotum,
barbarico postes auro spoliisque superbi.'   (II.503–4)

Aeneas pauses as a climax approaches, then turns again to his audience; the break marked by *"Forsitan et Priami"* can mean nothing else. Then he relates the fall of Priam. This episode, climactic and symbolically central, is rich with drama, irony, and pathos. In Priam's

house, before his very eyes, is the reality Laocoon had foreseen: "medium in penetralibus hostem" (508); and the old man's response is as
futile as Aeneas's: "arma diu senior ... nequiquam" (509–10).
Aeneas sees Polites slaughtered in front of Priam; the butcher is Pyrrhus, son of Achilles: illusions of glorified heroism are shattered by
the horror and butchery. Priam compares Pyrrhus to the noble
Achilles he recalls:

> ' "at non ille, satum quo te mentiris, Achilles
> talis in hoste huit Priamo." '   (II.540–41)

The allusion to *Iliad* XXIV, while perhaps paying tribute to Homer, is
also an epilogue, the end to which even noble heroism inexorably
leads. Pyrrhus exults in savagery:

> ' "illi mea tristia facta
> degeneremque Neoptolemum narrare memento:
> nunc morere." '   (548–50)

" 'Be sure to tell my father about these shocking deeds of mine and how I
have disgraced him. Now die.' "

The vision has become one of harsh violence. In effect, this action
is beyond heroic prowess. Pyrrhus, associated by metaphor and simile
with the serpent, functions as an agent of Pallas. Pursuing and slaying Polites, he is *ardens* (*iam iamque manu ...,* 529–30); his
slaughter of Priam evokes the death of Laocoon:

> 'altaria ad ipsa trementem
> traxit et in multo lapsantem sanguine nati,
> implicuitque comam laeva, dextraque coruscum
> extulit ac lateri capulo tenus abdidit ensem.'   (II.550–53)

"Right up to the altar he dragged him [Priam], trembling and slipping
in the pool of his own son's blood; in his left hand he twisted Priam's
hair, while with his right he drew the flashing sword and buried it to the
hilt in his side."

Here, *implicuit* and *ensem* suggest the coiling and darting snake,
while *coruscum* echoes the first appearance of Pyrrhus:

'exsultat telis et luce coruscus aëna;
qualis ubi in lucem coluber mala gramina pastus,
frigida sub terra tumidum quem bruma tegebat,
nunc, positis novus exuviis nitidusque iuventa,
lubrica convolvit sublato pectore terga
arduus ad solem, et linguis micat ore trisulcis.'   (II.470–75)

"He exults in his armor, flashing with bronze; like a snake which has
spent a winter hidden under the ground, feeding on poisonous weeds,
but now it comes out into the daylight, sheds its old skin, and is new
and fresh in its youthfulness; raising its breast upward to the sun, it
rolls its coiling back and flickers its three-forked tongue."

For neither Polites nor Priam was the altar a protection; as Servius
remarked, "ostenditur latenter, nihil prodesse religionem" (*ad* 502).

All Troy falls as Priam dies; Aeneas quietly links the fate of the
king and the fate of the city, and both of these with the proud past.[7]
Then he concludes, in a rich, powerful, sudden image:

'iacet ingens litore truncus,
avulsumque umeris caput et sine nomine corpus.'   (II.557–58)

"His great trunk lies on the shore, the head torn from the shoulders, a
corpse without a name."

This image does not follow consistently, but its power and significance have nothing to do with such consistency. There is no surface
"justification" whatever here or elsewhere in the poem for the sudden
image. But Aeneas sees it thus: the *ingens truncus* (for the feeble old
man), the body on the shore, headless, nameless, just a Trojan corpse.
This image of Troy in ruin shows the strength of Aeneas's feeling better than any apostrophe could. It epitomizes the nightmare. The detached image, caught in the vision of Aeneas as he narrates, concentrates all the cumulative bitterness at fortune, fate, and the gods
which was expressed in text and reenforced in context. This is the *pietas* of the heavens; this is the enmity remarked on again and again.[8]
"*Dis aliter visum*" Aeneas comments on the death of Phipeus, "iustissimus unus/ qui fuit in Teucris et servantissimus aequi" (426 f.): as
in the case of Panthus, his justice, goodness, and loyalty meant nothing to the gods. Again, Aeneas sees himself moved to fight *numine*

divum (336). At the turning point of their escapade in Greek disguise, he cries,

'Heu nihil invitis fas quemquam fidere divis!'   (II.402)

"When the gods are against you, you are forbidden even to trust them."

But it remains for Venus to present the full measure of divine enmity. She comes to Aeneas as he is about to slay Helen, for he considers her the cause of the whole disaster: *"Troiae et patriae communis Erinys"* (573). Venus intervenes, in a flood of light; the death of Helen would be beside the point (and, perhaps, a blow at Venus herself). Neither Helen nor Paris is truly guilty; the cause is elsewhere: *"divum inclementia, divum"* (602).

What follows is one of the most powerful scenes in the poem, embodying the *Troiana fortuna*. Venus removes the cloud of humanity from Aeneas's vision and shows him the reality beyond warriors, Greeks, dead Priam, and cowering Helen.

' "hic, ubi disiectas moles avulsaque saxis
saxa vides, mixtoque undantem pulvere fumum,
Neptunus muros magnoque emota tridenti
fundamenta quatit totamque a sedibus urbem
eruit. hic Iuno Scaeas saevissima portas
prima tenet sociumque furens a navibus agmen
ferro accincta vocat.
iam summas arces Tritonia, respice, Pallas
insedit nimbo effulgens et Gorgone saeva.
ipse pater Danais animos virisque secundas
sufficit, ipse deos in Dardana suscitat arma." '   (II.608–18)

" 'There, where you see masses of masonry scattered, stones wrenched from stones, and smoke and dust billowing upwards together, there Neptune himself is at work shattering the walls and the foundations dislodged by his mighty trident, and tearing the whole city from its site. Over there stands Juno most furious in the van before the Scaean Gates, and with her sword at her side and violence in her heart she is calling the marching ranks of her friends from the Greek ships. Look around! On the citadel's height sits Tritonian Pallas, light glaring from her garment of cloud and the merciless Gorgon-head on her breast. Even the Supreme Father gives renewed courage, strength and victory to the Greeks, and inspires the gods themselves to fight against the arms of Troy.' " (Tr. Knight)[9]

Venus presents this apocalyptic vision with an assumed calm, a quasi-didactic air. First, Neptune, tearing down the walls he himself had built: the irony of *Neptunia Troia* (625) is bitter. Then, Juno, *saevissima* and *furens,* spurring on the Greeks to slaughter and plunder and destruction. Next, Pallas, effulgent, atop her citadel. Finally, *ipse pater.* Having presented the vision, Venus adds two hasty lines and vanishes.

The four gods play their roles with a vengeance. Neptune, sober and businesslike, rocks the city at its very foundations. Jupiter, at the other end, is *hominum sator atque deorum;* vitalizing and sustaining the Greeks, he leads on the gods also. Juno, at the legendary Scaean Gates, is her fierce and destructive self; the unusual detail of *ferro accincta* underscores the destructiveness. But Pallas, in contrast to the fiery Juno, *occupies* the citadel. Less frenetic than Juno, she shows the same power and control that Juno herself noted at the beginning of the poem (1.39 f.).

Each of the three sites chosen here—walls, gates, and citadel —is important both strategically and mythologically. The citadel is the most crucial, both as the refuge for the serpents that destroyed Laocoon and any chance of averting the success of the Wooden Horse, and as the abode of Pallas for whom the Horse was a gift. We cannot rearrange the hierarchy of the gods, but we must recognize that the figure of Pallas stands central, embodying in a serpentlike image the ineluctable quality of Fate. Pallas suggests form, Juno energy; Pallas knowledge, Juno passion and will; Pallas vision, Juno force and fury. These are not categorical distinctions, but the polarity between form and energy, knowledge and will, marks Book II and much of the poem. Juno, not Pallas, is the implacable foe of Aeneas and his Trojan remnant.

Venus's abrupt disappearance plunges Aeneas back into the heavy night and its now phantasmagoric atmosphere:

> 'apparent dirae facies inimicaque Troiae
> numina magna deum.' (II.622–23)

Neptunian Troy falls like a great tree in utter and final collapse. Image piles upon image, almost paralyzing the hero.

At his father's house, Aeneas finds Anchises in despair—

appropriately, for Anchises vividly figures the wrath of the gods, the
fire of Troy, and the ancient guilt that propelled Troy to this destruction. Witness of its earlier fall, victim of Jove's envious thunderbolt,
he now is immobile (*fixusque manebat; sedibus haeret in isdem*), a
grim parody of Pallas. He has seen Troy ruined once before, has lived
through one captivity. "Bid me farewell and leave this dead body":

> ' "satis una superque
> vidimus excidia et captae superavimus urbi.
> sic o sic positum adfati discedite corpus." '   (II.642–44)

Aeneas counters by describing the fate of Priam and Polites: Pyrrhus
is an expert at butchering sons and fathers [10]—

> ' "iamque aderit multo Priami de sanguine Pyrrhus,
> natum ante ora patris, patrem qui obtruncat ad aras." '   (II.662–63)

But anger, fear, and piety avail nothing. Anchises will not be moved
until heaven has twice signaled its benediction. That double benediction will be less sanction for Aeneas's concern than emblem of the
destined enterprise of Anchises' posterity. The signs mark clearly what
commentators overlook; though it is Aeneas who shoulders the
human burdens of the future, that future carries a price and reward
beyond his knowing. Anchises will be saved for his role, during the
wanderings between Troy and Carthage, as guardian of the enterprise.
     Anchises knows already what Aeneas has barely begun to learn
—that the gods, not the Greeks, are destroying Troy; that *fatum*
transcends human endeavors and ignores human *pietas*. Behind this
querulous old man, bumbling and pathetic in his overbearing dignity
during the wanderings, is the figure marked by Venus, by Jupiter, and
by Fate, and removed beyond the ordinary rules of life. He is detached from Troy and from common humanity in a way Aeneas cannot comprehend. Once again, Aeneas responds pitifully and futilely:

> 'rursus in arma feror mortemque miserrimus opto....
> "arma, viri, ferte arma; vocat lux ultima victos.
> .... numquam omnes hodie moriemur inulti." '   (II.655, 668, 670)

"Once again I am impelled to fight, yearning only for death in my misery. . . . 'Arms, men, bring me my arms! The final hour summons the vanquished. . . . We shall not all die this day unavenged!' "

The lust for vengeance coheres with his earlier desire for death. Here, both impulses are rendered more futile than the intent to take unholy vengeance on Venus's Helen. In each case, the divine hand restrains him.

The gods send two signs. First, the tongues of flame over the head of little Ascanius; the boy is marked, as Anchises perceives triumphantly, for great things. Then, in confirmation, there is a crash of thunder on the left, and a star shoots down from the sky, blazing a bright path through the darkness. They watch it hurtle over the rooftops and finally bury itself in the woods on Mount Ida, while all around the ground smokes with sulphurous fumes:

> 'intonuit laevum, et de caelo lapsa per umbras
> stella facem ducens multa cum luce cucurrit.
> illam summa super labentem culmina tecti
> cernimus Idaea claram se condere silva
> signantemque vias; tum longo limite sulcus
> dat lucem et late circum loca sulphure fumant.'   (II.693–98)

Servius explains the whole portent allegorically, seeing it as a précis of what is to come (including the death of Anchises: "*ex fumo autem mors Anchisae....*"). But, in total context, the ordering control of fire and light contrasts with the raging energy of the fires in the city. Dispatched by the same Jupiter who is overseeing destruction, the sign embodies the destructive power of the gods even while it presents, in its clarity, a vision of order.

The granted signs, both sharply visual, seem incongruous in their juxtaposition with the vision of Troy's destruction.[11] But that juxtaposition is relevant. In the first place, Aeneas does not react to the signs as signs. Rather, his reaction is almost automatic, part of the original momentum generated by the death of Priam and Polites, and recharged by Venus. In the second place, Aeneas could not absorb the fundamental meanings of his vision. So he takes his father on his back, pinpoints a landmark outside the walls as common goal by di-

verse paths, and sets out. Aeneas acts almost as if divine guidance is
not with them; he lays out a plan and follows it through; having lost
Creusa he rushes back into the city and patently invites death. The
pattern is dominated by the guiding presence of the gods and by
Aeneas's utter disregard for that presence.

His shouldering of Anchises is an act of instinctive humanity rich
with symbolism:

> ' "ipse subibo umeris nec me labor iste gravabit;
> quo res cumque cadent, unum et commune periclum,
> una salus ambobus erit." '   (II.708–10)

" 'I will carry you on my shoulders; this burden will not weigh me down.
However things turn out, we shall share one common danger, one common safety.' "

As he leads his family out, he is tender and fearful and alive to the
immediate perils. Every breeze, every sound increases his anxiety for
the safety of his family:

> 'nunc omnes terrent aurae, sonus excitat omnis
> suspensum et pariter comitique onerique timentem.'   (II.728–29)

We have here the feeling of the man whose first massive doses of ad-
renalin have drained off, who is limp but determined to go on.

Ths loss of Creusa shocks him the way the first sounds of Troy's destruction had shocked him, and he reacts as he did then, though the
context is changed:

> 'quem non incusavi amens hominumque deorumque,
> aut quid in eversa vidi crudelius urbe?'   (II.745–46)

Furiously blaming gods and men for this final horror that is more bitter than anything he had seen so far, he arms himself and rushes back
into the city. He is "resolved to reenact the whole adventure, to retrace his whole course through Troy, to face all those perils over
again":

'ipse urbem repeto et cingor fulgentibus armis.
stat casus renovare omnis omnemque reverti
per Troiam et rursus caput obiectare periclis.'   (II.749–51)

Within this cyclical texture, the next scene offers a microcosm of
Book II, leading to the pathetic last meeting with Creusa. The loss of
Troy is epitomized in the loss of Creusa:

'male numen amicum/confusam eripuit mentem.'   (735–36)
'coniunx ... erepta Creusa.'   (738)

Aeneas returns, retracing his steps and plunging back [12] to *muros,
limina,* and then his own house, now in flames; then to the home of
Creusa (as Austin suggests); thence to Priam's palace and the citadel,
where, at the sanctuary of Juno, Ulysses and Phoenix guard the
booty:

'huc undique Troia gaza
incensis erepta adytis, mensaeque deorum
crateresque auro solidi, captivaque vestis
congeritur. pueri et pavidae longo ordine matres
stant circum.'   (II.763–67)

"Here, the plunder from all over Troy was piled, looted from the burning
temples—tables for the divine feasts, bowls of solid gold, looted vest-
ments. Children and mothers were standing in a long line, shivering with
fear."

Here again are the *"pueri circum innuptaeque puellae"* (238), the
figure of Ulysses from Sinon's story. But now there is also a special
terror—*"simul ipsa silentia terrent"* (755), and then the hysteria:
"implevi clamore vias" and the echoes of his voice in the hauntingly
empty and desolate streets.

Creusa appears to him, an apparition that is *infelix* to Aeneas
(772). The numinous and sudden quality of the apparition is emphasized by sound and repetition:

'infelix simulacrum atque ipsius umbra Creusae
visa mihi ante oculos et nota maior imago.'   (II.772–73)

Creusa is *simulacrum, umbra,* and *nota maior imago;* the specter is
visa and *ante oculos.*[13] Not a word is superfluous; nor is any in the
next line, breathless and rushing—"obstipui, steteruntque comae et
vox faucibus haesit"—in contrast to the gentleness and calm of
Creusa:

> 'tum sic adfari et curas his demere dictis.'   (775)

Her memorable words begin and end tenderly: "o dulcis coniunx.
... iamque vale et nati serva communis amorem" (777, 789). But
counterpointed are the hard facts. These things are willed by the
gods, she says; they have taken me from you. There is some comfort
in her fate: she is not in Greek hands:

> ' "sed me magna deum genetrix his detinet oris." '   (788)

" 'Rather, the great Mother of the gods is keeping me on these shores.' "

As for himself:

> ' "longa tibi exsilia et vastum maris aequor arandum,
> et terram Hesperiam venies, ubi Lydius arva
> inter opima virum leni fluit agmine Thybris:
> illic res laetae regnumque et regia coniunx
> parta tibi; lacrimas dilectae pelle Creusae." '   (II.780–84)

" 'For you, there is long exile and a vast expanse of ocean to be furrowed.
Then you will come to the western land, where Lydian Tiber flows with
gentle current between the rich meadows of good men. There, prosperity
and a kingdom and a royal bride await you. Put by those tears for the
Creusa whom you loved.' "

The prophecy and the toil incumbent on Aeneas go somewhat further
than Hector's words; but, as then, he cannot take in the significance.
The imagery suggests earth and its richness, and the metaphor in
parta includes also birth, but the primary and operative meaning here
is approximately that suggested by Conington: "of things that are virtually, though not actually realized." The same forces that have taken
Creusa from Aeneas have taken her significance from his life, the sig-

nificance of wife and family, of labor and childbirth, of the human enterprise precisely as human enterprise. The word *dilectae* is not casually used; it is stronger and deeper than *carus* or most other words for human affection.

Aeneas attempts to embrace Creusa, even as she vanishes ("tenuisque recessit in auras"):

> 'ter conatus ibi collo dare bracchia circum;
> ter frustra comprensa manus effugit imago,
> par levibus ventis volucrique simillima somno.'   (II.792–94)

"Three times, then, I tried to put my arms around her neck; but three times my grasp was in vain, the shade slipped through my hands, like the light breezes or most like a fleeting dream."

As commentators note, the act is almost a stylized convention. But there is nothing of imitation here. The act springs from Aeneas's humanity, forcing itself out; more than "Don't go," it tries to deny or even reject what has been said, to turn away from the realities forced on him throughout this night. The nightmare now becomes reality, for when he tries to embrace Creusa—and, in her, Troy—she vanishes like a dream.

The same tension underlies the concluding passage. It is masterly in the climactic silence and in the release it provides. But there are telling contrasts and details. The freshly prophesied destiny loses its luster in the face of this *miserabile vulgus.* In the final lines, Aeneas sees the morning star rising above Ida, and sees also the burning city behind him. Whatever brightness or hope there might be in that star, it is dimmed by that other light in the sky: "nec spes opis ulla dabatur" (803).

Aeneas takes charge here, almost by default, but the charge itself should not be mistakenly termed leadership. "Cessi, et sublato montis genitore petivi" (804). The word *cessi* contains much. It means, in the first place, that he turned away, literally and figuratively, from the smoldering ashes of Troy; it means that he gave way, ceased fretting about what had happened—ceased, that is, for the moment; it means that he left his fatherland, as Servius remarks. But all the meanings are qualified by the final image, Aeneas carrying Anchises toward the mountains: an "action . . . almost mechanical. . . . The sight we have of Aeneas is that of a weary, defeated man carrying his father to exile" (Austin).

Infandum: the tale has been unbearably hard to tell. Mythic, ahistoric, the Night of Troy was, for Aeneas, a fourfold nightmare: a nightmare of deception by an enemy incredibly shrewd and clever; a nightmare of illusion and blurred reality; a nightmare of fate and divine intervention; and, less specifically, a nightmare in which a world and a way of life passed—not Troy itself so much as the heroic life, the life of glory and war and self-reliance, the world of honor and instinct and courage. The nightmare here is compounded partly of the shrill exposure of that life, partly of its obstinate continuance. Though dead, it will not stay buried; much of the struggle throughout the poem is to come to terms with the new life. Aeneas will. In the end, he will have knowledge. But that knowledge, releasing him from the nightmare of Troy and bringing him hope in the future—as at the end of Book VIII or his speech to Ascanius in Book XII—will bring no lasting joy.

CHAPTER THREE

THE WANDERER

> 'Postquam res Asiae Priamique evertere gentem
> immeritam visum superis, ceciditque superbum
> Ilium et omnis humo fumat Neptunia Troia,
> diversa exsilia et desertas quaerere terras
> auguriis agimur divum, classemque sub ipsa
> Antandro et Phrygiae molimur montibus Idae,
> incerti quo fata ferant, ubi sistere detur,
> contrahimusque viros. vix prima inceperat aestas
> et pater Anchises dare fatis vela iubebat,
> litora cum patriae lacrimans portusque relinquo
> et campos ubi Troia fuit. feror exsul in altum
> cum sociis natoque penatibus et magnis dis.'   (III.1–12)

"After the gods had seen fit to destroy Priam's Asian empire and his people, though innocent, and proud Ilium had fallen and the whole of Neptunian Troy lay in smoking ruins, we were scattered into exile by signs
from the gods, forced to explore deserted regions. Below Antandros, in
the foothills of Phrygian Ida, we labored to build a fleet, uncertain where
the fates would lead us or where we should be allowed to settle, and we
gathered our company together. The summer had just begun, when father
Anchises bade us spread our sails before the fates. In tears I left the shores
of my fatherland, the harbor, and the plains where Troy had been. I was
borne away, an exile on the deep, with my comrades and my son, with
the household gods and our great gods."

Less conspicuous than other opening passages (*Postquam* seems almost prosaic), these lines suggest both the adventures and the implications of Book III. The narrative structure moves from the general to

the strikingly particular, from the summary of their fall and condition
to the description of the building of the fleet ("we"), and then the departure, marked by the picture of Aeneas, virtually helpless, being
carried to sea: *feror exsul in altum.* Imagery and texture enrich
meaning. The shape of line 3, bracketed by *Ilium* and *Troia,* and the
ironic echoes of Book II ("Neptunus muros magnoque emota
tridenti/ fundamenta quatit," II.610; "Ilium et ex imo verti Neptunia Troia," 625) indicate the meaning of the elusive words in line 4.
Diversa exsilia and *desertas* have given commentators needless headaches; the words are connotative, suggesting the uncertainty and
vagueness in the gods' auguries. The Trojans will make wrong starts,
run into dead ends, be generally subject to the wrongheadedness both
divine and human that pervaded Book II. The distant exiles and deserted lands are vague, as vague as the uncertain fates which they trust
only under duress. So *molimur* (6), which usually would connote an
organized, deliberate effort on behalf of a large enterprise, is undercut
by *incerti* (7). The unusual rhythm of *dare fatis* in line 9 and its use
are quite ominous. The images are also important: for example, smoking Troy, the smoke continuing, lasting, though the night of ruin was
short. *Fumat* may be intended to suggest how *Troia* will remain with
Aeneas during his journeys. The uncertainty underlined in the passage gives *feror exsul in altum* the tone and impact of *maria omnia
circum* (I.32).

Beyond the uncertainty are the obsessive and mysterious burden of
Troy and its *fortuna* (16), the conflict of humanity and destiny, the
human dimension of the divine intrusion. Thematically, the passage
hinges on the varied faces of the divine manifested here; *visum su-
peris* suggests the recurrent *vis superum* as well as *dis aliter visum*
(II.428), and defines the vision of Troy's destruction by the gods; *incerti quo fata ferant* explains *auguriis agimur divum* and is reinforced
by *dare fatis vela.* Whatever the precise theological and historical
meaning of *magnis dis* (about which scholars have despaired), the
phrase is heavy with ambivalence and unresolved doubt.

Aeneas makes some of this explicit in his prayer. He asks Apollo to
give them a true home, a lasting city, a second Troy for this weary
remnant that survived Achilles and the Greeks:

' "da propriam, Thymbraee, domum, da moenia fessis
et genus et mansuram urbem; serva altera Troiae
Pergama, reliquias Danaum atque immitis Achilli.
quem sequimur? quove ire iubes? ubi ponere sedes?
da, pater, augurium atque animis inlabere nostris." '   (III.85–89)

"Who is to guide us? Where do you bid us go, where settle? O father, give us a sign, and take possession of our hearts." The prayer bespeaks eloquently the sense of exile, their weariness, the vagueness of their goal. Aeneas refers to *altera Troiae Pergama,* but not with any certainty. He concludes the prayer by begging Apollo *animis inlabere nostris.*

Apollo's response is cloaked in mystery:

' "Dardanidae duri, quae vos a stirpe parentum
prima tulit tellus, eadem vos ubere laeto
accipiet reduces. antiquam exquirite matrem.
hic domus Aeneae cunctis dominabitur oris
et nati natorum et qui nascentur ab illis." '   (III.94–98)

" 'Long-suffering sons of Dardanus, the very land which first gave birth to your stock, that same land will take you back to her abundant breast. Seek out your ancient mother. Here shall the house of Aeneas rule, from shore to shore—and your sons' sons and all their descendants.' "

Neither here nor later, when the Penates explain more in detail, can we perceive the kind of mandate that clarifies and justifies everything, and that gives Aeneas the resources to rise above the problems and vexations which the gods see fit to impose on him. The promise of *ubere laeto* and the details provided by the Penates may be encouraging, but the promises contrast grimly with their sea-tossed experience. Poetic reality here resides not unilaterally in the words of Apollo and the Penates but in the continuing totality of action, character, symbol, texture, and tone. For instance, the pathetic blindness of Anchises as he misinterprets Apollo and the bitter episodes that follow swiftly —plague, storm, Harpies.

As presented in Book III, the voyage from Troy to Carthage is part of the larger journey of Aeneas that dominates the greater part of the

poem. But these two kinds of journey are not to be separated; such
would be the same kind of uncritical procedure whereby readers discover "intended" meanings (about Augustan Rome, for instance) or
allegories which are plainly not there. Nor can we separate the goal
from the journey itself; just as the journey is qualified by its starting
point—the divine destruction of Troy—so its end gives meaning
to the journey and itself receives meaning.

Aeneas encountering the power of Juno and the intrigues of Venus
in I, Aeneas slipping into passivity and the delusion of making a city
in IV, Aeneas presiding over the games, Aeneas entering into the life
of Hades, Aeneas attempting a rapprochement with Latinus, Aeneas
retiring to Arcadia away from the war and the actual issues he must
face—these are some of the episodes in his journey, which bears
only a superficial resemblance to the Homeric paradigm, whether
considered in *Odyssey* IX–XII or in the allegories of the whole
poem. The time-honored observations about the Odyssean and Iliadic
halves of the *Aeneid* do credit to neither Homer nor Vergil and ignore the realities of both poems. Vergil's hero travels a difficult and
often senseless journey into the unknown; that he places upon his
journey the attributes of his past experience does not make it any less
unknown and sometimes only compounds his troubles. What guidance Aeneas receives tells him less than it tells the reader, who sees
Jupiter and Juno closer up than Aeneas ever can and who may easily
confuse himself with the hero.

The journeys of Odysseus and Aeneas are radically different in
character. Odysseus's journey occupies only a small (though admit-
tedly very popular) part of the *Odyssey,* a part that some critics consider irrelevant to the major action, the reestablishing of order in Ithaca. Odysseus travels, without evident purpose, generally outside the
world of men; in the last stages from Ogygia to Ithaca by way of
Scheria, Odysseus goes from the unknown to the known, from the
mysterious to the market place. Aeneas's journey—even that part
which is supposedly "imitative" of Homer—occupies a substantial
part of the *Aeneid.* If we ignore the spurious notion of imitation, the
larger journey of Aeneas occupies most of the poem. It has a purpose,
though part of the journey is discovering what that purpose might be.
In virtually every stage, Aeneas goes from the known to the un-

known. From the first action (the departure of the Greeks from Troy) to the last action (the slaying of that last hero Turnus), every stage is not only relevant to the purpose but is part of the purpose.

If the paradigm of Odysseus's journeys, fantastical or allegorical, does apply to the *Aeneid* (to Book III or to the poem as a whole), it does so in ambivalent ways—by contrast, by irony, by paradox, and by evocation. Thus, for instance, one may compare the strong certainty of Odysseus's statements to Alcinous about going home to Aeneas's statements to Dido in Book I: Odysseus is definite and clear and confident; he is now really on the way home; Aeneas is hopeful, uncertain, a little vague about where he is going; his fall into Dido's arms belies any certainty or clarity about either his goal or his desire to reach it. Odysseus begins the narrative of his wanderings with this warm certainty of getting home; Aeneas begins III with the heavy image of still-smoking Troy. Compare too the departing words of Odysseus to Calypso and those of Aeneas to Dido. Only if one looks at such scenes as these in context, as part of a whole poem, not as detached episodes, can the relationship between Homer and Vergil be fruitfully discussed.

During his wanderings, the cities of Troy and Carthage set off for Aeneas the uncertainties of sea and land. These cities seem massive in their reality; both hold Aeneas tenaciously, with bonds he finds hard to dissolve. Carthage eventually is subsumed under Troy, of which it is a kind of shadow; and old Troy is bitterly present in his wanderings in Books III, V, and VI, and throughout the Italian experience. Troy obsesses and besets him in Carthage, in Sicily, and in Hades; the attempts to stop at Crete, in Sicily, and in Hades are lingering expressions of what he lost at Troy and cannot regain. Each of his brief stops is, like Troy, a point marked no return. Each of these is part of his experience of the journey.

The story of Achaemenides, toward the end of III, returns Aeneas briefly to Troy. He hears again Sinon talking and sees again in the background the resourceful, elusive, ever-Greek figure of Ulysses, now *infelix*. Achaemenides' story is, of course, true, while Sinon's tale interwove strains of falsehood and truth. But there are many points of contact. Sinon and Achaemenides are both partially invented by Vergil. In both episodes, *clementia* and celestial signs operate. Achaemenides throwing himself on Anchises' pity is again Sinon beseeching Priam; the dire apparition of the Cyclops confirms Achaemenides' story as the snakes confirmed Sinon's. Ulysses, named in both cases as the agent of the speaker's fate, becomes here an indirect object of *clementia* in the repeated epithet *infelicis* (613, 691).[1] The tables have been turned; this hint of compassion contrasts sharply with the fear and hatred of Greeks expressed earlier in III. But this too is part of the Troy-obsession and the slow break from Troy, corollary to the painfully slow growth of knowledge. And at Carthage it becomes clear that (*a*) the final break is still far off and (*b*) Aeneas is only vaguely aware of the need to make that break.

The dominant episodes of III—Polydorus, the Cretan settlement, Epirus and Andromache—are variations on *Troia*. Polydorus embodies an important aspect of the old heroic world—the nexus between power, opulence, greed, and treachery; his message to Aeneas parallels the first half of Hector's statement in II.[2] The bizarre manifestation of Polydorus parodies the Fall of Troy. The Cretan episode hinges on Anchises' interpretation of Apollo's words. Anchises identifies the ancient mother as Crete, the *locus* of *mons Idaeus* and the *gentis cunabula nostrae*. From Crete, says Anchises (*"si rite audita recordor"*), came their great ancestor Teucer and the cult of Cybele. Led by Anchises, the Trojans settle at Crete. In lines recalling the description of Carthage, Aeneas tells of his high hopes, the happy activity of the Trojans, the beginnings of an organized society:

> 'ergo avidus muros optatae molior urbis
>
>   . . . .
>
> conubiis arvisque novis operata iuventus;
> iura domosque dabam.'   (III.132, 136–37)

But the settlement proves abortive, as a mysterious plague suddenly decimates the fields and the crops.

That terror, however, leads to a highpoint of III, the one occasion when Aeneas is granted by the Penates a relatively clear definition of the future:

' "est locus, Hesperiam Grai cognomine dicunt,
terra antiqua, potens armis atque ubere glaebae;
Oenotri coluere viri; nunc fama minores
Italiam dixisse ducis de nomine gentem:
hae nobis propriae sedes, hinc Dardanus ortus...." '   (III.163—67)

" 'There is a place—the Greeks call it Hesperia—an ancient land,
mighty in arms and possessed of a rich soil. The Oenotrians colonized it;
now it is said that their descendants have named it Italy, after one of
their leaders. Here is our true home: here was Dardanus born. . . .' "

Amid the clarity, there is the paradox that Aeneas must journey far
back into the *past,* a past which Cassandra had clearly seen but which
Anchises somehow could not see. She had often told him about it,
using these very names—"saepe Hesperiam, saepe Itala regna"—
but who would ever believe Cassandra? For Anchises, past and future are Troy, both the Troy he has known and the Troy he imagines,
as later in Hades he refurbishes it with his posterity. Here, the episode
contributes to the pattern of uncertainty—hopes dashed, frightful
warnings, mistakes, misunderstanding, and confusion.

At Epirus, the longest episode in III (294—505), Aeneas witnesses, and then leaves behind, a replica of Troy, with its own Xanthus and the Scaean gate:

'parvam Troiam simulataque magnis
Pergama et arentem Xanthi cognomine rivum
agnosco Scaeaeque amplector limina portae.'   (III.349—51)

While there are hints of a new stage in history—Priam's Helenus
reigning in Greek cities (295)—Andromache forces the return to
the past, where she lives with Troy and its context of fate, illusion,
and deception. Her reality is the false Simois, the empty tomb of Hector, and her own hovering between life and death. This also Aeneas
feels deeply; about to depart, he says:

' "vivite felices, quibus est fortuna peracta
iam sua: nos alia ex aliis in fata vocamur.
vobis parta quies: nullum maris aequor arandum,

arva neque Ausoniae semper cedentia retro
quaerenda.'' '   (III.493–97)

" 'Live happily, you whose fortune has run its course. As for us, we are
summoned ever onwards from fate to fate. You have won your rest; you
have no expanse of sea to plough, no receding fields of Ausonia to seek.' "

Dignity, courage, and resolve cannot obscure the pathetic uncertainty.
While he knows this *effigies* is a false city, like other false cities in III,
his journey to the true city is bounded by the juxtaposed *fortuna* and
fata. Aeneas's present reality is the *aequor arandum* and the *arva semper cedentia retro,* recurring phrases that fill out the expanding symbolic contrasts between firm land and turbulent sea. Though his land
experiences have reflected the experiences at sea, Aeneas thinks
mainly in terms of civil and domestic stability; the metaphor in *arva*
shows his feeling.

Miniature Troy and its primary exponent Andromache bracket the
discourse of Helenus. There is deliberate counterpoint here, even to
the details of Helenus and Andromache addressing Anchises and Ascanius (472 f.; naturally: honoring Priam and Astyanax). Helenus's
discourse is different from the prophecies of Jupiter in I, of Creusa and
Hector in II, or of Apollo in III; Helenus deals with specific problems
Aeneas must face, obstacles he must overcome, rites and ceremonies
he must perform, signs and oracles he must understand, all in the
near future. The counterpoint operates between miniature Troy, the
shadow life, on the one hand, and the practical exigencies of the journey on the other.

Helenus deals with various categories of perils and troubles:
human perils (396 f., the Greeks); natural and preternatural (384 f.)
and monstrous (410–32); and the divine peril (433–40, Juno).
He offers professional advice on ceremonies and on dealing with the
Sibyl. The advice fits within the over-all structure, for it implies the
objective divine order, its detachment from the human order. In the
divine order, sacrilege is sacrilege however it occurs; as at Sophocles'
Thebes, motive does not affect the exercise of divine power. The gods'
thoughts are not those of men: Pallas repudiates the Trojan women,
Jove ignores the prayers of some suppliants, Neptune destroys the city
he built.

In this context, it may seem surprising that Juno receives little attention in Book III. But Aeneas is simply narrating; there is much he cannot know. Any reference to Juno thus becomes quite crucial. Helenus gives her special attention. First, he juxtaposes her with the monstrous Scylla. Further, he departs from the pattern he had followed, of presenting the peril and its precise elements, and then giving his advice; here, he replaces the specifics of the peril with a solemn prologue about its enormity:

> ' "praeterea, si qua est Heleno prudentia vati,
> si qua fides, animum si veris implet Apollo,
> unum illud tibi, nate dea, proque omnibus unum
> praedicam et repetens iterumque iterumque monebo,
> Iunonis magnae primum prece numen adora,
> Iunoni cane vota libens dominamque potentem
> supplicibus supera donis: sic denique victor
> Trinacria finis Italos mittere relicta." '   (III.433–40)

" 'Further, if I have any foresight as a prophet, if I deserve any trust at all, if Apollo inspires my spirit with truth, O goddess-born, one thing I solemnly tell you, one thing over and above all the rest, I would repeat this warning again and again and again: You must worship first of all the godhead of mighty Juno with prayer; to Juno you must offer your vows willingly; that great deity you must win over with the offerings of supplication. Do this, and at last you will leave Sicily behind you and reach the borders of Italy.' "

By means of triple repetitions and a threefold rhythm throughout, he heightens the disquieting force of his words. Juno, the supernatural peril, is the most dangerous of all, but Helenus is silent about what she does, significantly revealing less than he knows.

The clarity and order of the details throughout the bulk of the discourse do not rule out mystery. While he defines what Aeneas must do, Helenus only implies the basis for his actions. But the fate that pervades the texture of his discourse transcends these metaphysical perils; this mysterious power Helenus can only hint at. Thus, at one point, he refers to the higher sanctions for Aeneas's divinely ordained journey, but elaborates this only by obscure references to Jupiter and fate, and to the cyclical yet fixed order of the world:

     ' "(nam te maioribus ire per altum
auspiciis manifesta fides, sic fata deum rex
sortitur volvitque vices, is vertitur ordo)..." '   (III.374–76)

Thus, too, he explains that some things the Parcae keep from him,
other things Juno forbids him to reveal:

     ' "prohibent nam cetera Parcae
scire Helenum farique vetat Saturnia Iuno." '   (III.379–80)

Nonetheless, somehow the fates will find a way and Apollo will help,
if he is called on:

     ' "fata viam invenient aderitque vocatus Apollo." '   (III.395)

All in all, Italy, though near, lies yet far off, at the end of a long voyage, by a way that is not a way:

     ' "longa procul longis via dividit invia terris." '   (III.383)

Not a rhetorical display, this last line connotes distance that is neither
physical nor measurable, and adds another dimension to *aequor arandum.* Helenus gives Aeneas no reason to believe that the fact of destiny means an easy or assured achievement of destiny. *Fata viam
invenient:* in Aeneas's experience thus far, these words can only mean
that perils lie ahead and that he will have to find some resources with
which to meet them.

    Priest of Apollo, Helenus is one of Apollo's agents in Book III.
While there is reason to connect Apollo with Troy and with the divinity of colonizers, neither is primary here. Rather, he is the mysterious figure, aloof, ambivalent, and often harmful. Like Fate itself,
Apollo impinging on humanity is at once creative and destructive.
The ambivalence is notable here in significant details and in the
structure of Helenus's discourse. The discourse does not alternate between hope and trouble, success and failure; rather, the promised
peace and order are premised on violence, chaos, and frustration, and
the great goddess-daughter of Saturn is cast as the Enemy. Both literally and symbolically, then, the destruction of Troy and the ashes of

Troy are prime requisites for the quest and the achievement. He who loses his life will find it.

While Helenus's discourse, then, is less grand and less charged emotionally than other prophecies in the poem, it bears important relevance to the dramatic movement of the poem. Within the framework of mystery, it outlines Aeneas's journey from Epirus to Cumae, presenting the exigencies of present reality to Aeneas and conveying something of the quality of that reality.

In this episode, Aeneas occupies the central place; Helenus's words are for his ears only, not those of Anchises. Elsewhere in the wanderings of Book III, however, Anchises is the central figure. This may be due to Aeneas's modesty as he tells his tale to Dido, but there are other elements as well. Aeneas defers constantly to his father, even when Anchises does not simply seize the initiative; Aeneas emphasizes his own weariness. These details argue that Anchises kept to the forefront as long as he was alive. The figure of Anchises is important enough in III, V, and VI to warrant some close examination. For one thing, he is significantly associated with Troy, particularly by way of Laomedon; for another, the relationship between Anchises and his son has important bearing on Aeneas's destiny.

At the point in Book II where Anchises enters the story, a great deal of momentum has been generated. For Aeneas the command to leave was inexorable, harshly defined by many voices and actions— Hector, Panthus, and Cassandra; the Greek victories and the desecrations, particularly in the deaths of Priam and Polites; Venus and the vision of the gods destroying Troy. But Anchises *refuses* to leave; his profound pessimism seeks death. Aware of what is really happening, he fatalistically wants to escape it by not running. Only oblivion can measure this final expression of the divine anger.

The startling omen of the tongues of flame does not suffice; he must have a second sign, partly because he does not understand the first, partly because he does. But only the Jovian blast of thunder on the left followed by the comet radiantly pointing to a new future persuades Anchises. The sequence of actions is important. While his pessimism is like Aeneas's first reaction, it springs from different sources. Aeneas, though certain of the Greek victory, judged it a *nefas* to desert the dying homeland. For Anchises, patriotism is irrelevant; the homeland and his life have become a *nefas*. But the double sign, illuminating the future of Anchises and his grandson Ascanius, shows that his guilt is also irrelevant. The cause of his pessimism is gone. Thus the image of Aeneas at the end of II—bearing his father on his shoulders out of Troy and toward the mountains bathed in the glow of the morning star—is misread if seen simply as conventional *pietas*. Though Aeneas formulates the plan and the route, Anchises is in charge. He directs the flight; panicky, he reroutes Aeneas, and they lose Creusa.[3] Weak as he is, he exercises the power but not the responsibility of leadership. This is a phenomenon not rare in the *Aeneid*—weakness exerting power from its perch on the shoulders of others.

Anchises embodies the past—the Trojan and Laomedontian heritage, the divine family, the *vis superum*—and also the future; his presence in the flight symbolizes how intricately past and future are intertwined. Anchises provides more headaches than help for Aeneas, but he is the historical pivot of the enterprise. While Aeneas, still bewildered and stupefied by the divine action on Troy, acts humanly and out of human motivation, Anchises is caught up in a complex of history, power, and the will of the gods.

In the journeys of Book III, Anchises is dominant. Aeneas's leadership (a role he accepted reluctantly) is subject always to Anchises' regency; the distinction is not idle, for it corresponds to the level of reality on which each operates. In III, Aeneas gradually learns of his new destiny; later events manifest his imperfect understanding and imperfect commitment. At any rate, while proceeding as best he can, he acts primarily as agent for the fleeing Trojans. He has a father and a son, and a horde of followers, for whom he must bear responsibility. Anchises plays a different role—reprieved by the gods, he exercises power. In the early stages, he exercises it too easily and even irresponsibly.

The opening lines of III highlight Anchises' authority: "pater Anchises ... iubebat,/ litora ... patriae ... relinquo." At Thrace, the grotesque affair is referred to Anchises for decision (*primumque parentem,* 58). In both cases, Aeneas seems incapable of action. In the next episode, Anchises interprets Apollo's prophecy, hitting quickly

upon Crete and proffering that decision with a haste remarkably unlike his reluctance at Troy. But the basis for decision is dubious: "tum
genitor veterum volvens monimenta virorum ..." (102). Pondering
the ancient traditions of his people, Anchises completely misses the
clue in Apollo's first words, *Dardanidae duri* (94). His own experience and knowledge force him to understand the *antiquam matrem*
(96) as the matrix of known Troy. The point is that Anchises misinterprets because he believes his family's fortune dependent on a duplication of past Troy. (It is a view he clings to after death: the preconceptions implicit here will be reasserted in Hades, when he shows
Aeneas selected aspects of their future.) When the plague decimates
them at Crete, Anchises facilely advises that they return to the oracle,
beg forgiveness, and seek clearer counsel.

At this point, Aeneas comes, briefly, stage-center. The Penates appear to him, in a vision whose authenticity he underlines, insisting it
was not a dream. Addressing him, perhaps pointedly, as "tu," they explain Apollo's words, thus rendering superfluous the trip that Anchises proposed. When Aeneas relates this to Anchises, with superb
delicacy and tact, Anchises is untroubled by his costly error. He offers
a bleak confirmation—Cassandra prophesied precisely this—but,
remaining totally insensitive to the irony here (Cassandra had *often*
told him of Hesperia: *saepe*), he excuses himself by writing her off:[4]

> ' "aut quem tum vates Cassandra moveret?
> cedamus Phoebo et moniti meliora sequamur." '   (III.187–88)

" 'But at that time, who would be influenced by Cassandra's prophecies?
Let us yield to Apollo and, now that we have been warned, follow the
better course.' "

From this point on, Anchises' authority is modified. At the Stro-
phades, he is spokesman only in the prayer after the Harpies' strange
prophecy (265 f.); it is Aeneas who leads the fight against them (234 f.).
At Epirus, Helenus delivers his discourse to Aeneas; Anchises and
Ascanius receive the obeisances, the gifts, and the ceremonial of departure. In this latter incident, the pattern resembles the earlier pattern,
beginning with the signs at Troy. What has changed is that Aeneas
has assumed full responsibility for the safety and welfare of his people. Anchises speaks for them again when they sight Italy, utters a

command as they pass Scylla and Charybdis, and assumes the Priam-role when they encounter Achaemenides, but he is not again in a po-sition to impose his decisions.

While I would hardly deny the nexus of *pietas* between Aeneas and Anchises, or argue that their relationship is modeled on that be-tween Agamemnon and Achilles in the *Iliad,* I think we must recog-nize that at least one aspect of Aeneas's *pietas* is his endurance of An-chises. This emerges clearly in Book III, no matter how hard Aeneas the narrator strives, as he evidently does, to present Anchises in the best possible light. It seems obvious that Aeneas, arrived at Dido's palace, has little to thank either father or mother for. Venus's two no-table actions thus far have been her revelation of the true horror of Troy and her rejection of Aeneas in the middle of his troubles. She is, indeed, true to form: the impassioned goddess could hardly be ex-pected to show compassion. Whatever his authority, Anchises was al-ways an integral part of the wanderings. With his death, the charac-ter of the journey seems to change. However, the symbolism of Aeneas carrying Anchises continues, in new contexts. Note that the entire narrative of II and III is framed by *pater Aeneas.* But the An-chises section of II begins with *cari genitoris imago* (II.560) and ends with *sublato genitore* (II.804); while III begins with *pater Anchises* (9) and ends with *genitorem Anchisen* and *pater optime* (709–10). The distinction between *pater,* the figure of authority, and *genitor,* the begetter, applies here. Thus, the ambiguous *meta* (III.714).[5]

Anchises dies in Sicily (where later another replica of Troy will be established). About this final episode before the storm and Carthage, Aeneas says little. Perhaps the death of his father made this Sicilian interlude too painful to recall; perhaps also the narrative has gone long enough. The subdued apostrophe to his father brings his whole narrative to a quiet, ambiguous close; it is almost a private outcry overheard:

> 'heu, genitorem, omnis curae casusque levamen,
> amitto Anchisen. hic me, pater optime, fessum
> deseris, heu, tantis nequiquam erepte periclis!'   (III.709–11)

"Alas, I lost my father Anchises, the solace in every misfortune and trou-ble. Here, best of fathers, you forsook me in my weariness—you, res-cued from so many perils, for nothing."

The recurrent *fessum* [6] and the tone of *deseris* and *nequiquam* indicate his numbness and weariness. He does not refer to the nearly disastrous storm (which Dido has already heard of anyway). But he does recognize that he has reached an important turning point. His concluding lines, while offering a gracious compliment to Dido, are also obscure:

'hic labor extremus, longarum haec meta viarum.
hinc me digressum vestris deus appulit oris.'   (III.714–15)

"This was my last blow, this was the turning point of these long journeys. From there, I was setting out when a god drove me onto your coasts."

The force Anchises brings to bear after his death is neither negligible nor substantially different. The reference to him in IV will be discussed shortly. In V to VIII, Vergil moves the action into the new world. Books V and VI are heavy with the old Troy and its major exponent here, Anchises. In VI, Anchises shows his family's future; in VIII, mother Venus presents the shield of victory, which, like Elysium, bears the images of the family's dynasties.

At Carthage, trying to explain to Dido why he must leave, Aeneas says:

'me patris Anchisae, quotiens umentibus umbris
nox operit terras, quotiens astra ignea surgunt,
admonet in somnis et turbida terret imago;
me puer Ascanius capitisque iniuria cari,
quem regno Hesperiae fraudo et fatalibus arvis.'   (IV.351–55)

"As often as night covers the earth with its dewy shades, as often as the stars rising light the skies, the troubled figure of my father Anchises warns me in my dreams and frightens me. My son Ascanius also—the wrong I am doing to his dear self, whom I am defrauding of his kingdom in Hesperia and the fated fields."

In itself or taken together with the following account of Mercury's appearance, the argument is not impressive. But the vivid terror in Aeneas's description of those nightly visitations is striking. The structure of the first three lines sharpens them; the clause is periodic, *patris Anchisae* holding us until its subject appears in the last word, *imago*.

The darkness of night and the clarity of the fiery stars parallel the two phrases of line 353. The next two lines are linked to these three by syntax (the verbs of 353 are understood) and by rhythm: *me patris Anchisae* ..., so that the interests of Anchises and the interests of Ascanius weigh equally on Aeneas's heart. The final line echoes 350:

> 'et nos fas extera quaerere regna.'

"It is no sin for us to seek a kingdom in a foreign country."

Here, *fas* is taken to mean "no sin" (Austin). But that hardly seems adequate. It is not a question of rightness—this, Dido, is what you are doing; why can't we? The "rightness" of it is irrelevant. The chiastic echo of *fas* and *regna* in *regno* and *fatalibus* (355) suggests quite otherwise. *Fas* means the will of the gods, as opposed to human will and human desire. This large reality epitomizes Aeneas's speech; he is struggling painfully to make it clear both to Dido and to himself. His journey is on behalf of a future which the gods have pledged to Anchises and Ascanius. He *must* go, at whatever cost to Dido and to himself. Any other course was ruled out at the moment that Mercury exposed him to the truth about himself. Some of the cost to Aeneas is suggested in Book v.

Leaving Carthage, Aeneas is again beset by weariness. In both Books III and v, the word *fessus* often describes Aeneas's condition either specifically or as reflecting the whole Trojan condition. The word occurs thirty-two times in the poem, but half of these occurrences are in III and v. In III, for instance, the weariness implied in the opening lines is stated explicitly in the landing at Delos: "haec fessos tuto placidissima portu / accipit" (78 f.), and in Aeneas's prayer to Apollo: "da moenia fessis / ... et mansuram urbem" (85 f.). When they sight Actium,

> 'hunc petimus fessi et parvae succedimus urbi;
> ancora de prora iacitur, stant litore puppes.'   (III.276–77)

"We made for it, weary, and reached the small city. The anchors were thrown from the prow, the ships stood at the shore."

Here, as in the earlier illustrations, the image of the desired city reinforces the suggested feeling, as do contrasting words like *petimus*
and *stant*. After leaving Helenus, they pause briefly on the way to
Italy and rest briefly—"fessos sopor inrigat artus" (511)—until
Palinurus summons them back to their ships. At dawn they see
Italy for the first time and see also the ambivalent omen of the four
white horses, *bellum ... spes et pacis*.

The most striking occurrence of the word comes, of course, in the
apostrophe to Anchises: "hic me, pater optime, fessum/deseris" (710 f.).
Its force depends on the cumulative effect of the variations on the
motif of uncertainty. Aeneas's outcry implies more than the loss of a
staff on which to lean (*curae levamen*); it conveys also his sense that
the enterprise has lost its meaning: *"heu tantis nequiquam erepte
periclis!"* Seen retrospectively as the result of his entire experience,
from the Wooden Horse to the storm, this weariness betrays his vulnerable condition on landing at Carthage. That landing scene, in Book
I, begins with *Defessi Aeneadae* (157) and ends with another description of the Trojans as *fessi rerum* (178). Central to it is the
famous description of the harbor, womblike, recessed and secluded,
withdrawn from the strenuous activity of the open sea—a place where
tired ships could pause, without need even for cable or anchor:

> est in secessu longo locus: insula portum
> efficit obiectu laterum, quibus omnis ab alto
> frangitur inque sinus scindit sese unda reductos.
> . . . .
> ... hic fessas non vincula navis
> ulla tenent, unco non alligat ancora morsu.   (I.159–61, 168–69)

All of this is relevant when, at the beginning of Book v, the Trojans are forced off course by a storm. Both ships and men are described as weary (29, 41); the condition, less physical than emotional,
applies particularly to Aeneas. Later on, Aeneas is urged by Nautes,
the sailor nearly anonymous, to leave behind those who are overcome
by weariness, mostly the women (*tot vada fessis,* 615). Sick of the sea
and the endless journeys, they have been begging for a home: "urbem
orant, taedet pelagi perferre laborem" (617). Nautes' advice is quite
specific. Aeneas should leave some Trojans with Acestes, especially

those who are fully disheartened—the old men, the women exhausted by the sea (*fessas aequore matres*, 715), the timid, and the
frail. For them, Nautes says:

> 'his habeant terris sine moenia fessi;
> urbem appellabunt permisso nomine Acestam.'   (v.717–18)

"Let these weary ones have their city right here; if Acestes agrees, they
will call this city by his name, Acesta."

This eminently practical advice transcends practicality, as Nautes
himself knows. He is privy to the secrets of the other world, for Tritonian Pallas herself has instructed him: "unum Tritonia Pallas/
quem docuit multa ... arte" (v.704–5). He reminds Aeneas that
he is not his own man, and that the troubles fostered by both fate and
fortune must be met with stern resolve:

> 'nate dea, quo fata trahunt retrahuntque sequamur;
> quidquid erit, superanda omnis fortuna ferendo est.'   (v.709–10)

"Goddess-born, let us follow wherever the fates lead us and lead again.
Whatever happens, we can conquer fortune only by enduring it."

One implication certainly of Nautes' advice is that men must not in-
quire too deeply into the ways of the gods; their *ira* and the *fatorum
ordo* are sometimes indistinguishable (706–7).

Characterizing the sea-weariness of Aeneas and his Trojans, this
rich though minor motif implies the elusiveness of the enemy.
Aeneas's uncertainty arises from the *ordo fatorum* and the *ira deum;*
neither can be easily dissociated from the other, whether at Troy, in
the wanderings, in the storm, or at Carthage. Here is, if you will, the
quiet at the eye of the hurricane. Later on, in the war in Italy, Aeneas
shows few such symptoms; even "weariness" is never associated with
him. Not that he has been perfected in his heroic mission; at this
point, we can only say that the enemy becomes more distinct, better
defined, thus perhaps more manageable. Why and how remain also to
be seen. Aeneas is slowly learning the nature of reality even while he
resists such knowledge.

After the exertions of will to which Mercury goaded him, and perhaps after the shame and remorse consequent on his moment of truth in Book IV, Aeneas does exhibit firmness in Book V. In the context of uncertain weariness, this firmness is hardly a mindless strength or a power that penetrates very deep. Forced to land in Sicily again and make yet another stop before the dreaded and desired arrival that is to mean Hades, he puts a good face on it; to his *Dardanidae magni* he says,

> 'iamque dies, nisi fallor, adest, quem semper acerbum,
> semper honoratum (sic di voluistis) habebo.'   (v.49–50)

"Now, unless I am mistaken, the day has come which I will always count bitter and always honored—such was your will, gods."

The hint of bitterness remains only a hint, both in the speech and in the subsequent games. Here, the emphasis is on *honoratum,* while in the elaborate funeral games on the ninth day, the emphasis is on the fullness of celebration.

During the games, Aeneas is confidently in charge. He reflects the unrestrained pleasure of the Trojans engaged in contests of brawn and skill, though he does not himself participate. He dispenses prizes with a prudent largesse that heads off some incipient crises. Like a wise father he handles the crises adroitly, soothing ruffled feelings and preventing frictions from becoming serious.

The boatrace and the footrace are lively, even humorous and touching at times. Vergil's artistry in manipulating detail and incident and in exploiting the human qualities of the events is superb but unobtrusive. In the detail of Gyas chucking Menoetes into the water (172 f.) or of Nisus blocking Salius (335 f.), he adds color to athletic excitement and thoroughly humanizes the convention.

The primary characteristic of the first two contests is heroic energy. In their way, these games are innocent tributes to the past. Aeneas presides over them as celebrant of the rites in honor of dead Anchises; Vergil celebrates them as a tribute, delicately conceived, to an older, seemingly simpler world. Not the world where the best man wins —in the footrace, the best man definitely does *not* win—but the

world where heroism, whatever the outcome, was not complicated by
the hiatus between divine order and human morality. Like many
other passages, the climax of the boatrace, totally Vergilian, sounds
Homeric:

> tum vero ingeminat clamor cunctique sequentem
> instigant studiis, resonatque fragoribus aether.
> hi proprium decus et partum indignantur honorem
> ni teneant, vitamque volunt pro laude pacisci;
> hos successus alit: possunt, quia posse videntur.   (v.227–31)

Now the din redoubled; the spectators all urged on the pursuer; the sky
resounded with their cries. One crew was angered by the fear that they
might lose the prize which they thought already won, and they were willing to sacrifice their very lives for glory. The other crew was heartened by
their success: they could do it because they believed they could.

The boxing match and the archery contest assume different proportions. In each, interest is heightened by size, by atmosphere, by the
unusual and the unexpected. But neither has quite the air of heroic
excitement or the athletic vigor the two races had. The two boxers,
Dares and Entellus, are drawn larger than life in extraordinary passages which never seem as lengthy as they are. The match proper is
quickly ended, but it is highly effective because of the careful preparation and the unexpected aftermath. Throughout, our interest is engaged by the two contestants, superhuman figures of vast strength,
whose origins seem surely a distant world or the legendary past. As
Williams suggests (pp. 116 f.), Vergil gave this episode a mythic
cast in order to distance the bout suitably. Perhaps for the reason
which Williams offers, Vergil's distaste for such bloody affairs, but
perhaps for other reasons too.

The episode has a distinctly ritual tone. Entellus (a kinsman of
Aeneas) and Dares clearly have more at stake than the winning of a
prize. Some of the details are overt allusions to the story of Troy—
particularly the notable similes. In one simile, Dares is compared to
an invading general (*celsam oppugnat qui molibus urbem,* 439), who
tries in every way to conquer his enemy. Entellus is the city under
siege; earlier he was described as *membris et mole valens* (431 f.),

and the word *molibus* (439) has, as Servius suggested, two meanings
syntactically, either siege engines or the ramparts of the city. Dares,
on the other hand, is *pedum melior motu fretusque iuventa* (430).
Entellus is old and indigenous, while Dares, the younger man, is the
newcomer. In 449–50, Entellus falling to earth is compared to a
great tree crashing: the simile recalls the crashing tree in
II.626–31.

The pattern is almost allegorical, Entellus representing Troy, and
Dares Greece. Entellus rises to crush Dares (perhaps prophetic of the
Trojans' future). But the allegorical pattern is unnecessary. The paradigm of the besieged, falling, and rising hero-and-city suggests the cycles of rise and fall. It reenacts Troy to some degree, but with willed
change: the victory of Entellus is also his last victory.

Occasionally, the narrative transcends its matter. Passages like the
following might be part of a battle in war:

> at non tardatus casu neque territus heros
> acrior ad pugnam redit ac vim suscitat ira;
> tum pudor incendit viris et conscia virtus,
> praecipitemque Daren ardens agit aequore toto
> nunc dextra ingeminans ictus, nunc ille sinistra.   (v.453–57)

But the hero [Entellus], not slowed or unnerved by his fall, went back
more fiercely to the fight, his violence aroused by rage. His shame, plus
his confidence in his own courage, kindled his strength; blazing with fury,
he drove Dares headlong across the field, battering him now with his
right and now with his left.

This could well describe a conflict to the death. In fact, it almost is
one, and *pater Aeneas* has to step in and stop it. We recall also that
Entellus was goaded into the fight by Acestes, who called him, among
other things, *"heroum quondam fortissime frustra"* (389). When Entellus exits, he does so with the grandiose flourish of the great hero
who has made his splendid comeback and now can fade:

> 'nate dea, vosque haec' inquit 'cognoscite, Teucri,
> et mihi quae fuerint iuvenali in corpore vires
> et qua servetis revocatum a morte Dareta.'   (v.474–76)

"Goddess-born and all you Trojans, learn now what strength of body I had when I was young, and from what death you have rescued Dares, now safe."

Acestes taunted Entellus also with the sarcastic reminder that his goddess-born master Eryx used to be the pride of Sicily: *"magister / nequiquam memoratus."* At the end, Entellus pointedly offers sacrifice to Eryx:

> 'hanc tibi, Eryx, meliorem animam pro morte Daretis
> persolvo; hic victor caestus artemque repono.'   (v.483—84)

It is emphasized that the victim, a bullock, is sacrificed vicariously (*pro*) for Dares—a symbolic sacrifice ending a symbolic ritual. Now, Entellus can put away his gloves and close his career.

The sum of these motifs is a kind of staged tribute to the superb, though fading, world of heroism. The whole action of the first three games offers detached but warm tribute to the past, detached because the games are self-contained, there is no ulterior effect so far, they exist in a well-defined world of their own.

The pace of narrative changes at this point. The archery contest and the Game of Troy may follow in order, but they distinctly lack the self-containment visible so far, their design differs from that of the earlier games, and there is no clear end to them. Both the archery contest and the Game of Troy are much shorter than the other three events. Extraordinary and nonathletic elements occupy a good portion of the narrative—the phenomenon of the flaming arrow, which comes *after* the contest is technically over, and the excursus on the later development of the Game of Troy. Even while Ascanius is riding on his horse as leader of the Trojan youth in their display, word comes of the burning of the ships, and we realize with a shock that that burning was simultaneous with the archery contest and the pageant.

Clearly, any consideration of these two games must keep in view the effective conclusion of the funeral ceremonies—the outbursts of the Iris-led Trojan women at the shore and the burning of the ships. The flaming arrow, while it may be linked to the fiery omens of Book II, is surely linked also with the burning of the ships. In the sequence of events, the center of narrative moves from the games proper to other Trojan activities (the women at the shore) and other activities (Juno and Iris), and relocates on the beach.

In the archery episode, some confusion develops when the dove-target is accidentally lost and Acestes impulsively and self-assertively (*pater,* 521) shoots at empty space. The arrow bursts into flame. Seizing on this, Aeneas, with fine tact, recognizes Acestes' act of assertion and presents him a precious bowl from among the personal treasures of Anchises:

> 'sume pater; nam te voluit rex magnus Olympi
> talibus auspiciis exsortem ducere honores.'   (v.533–34)

"Father, take this. The great king of Olympus has willed, as these signs manifest, that you should be distinguished in the winning of honors." [7]

Thus, Aeneas both limits the possibilities of mystery here and effectively restores order.

The Trojan Game reflects the order imposed by Aeneas's will. Planned as the climax of the ceremony, this display is marked by admirable design and symmetry. The symmetry is brought out even in narrative, which moves unobtrusively from the youths themselves to the audience and the effect of the display on them (*veterumque agnoscunt ora parentum,* 576), and finally to the historical excursus. The similes both express and make ambiguous this order and design, particularly the labyrinth simile:

> ut quondam Creta fertur Labyrinthus in alta
> parietibus textum caecis iter ancipitemque
> mille viis habuisse dolum, qua signa sequendi
> frangeret indeprensus et inremeabilis error: (v.588–91)

It was like the Labyrinth of old in mountainous Crete, which was fabled to have a path weaving between blind walls, a maze treacherous with its thousand alleys; so that no one could find the clues to retrace his way.

The labyrinth is not a simple natural phenomenon. Its details do not function as illustration or ornament. The words—*textum, caecis, dolum*—suggest far more than the intricate organization of the labyrinth; they connote deception, blindness, and frustration. The last two words—*inremeabilis error*—climax a masterful line in which rhythm expresses "monotony and sameness," the long words convey "the feeling of being lost in an interminable maze" (Williams). *Inremeabilis* suggests sea-travel. Once crossed, the sea cannot be recrossed; *error* of course enlarges that meaning, in its obvious connection with the Trojans' wanderings.[8]

The labyrinth suggests order and design transcending human order; thus the illusion, the blindness, and the frustration. This is one of those points at which we are permitted to glimpse the intersection of the human and the superhuman. The auctorial excursus on the later history of the Game of Troy—spoken in a *social* voice that is rare in the poem—can hardly be taken, then, as indicating purely historical relevance for the *Ludus*.[9] Any judgment that the author "intends" in the concluding lines to buoy the reader with confidence for Aeneas's enterprise is surely undermined by the simile of the labyrinth. The labyrinth cannot be ignored. And what is happening simultaneously on the beach cannot be ignored either.

The episode of the burning of the ships (604–99) abruptly ends the funeral ceremonies, turning the splendid symmetry of the pageant into a scrambling disorder. Whatever relief from tension the games had offered now fades abruptly: *Fortuna fidem mutata novavit* (604). *Fides* here must mean, among other things, the hope contained in the celebrations: the easier feelings during the interlude, the absence of pressure. But even in the old world, such activities were prey to the mutations of *Fortuna;* here, Saturnian Juno manipulates such *Fortuna* for her own ends. Her ancient, abiding enmity pressing her, Juno dispatches Iris, who comes unseen along her rainbow (*per mille coloribus arcum,* 609). The rainbow recalls the simile used for the serpent at Anchises' tomb, the serpent whose meaning Aeneas could not then understand (88 f.).

The Trojan matrons are bewailing *amissum Anchisen* (614), *as if* that loss and their personal grief are the same thing. The absence of Anchises seems causally related to their troubles; not *Fatum* but *Fortuna*—an aspect of *Fatum*—underlies their weariness, as

Iris-Beroe exclaims: "o gens/ infelix, cui te exitio Fortuna reservat?" (624 f.). This combined yearning for Anchises and for rest is exploited by Iris-Beroe, in words which parody Aeneas's own:

> 'quis prohibet muros iacere et dare civibus urbem?
> o patria et rapti nequiquam ex hoste penates,
> nullane iam Troiae dicentur moenia? nusquam
> Hectoreos amnis, Xanthum et Simoenta, videbo?'   (v.631–34)

"Who stops us from laying our walls here and giving our people a city? O fatherland, O home-gods, rescued from the enemy in vain, shall no walls ever again be called walls of Troy? Am I never to see a Xanthus and a Simois, the rivers of Hector?"

And when they hesitate, Iris overawes (*dea*) and panics them, again with the ambivalent rainbow:

> ingentemque fuga secuit sub nubibus arcum.   (658)

The result is possession, and havoc, until Ascanius comes from the interrupted games (*belli simulacra*). They do serious damage, and all the heroic strength and prowess (*vires heroum*, 684) manifested in the games are inadequate.

Aeneas cries out to the gods; the formulaic words do not obscure his deep bitterness:

> 'Iuppiter omnipotens, si nondum exosus ad unum
> Troianos, si quid pietas antiqua labores
> respicit humanos, da flammam evadere classi
> nunc, pater, et tenuis Teucrum res eripe leto.
> vel tu, quod superest, infesto fulmine morti,
> si mereor, demitte tuaque hic obrue dextra.'   (v.687–92)

"Almighty Jove, if you do not yet hate the Trojans one and all, if ancient piety has any regard for men's sufferings, permit our fleet to escape this fire now, O Father, and save the frail hopes of the Trojans from destruction! Or else, if this is what I deserve, blast this remnant with your lightning and destroy me right here by your own hand."

It is a harsh and desperate outburst, belying the confidence he professed and displayed during the games. Jupiter sends a storm that puts out the fire, but Aeneas's misery lingers: *At pater Aeneas...*

> pectore curas
> mutabat versans, Siculisne resideret arvis
> oblitus fatorum, Italasne capesseret oras.   (v.701–3)

But father Aeneas . . . turned over his cares in his breast, vacillating—should he forget the fates and settle down here in Sicily, or should he set out for the Italian shore?

—and the advice given him by Nautes (discussed earlier) is not wholly relevant, in its practical details, to his feelings. Thus, having received the advice, he is torn even more by every kind of anxiety:

> Talibus incensus dictis senioris amici
> tum vero in curas animo diducitur omnis.   (v.719–20)

The bitterness clearly goes back to the beginning of v, and to the Carthage episode. In retrospect, the words at Anchises' tomb gain meaning: Aeneas addresses

> '...recepti
> nequiquam cineres animaeque umbraeque paternae.
> non licuit finis Italos fataliaque arva
> nec tecum Ausonium, quicumque est, quaerere Thybrim.'
> (v.80–83)

". . . ashes recovered in vain, and the spirit and shade of my father. It was not granted that I should have you with me in my quest for the Italian boundaries or the destined fields or Ausonian Tiber, wherever that is."

Nequiquam, echoing III.711 ("tantis nequiquam erepte periclis"), is inseparable from *recepti.* The rescue of Anchises was futile, because all it amounted to was moving his remains (*cineres*) from burning Troy to Sicily.[10] At the same time, Aeneas feels Anchises' death as both a personal failure and something that complicates all his own problems, for the old man was pivotal to the whole undertaking, yet debarred from it.

The night after the burning of the ships, Anchises appears to Aeneas (721 f.). In the economy of the supernatural, the apparition is not Anchises' shade but merely an image (*facies,* 722) of that shade, apparently sent by Jupiter (*caelo delapsa*); but these puzzling distinctions have no meaning for Aeneas. His father's words are unusually affectionate:

> 'nate, mihi vita quondam, dum vita manebat,
> care magis, nate, Iliacis exercite fatis....'   (v.724–25)

"My son, once dearer to me than life itself, while life remained, my son, heavily burdened by the fates of Ilium. . . ."

The rest of the discourse, however, is dominated by the other world, including the description of Nautes' counsels as *pulcherrima* (728)—they are, of course, since they conform to the rigid but unfathomable requirements of the divine—and Anchises' parting words, reflecting the other world's inexorable rules. These details surround the ghostly counsels:

>   'Ditis ...
> infernas accede domos et Averna per alta
> congressus pete, nate, meos. non me impia namque
> Tartara habent, tristes umbrae, sed amoena piorum
> concilia Elysiumque colo.'   (v.731–35)

"You must enter the infernal world of Dis, cross deep Avernus, and come to meet me, my son. I am not confined in damned Tartarus or among the mourning spirits; rather, I dwell in Elysium among the happy throngs of the good."

Presumably Aeneas takes in most of this, but his immediate spontaneous reaction is another pathetic attempt at human contact; as the apparition dissolves like a wisp of smoke, he tries to embrace it, just as he tried to embrace Creusa's shade and as he wished to touch the fleeting Venus in Book I:

> 'quo deinde ruis? quo proripis?...
> quem fugis? aut quis te nostris complexibus arcet?'   (v.741–42)

"Where do you rush? Why such haste? Whom do you flee? Who bars you from my embrace?"

The orderly ritual that follows allays emotional excitement, and the surface becomes calm once more. But the underlying problems have merely been deferred.

The next few days are days of controlled activity and accomplishment. Acestes agrees to the city and Aeneas lays it out, in a manner inevitably recalling the building of Carthage in I and the settlement of Crete in III. The nine-day period celebrating the founding of this city parallels the nine-day period in honor of Anchises. Then Aeneas and his diminished band leave behind yet another replica of Troy, *"hoc Ilium et haec loca Troiam ..."* (756).

Again, the scene then shifts abruptly to Venus and Neptune. Venus complains to Neptune about Juno's implacable hatred. Recalling the former trouble, she again characterizes *Iunonis gravis ira* (781), but this time, her references to Troy and its trouble are surprising:

> 'non media de gente Phrygum exedisse nefandis
> urbem odiis satis est nec poenam traxe per omnem
> reliquias Troiae: cineres atque ossa peremptae
> insequitur.'   (v.785–88)

"It is not enough for her unspeakable hatred that she has devoured the Phrygian city from the midst of its people, or that she has dragged the remnant of Troy through punishments of every kind; she is persecuting the very ashes and bones of the ruined city."

The *cineres atque ossa* of destroyed Troy is a startling hyperbole. However, the sense of annihilation was implicit in Aeneas's outburst to Jupiter and recurs (VI.62) in Aeneas's prayer to Apollo. It is implicit too in the characteristically Trojan establishment that Aeneas leaves behind at every stage of his journey.

On his side, Saturnian Neptune extracts a price, for whatever reason. In his speech, he goes out of his way to assert his power, echoing Juno's own assertions. Unlike Juno, he holds no grudge against Aeneas himself. He reminds Venus that he had saved Aeneas once during the war by hiding him in a cloud (*"nube cava rapui"*)—and

this at a time when he was himself bent on destroying the very walls
he himself had built:

> 'cuperem cum vertere ab imo
> structa meis manibus periurae moenia Troiae.'   (v.810–11)

He promises Venus that Aeneas will reach Avernus safely, but there
is a price:

> 'unus erit tantum amissum quem gurgite quaeres;
> unum pro multis dabitur caput.'   (v.814–15)

"There will be only one man lost at sea, whom you will mourn; one life
will be given for many."

The chilling lines show Neptune—elemental, strong, the god of
the forces of nature—dispensing good and ill without distinction.

And Venus is *laeta* (816). Naturally enough, for Neptune's promise seems to bode well for Aeneas; who cares about Palinurus? But
this too is chilling; Venus's earlier intrigue with Saturnian Juno was
marked by the same kind of indifference for Dido. The human sacrifice itself may come easily here, without a storm, without the threat
of further catastrophe; yet it is no different from the human sacrifice
extorted by Juno earlier in her assertion of power. Orontes or Palinurus, both are part of the price of Aeneas's enterprise.[11]

The episode of Palinurus's death, concluding Book v, is a masterpiece. It was foreshadowed at the beginning of v, as the ships were
sailing for Italy. Crying out at the stormy sea, "quidve, pater Neptune, paras?" (14), Palinurus says to Aeneas:

> 'magnanime Aenea, non, si mihi Iuppiter auctor
> spondeat, hoc sperem Italiam contingere caelo.'   (v.17–18)

"Great-hearted Aeneas, even if Jupiter himself guaranteed it, I would not
have any hope of reaching Italy under such a sky."

In retrospect, what might have seemed straightforward narrative—
the landing at Sicily and the opportunity to honor Anchises by funeral games—accrues a context of foreboding. The story of Palinu-

rus eludes any simple reading. Suspended between Sicily and Italy, Palinurus seems an integral part of Aeneas's journey.

The superb structure of the episode is marked by unobtrusive symmetry and design that reinforce smaller and larger meanings:

827–29: The figure of Aeneas
  830–34: Fleet proceeding, with Palinurus in lead
    835–41: Night; men asleep; descent of Somnus
      841–53: Encounter between Palinurus and Somnus disguised as Phorbas
      854–61: Overcome by sleep, Palinurus falls into the sea; departure of Somnus
  862–68: Fleet proceeding, without Palinurus
869–71: The figure of Aeneas

The sustained intensity of the episode is distilled in memorable lines like the following:

> cum levis aetheriis delapsus Somnus ab astris
> aëra dimovit tenebrosum et dispulit umbras,
> te, Palinure, petens, tibi somnia tristia portans
> insonti; puppique deus consedit in alta....   (v.838–41)

Then the god Somnus, slipping down lightly from the stars of the sky, displaced the dark air and dispelled the shadows; he was in search of you, Palinurus, carrying sad dreams to you, though you were innocent. The god took his seat high on the stern.

All this is soothing and disturbing at once. *Insonti,* innocent, is emphatic by meaning and position; but the word is rendered poignantly helpless as the narrative proceeds. The certainty of Palinurus's control, implied in *gubernator,* is underlined by detail and diction: the fleet proceeds like a column of troops, with Palinurus leading: "princeps ante omnis densum Palinurus agebat/ agmen ..." (833 f.). Disguised as Phorbas, the god Somnus descends and addresses soft but compelling words to Palinurus:

> 'Iaside Palinure, ferunt ipsa aequora classem,
> aequatae spirant aurae, datur hora quieti.
> pone caput fessosque oculos furare labori.
> ipse ego paulisper pro te tua munera inibo.'   (v.843–46)

"Palinurus, son of Iasus, the seas themselves bear the fleet forward, the breezes blow evenly, and you have time for rest. Lay your head down and steal those tired eyes from their labor. I will take over your duties for a little while."

The soporific words tempt to complacency, but Palinurus, tough, realistic, immune to the temptations of overconfidence, rejects the offer. Barely raising his eyes from his task, he answers with a vehemence hardly appropriate to Phorbas, but certainly keyed to his suspicions:

> 'mene salis placidi vultum fluctusque quietos
> ignorare iubes? mene huic confidere monstro?'   (v.848–49)

"Would you have me forget the face of the quiet sea and the sleeping waves, and trust myself to such a monster?"

Palinurus knows the sea and its gods only too well (*fallacibus auris / et caelo,* 850 f.). His suspicions are immediately confirmed:

> ecce deus ramum Lethaeo rore madentem
> vique soporatum Stygia super utraque quassat
> tempora, cunctantique natantia lumina solvit.   (v.854–56)

But suddenly the god shakes over both his temples a branch dripping with the dew of Lethe and heavy with power, and now, though he struggles, his swimming eyes are closing.

The two words *ecce deus* pack in the compressed details of narration, Palinurus's reaction, and his final shocked realization of what is happening. It is all quickly over. Palinurus resists heroically, so unyielding that when the god throws him overboard, Palinurus keeps his grip on the tiller and carries it with him, meanwhile calling loudly but futilely to his human friends for help:

> cumque gubernaclo liquidas proiecit in undas
> praecipitem ac socios nequiquam saepe vocantem.   (v.859–60)

But Aeneas and the rest of the fleet are at the outer fringes of this episode, unaware of either the aid provided or the human sacrifice

claimed by the gods. At the very beginning, the anxious father
Aeneas felt seductive joys flooding him:

> Hic patris Aeneae suspensam blanda vicissim
> gaudia pertemptant mentem.   (v.827–28)

The unusual *blanda* includes here two related meanings: "calm" but
also "flattering, seductive, caressing."[12] Aeneas feels a complacent joy
that things are now under control. At the end, saddened by the loss of
Palinurus, both as leader and as comrade, Aeneas assumes that overconfidence caused his death. Ironically, it was precisely such overconfidence that Palinurus sternly and vehemently rejected: "mene huic
confidere monstro?" The irony reflects both Aeneas's *blanda gaudia*
and the total situation as well—the two levels of the action and
Aeneas's ignorance of those levels or their relationship.

But the irony is broader still; the final image of Book v is called up
by Aeneas, a free image out of his imagination:

> 'o nimium caelo et pelago confise sereno,
> nudus in ignota, Palinure, iacebis harena.'   (870–71)

"O Palinurus, trusting too easily in the calm sky and sea, you will lie
naked on an unknown strand."

Palinurus, naked, dead on a strange shore—the image inevitably
evokes both Dido's curse and the earlier vision of dead Priam:

> 'iacet ingens litore truncus,
> avulsumque umeris caput et sine nomine corpus.'   (II.557–58)

Both images are detached from immediate context and spring naturally to Aeneas; the intuitive guess is a compelling insight. Yet in
neither case does Aeneas perceive the nature of what he must contend
with. Telling his tale, Aeneas could not articulate the terrible connection between the heroic figure of Priam and the exigencies of his mission as the sequences of visions and actions indicated. Palinurus's
death, like Priam's, is necessary to his enterprise. That Aeneas could
barely understand how and why Palinurus died only heightens the

effect of these final lines. Like Palinurus, like Priam himself, Aeneas has been displaced by powers whose measure he is not able to take. But one suspects that he can no longer "trust the calm sky and sea."

While the funeral games provide some relief for the Trojans, they manifestly do not do so for Aeneas. Covertly and overtly, lingering images of Troy and the old world abound during the wanderings, in both III and V. The temptation to stop and be satisfied with permanence in a false city is strong. Overcome by one means or another, nonetheless these temptations take their toll of Aeneas.

As Aeneas finally approaches Italy, we cannot say that he has recovered from either Carthage or Troy. But "recovery" is irrelevant. The Carthage episode was, in large part, the sum of the previous years, not so much in their incident as in their significance. To attempt to define precisely Aeneas's state at any and every given stage of his journey would be foolhardy. The enemy is not nostalgia or ordinary weakness or indecision or the lower passions; indeed, in an important sense, the enemy is in part the very enterprise to which Fate has committed Aeneas.

What we must try to understand are the terms of Aeneas's enterprise. His journey is itself a voyage in understanding. The outcome of the journey depends heavily on the quality of that understanding. In the long run, the poetic "moral" for Rome, and the meaning of the poem, will also depend on this. Thus the effort to mediate between a given line, passage, or episode and the whole work becomes one of the most difficult yet crucial efforts the reader can make as he confronts the poem.

Aeneas has come a very long way from Troy, partly by virtue of lesser, shadowy Troys. He will never again be quite so weary as he has been in these wanderings, but the journey is far from over. Too many problems remain unresolved, too much that has happened to him (particularly at divine hands) must yet be reconciled, the "goal" is still, spiritually, far off. Much as he may have reason to dislike travel, he must go on, this time, to the other world.

CHAPTER FOUR

HADES: JOURNEY THROUGH THE WOOD

🌿

The fleet arrives at Cumae; the Trojans disperse into the woods; Aeneas goes in search of the Sibyl. Narrating these actions, the opening lines of Book VI range from defined activity to hazy mystery, from smooth accomplishment to restless probing. In lines 1–8, the fleet makes an easy landing (*adlabitur oris,* 2) and is securely anchored (*dente tenaci / ancora fundabat navis*). The Trojans pour out onto the *litus Hesperium* and go about their business, routine matters of starting a fire and finding water. They are energetic and excited (*iuvenum manus emicat ardens*);

> pars densa ferarum
> tecta rapit silvas inventaque flumina monstrat. (VI.7–8)

Some [of the Trojans] raid the woodlands, the tangled hiding-places of the beasts, and show the streams they have found.

Counterpointed with *tecta,* the word *monstrat* contains also the hint of *monstrum,* an unnatural phenomenon which both reveals and conceals. The overtones in the poetic texture lead into the next passage, presenting Aeneas and his business.

Aeneas's immediate goal is less certain. Tone, texture, and movement in the next lines indicate another sphere of existence, before which the opening activities yield:

> at pius Aeneas arces quibus altus Apollo
> praesidet horrendaeque procul secreta Sibyllae,

antrum immane, petit, magnam cui mentem animumque
Delius inspirat vates aperitque futura.
iam subeunt Triviae lucos atque aurea tecta.   (VI.9–13)

But the pious Aeneas seeks the shrine where Apollo rules, enthroned on
high, and that vast cavern beyond, the hidden lair of the awe-inspiring
Sibyl. The Delian god pervades her mind and spirit with great power of
vision, to her he reveals the future. Now they draw near the grove of Hecate and the golden-roofed temple.

What were simply natural phenomena now become conditions of
reality. *Tecta* (13), not merely an "epic-type" word, looms over the
densa ferarum tecta (7 f.), while *aperit futura* (12) exploits the possibilities in the word *monstrat* (8). This sphere is dominated by Apollo
and Hecate, whose priestess and representative throughout Book VI is
the Sibyl. The golden roof of Apollo's temple may be the immediate
object of Aeneas's quest (*petit*), but linked to it are the groves of Hecate and the *antrum immane* of the Sibyl. Aeneas will move from the
citadel of Apollo to the twin gates of dreams, from the dead Misenus
to his own rebirth, in an elusive and shadowy world of flux against
the backdrop of historical and divine permanence.

The Sibyl is priestess of both Apollo and Hecate, *Phoebi Triviaeque sacerdos* (35). Earlier, in memorable similes, Vergil had paired
Apollo and Diana (one of the faces of Hecate) with Aeneas and
Dido; the pairing makes it impossible for us to ignore the emphases
here. In this context, the next passage gains particular force. Without
saying explicitly that Aeneas and other Trojans were studying the
sculpture on the temple doors, Vergil narrates the famous story of
Daedalus. Dedicated to Apollo, Daedalus's temple emerges out of a
distant, legendary past. It is there, and the sculpture on the portals is
there; only gradually do we realize (33 f.) that Aeneas and the Trojans are also there. They fade into the scene, so to speak.

But before they do, we have an uninterrupted look at temple and
ecphrasis (14 f.). Daedalus is of course a DP (like Aeneas, in many
ways); *fugiens,* he was forced to an *insuetum iter;* the metaphors of
sea travel define his journey—*enavit* (16), *remigium alarum* (19).
Many details presume the earlier simile of the labyrinth; in v.588 f.,
the maze of the labyrinth was described. The reliefs on the portals of

the temple at Cumae have much broader scope. They offer a contrast
with the exuberant Trojan youth, in Androgeos and the sacrificial victims, and perhaps a foreshadowing of Marcellus, in Daedalus's two
pathetic attempts to portray his Icarus. Also, the panels elaborate the
genesis and substance of the labyrinth:

> hic crudelis amor tauri suppostaque furto
> Pasiphae mixtumque genus prolesque biformis
> Minotaurus inest, Veneris monimenta nefandae.   (VI.24–26)

There he depicted Pasiphae's brutal passion for the bull, and her secret
union with him, and the monstrous offspring, hybrid fruit, the Minotaur,
a memento of this unspeakable love.

Numerous echoes of the latter part of Book I resound here, as they
did during the Game of Troy; for example, *sui ... monimentum et
pignus amoris* (V.572), describing the horse Dido had given Ascanius,
and which he rode in the fateful hunt in IV and on the beach at Sicily.[1]

All these details, and more, are context for the renewed description
of the labyrinth—*hic labor ille domos et inextricabilis error*
(VI.27)—and of its particular function, the slaying of the Minotaur.
Norden's suggestion that Vergil supposed an etymological connection
between *labor* and *labyrinthus* seems here well founded.

But meaning is elusive. There are suggestions of encounter with
the past, of the cost of greatness, of human tragedies divinely
wrought. Too, this moving passage seems prologue to the whole
Hades episode and to its parts—the meeting with Dido, for instance, the involvement with Fate, the brief return to the past in the
Deiphobus episode. And the labyrinth image itself surely suggests, as
Knight and others have argued, the rites of initiation and the pattern
of rebirth.

But Aeneas is not allowed to tell us what his reactions are, either
to the panels themselves or to the mysterious surroundings, for the
Sibyl suddenly appears, shocking Aeneas out of his meditation. She directs him to sacrifice to Apollo and Hecate, leads him to the *antrum,*
and there, seized with vatic frenzy, harshly orders him to pray.

Gripped by cold fear, Aeneas prays to Apollo:

'iam tandem Italiae fugientis prendimus oras,
hac Troiana tenus fuerit fortuna secuta.
vos quoque Pergameae iam fas est parcere genti,
dique deaeque omnes, quibus obstitit Ilium et ingens
gloria Dardaniae.'   (VI.61–65)

"Now that we have finally caught the elusive coasts of Italy, may the Trojan evil fortune have followed us only thus far, no further. And you, all
you gods and goddesses, it is right that you now spare the race of Perga-
mum, you deities who were offended by Ilium and the great glory of Dar-
dania."

Fas: in the divine economy, this *must* be right. It is almost assertion
more than petition. Aeneas here is calling upon all the gods, including those who favored the Greeks. The echo of Book II in these latter
lines is important:

'"fuimus Troes, fuit Ilium et ingens
gloria Teucrorum."'   (II.325–26)

The curse of Troy's grandeur has dogged them far enough.
    Then he turns to the Sibyl and asks for some confirmation: at last,
he would settle the Trojans in Latium, as well as the wandering deities and harassed powers of Troy:

'... Latio considere Teucros
errantisque deos agitataque numina Troiae.'   (VI.68–69)

He needs to have some certainty of the future, some hope that the
journey will end. Following the advice of Helenus, he concludes with
the request that the Sibyl speak directly to him, not commit her
prophecies to the leaves where they might easily become the play-
things of the winds:

'foliis tantum ne carmina manda,
ne turbata volent rapidis ludibria ventis:
ipsa canas oro.'   (VI.74–76)

    The Sibyl does not really grant his wish, nor does the journey
through Hades afford him certainty. While she does speak directly to

him, what she tells him he already knows, in the sense that other
prophecies, omens, revelations have already revealed as much—or
as little. And her words are wrapped in riddles. Her evasion is one
with the earlier prophecies he could not assimilate; it deepens the gap
between revelation and action. The allusive paradoxes in the Sibyl's
words may provide the reader with a conclusion to the series of
prophecies first of the long journey over the great sea and then of the
war to be fought. For Aeneas, however, they remain a puzzling part
of an obscure pattern.

She warns him that, though he has been through grave perils at
sea, worse ones await on land; though the sons of Dardanus will
reach Latium, they will wish they had never come: "Dardanidae ve-
nient .../ sed non et venisse volent" (85 f.). And she prophesies
war: "bella, horrida bella." By now, Aeneas is not unused to such orac-
ular pyrotechnics; he may well be tired of them. The Sibyl's words
so far have not met his question. Are they at last free of the *Troiana
fortuna?* She goes on:

> 'non Simois tibi nec Xanthus nec Dorica castra
> defuerint; alius Latio iam partus Achilles,
> natus et ipse dea; nec Teucris addita Iuno
> usquam aberit.'   (VI.88—91)

The negatives piled up are devastatingly emphatic. They will find another Simois, another Xanthus, another Greek camp, even a new
Achilles, this one also a goddess's son. Perhaps worst of all, they will
find there too the abiding enemy Juno. Then, climactically, she cries
out that this repetition of the nightmare of Troy will spring even
from the same cause:

> 'causa mali tanti coniunx iterum hospita Teucris
> externique iterum thalami.'   (VI.93—94)

"The cause of this terrible evil for the Trojans will again be a bride from
the family of a host, again an alien bridal chamber."

The corollary is that *Troiana fortuna* is not merely chance or accident
or a kind of jinx. Rather, it belongs somehow in the sphere of *fatum,
pietas,* and *labor.* Lavinia and Turnus will be part of it, just as Helen

and Dido were. So will Greek power—the one clear word of comfort the Sibyl can give invokes this paradox:

> 'tu ne cede malis, sed contra audentior ito
> qua tua te fortuna sinet. via prima salutis,
> quod minime reris, Graia pandetur ab urbe.' (vi.95–97)

"Yet do not yield to those evils; rather press on against them, even more boldly, along the way that your fortune allows you. Your road to salvation will open up where you least expect it—from a Greek city."

If, in a sense, the Trojan *fortuna* is behind them, in another sense it will be right there. The help from a Greek city takes two forms: directly, the assistance of Evander; indirectly, Diomedes' acknowledgment that Aeneas's cause is just. This help derives meaning from Book II with its emphasis on the divine, not Greek, destruction of Troy. The gods are blind to the human ironies of history. Certainly, too, it would be reckless to extrapolate here a foreshadowing of the more startling developments in Western civilization, with the alliances and counteralliances of one generation mocking the crusades of the previous generation. Rather, these lines hinge on the content of *fortuna,* and their relevance to Aeneas himself depends on the Sibylline counsel and its circular meanings: "tu ne cede malis, sed contra audentior ito" (95). As always, Aeneas is thrown back upon his own resources.

Aeneas's response to the *horrendas ambages* is surprisingly firm:

> ut primum cessit furor et rabida ora quierunt,
> incipit Aeneas heros: 'non ulla laborum,
> o virgo, nova mi facies inopinave surgit;
> omnia praecepi atque animo mecum ante peregi.' (vi.102–5)

When finally her frenzy passed and her raving mouth was still, the hero Aeneas began: "Maiden, no new trial, no unexpected burden arises before me. I have foreseen all these things and gone over them in my mind already."

Aeneas has been here before; he has lived with peril and with the peculiar trials of truth mixed with mystery. The use of *heros* underlines this firmness, but there is more. Recognizing another divine evasion,

he brushes it aside and turns away from the glowing fringes of the Sibylline vision to a symbol of Troy nearer his heart. We remember
that at the critical point of Book II, the death of Priam and the floating image of that headless trunk called up the figure of his own
father—*subiit cari genitoris imago* (II.560). Now, after another
glimpse of a fallen Troy, he asks of the Sibyl just one thing (*unum
oro*):

> 'ire ad conspectum cari genitoris et ora
> contingat; doceas iter et sacra ostia pandas.
> illum ego per flammas et mille sequentia tela
> eripui his umeris medioque ex hoste recepi;
> ille meum comitatus iter maria omnia mecum
> atque omnis pelagique minas caelique ferebat,
> invalidus, viris ultra sortemque senectae.'   (VI.108–14)

"Allow me to go and see the face of my dear father. Throw open the sacred gates and show me the way. On these shoulders I carried him,
through the flames, through a thousand pursuing weapons, and rescued
him from the midst of the enemy. He accompanied me on my way
through all the seas and endured every threat of sea and sky, weak as he
was and taxed beyond his strength, beyond the lot of old age."

The words are movingly compassionate; with full *pietas,* Aeneas pictures the weak, aged Anchises as the object of pity and love. This is
the first time in the poem that Aeneas has spoken about his father in
quite this way. Given the pervasive humanity of Aeneas, it is startling
to realize that only now does he spontaneously express such affection.
His words are quite different from the lines about Anchises' death
(III.709 f.) or at the grave (v.80 f.): both of those passages express
frustration; in both, the recurrent *nequiquam* voices the sense of partial failure in not having brought Anchises to *his* destination.

Anchises also provides the link with the future, with the *Auso-
nium, quicumque est …, Thybrim* (v.83). Aeneas defines his journey
through the underworld as an *iter* (109) that is not unlike the *iter*
(112) from Troy to Sicily; no translation can convey the force or the
implications of these lines. *Eripui his umeris* (111) calls up the dominating image at the end of II, Anchises on Aeneas's shoulders. But
now,

'ille meum comitatus iter maria omnia mecum....'   (112)

The hint of *maria omnia circum* (1.32), that image of circular wanderings, is subsumed in the phrase *maria omnia mecum*. Anchises has
long ceased to be the proximate reason for his destiny. *Invalidus* and
ultra (114) may recall Anchises' self-description in Book II (647 f.),
but the divine thunderbolt emphasized there is totally ignored.

In the next lines, Aeneas recalls that his father, in the apparition,
pointed the way to the next stage of his journey—literally Hades,
metaphorically the meeting with death and the past to prepare him
for life and the future. The terms he uses affirm life over death. (The
boldness of his request makes the Sibyl hesitate.) He calls to witness
all those others who have gone below, and asserts in a powerful conclusion: *"et mi genus ab Iove summo"* (123). Besides an affirmation
of life, his words are also an affirmation against all the powers, the
gods, the fortunes that have been dogging him, taking without giving, demanding without providing resources, pushing him to the very
extremes of endurance.

The Sibyl's answer comes, slow, a little harsh, and cautious. The
way down to Hades may be easy; the return is not:

'facilis descensus Averno...,

. . . .

sed revocare gradum superasque evadere ad auras,
hoc opus, hic labor est.'   (VI.126–29)

Calling him *sate sanguine divum* (125), the Sibyl deals carefully with
the authenticity of his claim—not its factual authenticity, but
whether Jove will honor it so far. Can the proposed trip be made
without the usual "easy descent" of death? One test will be whether
or not Aeneas is granted the golden bough which can neutralize *Iuno
inferna*.[2]

The Sibyl's characterization of Aeneas's intention—

'si tantus amor menti, si tanta cupido est

. . . .

... et insano iuvat indulgere labori....'   (VI.133, 135)

"If your desire is so great, your passion so strong . . . and you want to indulge in this foolish adventure. . . ."

—echoes Creusa's words at Troy (II.776):

' "quid tantum insano iuvat indulgere dolori?" '

" 'Why do you want to indulge in such needless grief?' "

The words are uttered by the official voice of the other world, free of contingency, immune to human affections, absolute in devotion to true *fatum* and true *labor*. The Sibyl's words are modulated by her experience of the other world; her hardness is not unlike that of Anchises in Book II, to whom human life, and therefore mutability, had become irrelevant. Creusa's words, though dictated no less by the conditions of the other world, were gentler, more understanding; yet the dichotomy is sharply felt in the ironic reversal in II. Creusa, who manifested the strongest attachment to life when Anchises despaired becomes the calm figure larger than life while Anchises turns panicky during the flight.

In a limited sense, the Sibyl is of course right. Aeneas as hero is struggling to be on the one hand a proper son, a proper worshiper of the gods, a proper Trojan leader; on the other hand he tries to remain a free agent. Though not a journey of self-discovery, Aeneas's journey involves the effort to discover and understand his proper role. To suggest that Aeneas never doubts, never is skeptical of gods, mission, or father, is to devitalize Vergil's poetry. Commentators speak of Aeneas's low morale or his discouragement or his lack of faith. All of these terms are inadequate and misleading. The *vis superum* has never shown itself an unmixed blessing; Aeneas's complaint about the *Troiana fortuna* is highly justified, for Fate and the gods, his mother included, have shown too much of their harshness.

Aeneas's passport to Hades is to be the golden bough:

'latet arbore opaca
aureus et foliis et lento vimine ramus,
Iunoni infernae dictus sacer; hunc tegit omnis
lucus et obscuris claudunt convallibus umbrae.'   (VI.136–39)

"Concealed in a tree's thick shade is a golden bough, with golden leaves and stem of gold; it is dedicated as sacred to Juno of the lower world. The whole forest hides the bough and shadows enclose it in dark valleys."

The play of light and darkness provides rich contrasts; the bough is artificial and unnatural. Brittle, glittering in the shadowy grove, the golden bough seems to reflect the golden roof of Apollo's temple gleaming above the dark grove of Hecate. The imagery belongs to the cave and wood imagery that dominates the first third of Book VI and continues in the first half of the journey through the underworld. Only when they reach Elysium is the air more free.

Aeneas's journey through the underworld takes us as much back to the past as it does forward to the future. For Aeneas himself, the journey seems at times to lay the past to rest—a fact that suggests the shallowness of the equilibrium he has achieved. His journey has a forward thrust, an urge ahead; it lacks the fear and terror we should have expected and is, in these respects, almost anticlimactic at times. The harshest test, "revocare gradum superasque evadere ad auras" (128), is over before the journey begins, for, as the Sibyl says, the golden bough will come easily, if the fates are truly calling him: "namque ipse volens facilisque sequetur,/ si te fata vocant" (VI.146–47).

Yet the journey is a new kind of *via invia* (see III.383)—now the *regna invia vivis* (154). The groves of Hecate that shade Apollo's golden-roofed temple and the dark woods that shadow the golden bough [3] are metamorphosed into the *umbrae* of the house of Dis, the enormous *ulmus opaca* (283), and the small and great caverns of the nether kingdom. The precise location, in this divine subterranean geography, of the Gates of Sleep Vergil has left as uncertain as their meaning; and well, for the whole shadowy world thus retains the proper qualities of a dream-world. At Troy, Aeneas awakened to a nightmare which never came into focus for him; now at Cumae he proceeds, fully awake, into the vague, uncharted land of the dead and of the past.

He proceeds with calm. He has cast his lot. What matters now is getting to his father and continuing the appointed adventures. So they go, walking in the dark shadows of the night, through the kingdom of Dis:

> Ibant obscuri sola sub nocte per umbram
> perque domos Ditis vacuas et inania regna.   (VI.268–69)

These lines embody the shape of their movement: the dreamlike advance in the first two words, the slow spondaic movement of the first line, the vague unreality all about them, the empty homes, the shadowy kingdoms. This world will never do what Troy and Carthage might have done. As the dawn breaks, they descend into night:

> quale per incertam lunam sub luce maligna
> est iter in silvis, ubi caelum condidit umbra
> Iuppiter, et rebus nox abstulit atra colorem.   (VI.270–72)

So the path in a forest is lit by the grudging light of a fitful moon, when Jupiter has concealed the sky in shade, and dark night has stolen color from things.

The treacherous light is the light of Hecate-Cynthia, fitful, unreliable, hidden at Jupiter's whim, and hiding the contingent human realities.

In the underworld, Aeneas moves past the phantasms of human ills and preternatural monsters, past the throngs of ghosts waiting for the burial of their bodies, across the Styx with Charon's grudging aid and through the entrance with the drugged acquiescence of Cerberus. He sees suicides and victims of love, children and heroes, and the vast fortress of the damned. Only then can he come to Elysium, the Blessed Land, where Anchises is. In Elysium he finds the calm and tranquillity commensurate with the world he seems to have expected; elsewhere, there is restless longing—for example, the souls who wait beyond Styx:

> stabant orantes primi transmittere cursum,
> tendebantque manus ripae ulterioris amore.   (VI.313–14)

They stood there, begging to be taken across first, and held out their hands in yearning for the farther shore.

Among these is Orontes (334 f.), lost the year before off Carthage, and Palinurus, lost just the other night, a fresh arrival, yet very like Orontes. Palinurus pleads with Aeneas in the terms Aeneas used to Venus and will use to Anchises. Despite the change of context, the plea is still the fundamental plea for human contact: *"da dextram misero"* (370). But the Sibyl intervenes:

> 'unde haec, o Palinure, tibi tam dira cupido?
> . . . .
> desine fata deum flecti sperare precando.'   (VI.373, 376)

"Palinurus, what is this unholy desire of yours? . . .
Stop hoping that the decrees of the gods can be changed by prayer."

This *dira cupido* is meaningless in the divine economy. The parallel with Aeneas may be instructive. Aeneas will see desire in Elysium too and cry out *"quae lucis ... dira cupido?"* (721) at the straining souls; Aeneas can recognize the condition but the laws of the Sibyl's world will not.

Charon challenges the Sibyl and her charge:

> 'umbrarum hic locus est, somni noctisque soporae:
> corpora viva nefas Stygia vectare carina.'   (VI.390–91)

"This is the land of shades, of sleep and drowsy night; it is forbidden to carry living bodies in the Stygian boat."

He points out their folly in terms recalling the Sibyl's own warning to Aeneas (125–35). The Sibyl's disclaimer and her proclamation of Aeneas's pious intention—

> 'Troius Aeneas, pietate insignis et armis,
> ad genitorem imas Erebi descendit ad umbras.'   (VI.403–4)

"Trojan Aeneas, renowned for piety and prowess, is descending to the deepest shades of Erebos, to his father."

—are unavailing; then she plays her trump card: *"at ramum hunc ... agnoscas"* ("you must, however, recognize this bough," 406 f.).

There is nothing more to be said; Charon must back down before the bough. The Sibyl's tactic is deliberate, sharply offsetting the *"tantae pietatis imago"* (405) with the unnatural, divine symbol of supreme power; Aeneas's *pietas* itself she treats with irony.

The irrational and arbitrary order seen so far is reiterated in the next scene. The untimely dead, the children, the innocent, the suicides—all these are mournful, sad, trapped.[4] But Minos is ineluctable: *urnam movet* (432)—the image recalls the *urna* in Daedalus's carvings (22) and the young men arbitrarily doomed. Not unlike this is the dream of fair women now caught perpetually by the *curae* which *durus amor* inflicted on them. Again we are reminded of Daedalus's sculpture, prologue to this whole world.

The Dido scene (450–76), short but powerful, derives its force at least in part from this shape of reality in the underworld. Together with the meeting with Deiphobus (494–547), this is the most moving episode for Aeneas in this part of his journey.

In the Dido scene, the roles are reversed. Here it is Dido who wanders, not on the sea but in a great wood:

> recens a vulnere Dido
> errabat silva in magna; quam Troius heros
> ut primum iuxta stetit agnovitque per umbras
> obscuram, qualem primo qui surgere mense
> aut videt aut vidisse putat per nubila lunam....   (VI.450–54)

Her wound still fresh, Dido was wandering in the great wood. Now when the Trojan hero found himself near her, and recognized her dim form amid the shadows—like one who early in the month sees, or imagines that he has just seen, the new moon rising through the clouds. . . .

Aeneas recognizes her, *per umbras / obscuram*—the word is held off, a clause away from *quam* (451) and still another clause from *lunam* (454) to which it also belongs. The moon simile, used shortly before at the entrance to the underworld (270 f.), provides suspense, distance, and tone, but here it carries no threat. With its adumbration of dreamy illusion, the moon circumscribes this episode and dramatically conveys Aeneas's doubtful then certain sight as he feels again the old love, and his tears fall (455).

In words echoing IV.596, *"infelix Dido,"* Aeneas cries out, *"funeris heu tibi causa fui?"* (458: "Was it death, alas, that I brought you?"). *Funeris* hits just the right note: he knew and did not know. The expostulations that follow (as I argued in chapter 1) summarize the earlier attempt to defend himself, while corroborating the pain his departure cost. He is trying to explain both to her and to himself. Her coldness makes his pleas even more urgent: *"nec credere quivi ..."* (463). But she goes on. Whatever she may now know about the *iussa deum* driving him (*"imperiis egere suis,"* he cries) is irrelevant.

In his last words to her, he begs her to stop a moment, to let him at least look at her: because of fate, this is the last time he can speak to her:

> 'siste gradum teque aspectu ne subtrahe nostro.
> quem fugis? extremum fato quod te adloquor hoc est.'   (VI.465–66)

Both appeal and question are poignant, the question echoing Dido's own *"mene fugis?"* (IV.314).[5] Hard finality bears down in *fato* (discussed in chapter 1). No understanding can be permitted him. Certainly, Aeneas cannot hope to be let off, but here he is not even allowed the hope that he can explain. This too is denied, in a stringent mockery of justice. His pleas meet only the same hardness, the same detachment that he himself had to assume at Carthage. The difference is that Dido is stony not only by divine condition but by personal choice; she turns away:

> tandem corripuit sese atque inimica refugit
> in nemus umbriferum, coniunx ubi pristinus illi
> respondet curis aequatque Sychaeus amorem.   (VI.472–74)

Then finally she pulled herself away and, still hating him, fled into the shadowy wood where Sychaeus, her husband in former days, responds to her unhappiness and equals her love with his own.

The thin hope of *tandem* is crushed by the terrible *inimica;* the shadowy grove takes her, where Aeneas can dimly make out her husband Sychaeus. *Aequatque Sychaeus amorem* emphatically excludes Aeneas; the extended reverse-parallel with Carthage reaches its climax. Whatever guilt may be imputed to Aeneas—and it is not inconsiderable—the choice he was forced to make at Carthage did not provide him with a blessed oblivion; he could not forget Dido or put her aside. She can, and does, put Aeneas aside:*pristinus* ("former, first") has an emotional force that is appalling in the context.

> nec minus Aeneas casu concussus iniquo
> prosequitur lacrimis longe et miseratur euntem.   (vi.475–76)

Aeneas was shocked by her unjust fate; and as she went long gazed after her with tearful eyes and pity for her in his heart. (Tr. Knight)

The key word is *iniquo,* "unjust." The word rebounds off *aequat* in the preceding line. Aeneas will never be free of her. She goes, but the distance is only on her side; he follows, with the self-hatred of his pity and the tears he has been shedding throughout this scene.

While this brief meeting does not justify Aeneas or condemn Dido, it gives us another glimpse into the abyss between Aeneas and those he wanted to love most dearly. Like his past, his affections are shredded before his own eyes. This episode may end the Dido story, but it settles nothing. In her wood, Dido may come to rest and peace. For Aeneas: *Inde datum molitur iter* (477). The suggestion of great effort (*molitur*) and finality (*datum*) bitterly recalls the forced departure from Carthage.

The setting for the Deiphobus episode has its own paradoxes. This is the last place before Tartarus and Elysium. Here are the heroes, inhabiting the "arva/ ultima, quae bello clari secreta frequentant" (478). The brilliance of heroism is subdued by the engulfing darkness (see 534, 545) and the enforced segregation (*secreta*). However impressive the heroes of the war against Thebes (Tydeus, Parthenopaeus, and Adrastus), or the Trojan and Greek warriors who won fame at Troy, the note of reunion that quickens the Trojans—

> circumstant animae dextra laevaque frequentes:
> nec vidisse semel satis est....   (vi.486–87)

All around, to right and left, the spirits crowded about him, nor was it enough to have seen him once. . . .

—strikes cold fear into the Greeks. Some flee, some cry out: "pars tollere vocem/ exiguam: inceptus clamor frustratur hiantis" (vi.492–93). But the choked-off war cry mocks their gaping mouths. In its dreamlike quality, it is an effective reminder of the world of night and shadows. The story of Deiphobus which follows is, like all this, grotesque parody of fading heroism and the dying past.

Deiphobus's mangled shade epitomizes Troy. A son of Priam— the identification is underscored: *Priamiden* (494), *Priamides* (509)—he succeeded Paris in Helen's bed. He tries to hide the disgrace of his death—*inhonesto vulnere* (497)—referring to his wounds in passing as *monimenta*. Commentators have seized on some inconsistencies between Deiphobus's tale and Book ii, but the point may well reside in these details. Deiphobus's authority is not first-hand. He was asleep, drunk (513–14, 520); the fact conjures up the peculiar setting of the Trojan nightmare. Too, Aeneas would hardly receive Deiphobus's account at face value. There is, indeed, some irony in Deiphobus's call for revenge, and the echoing *fatum* that pervades the tale derides his outmoded heroism.[6]

The next stop should be Tartarus, but since that is forbidden, the Sibyl describes for Aeneas the fortress of the damned. Seemingly digressive, this passage functions in various ways. It is necessary to the moral structure of the journey and to the topography of the underworld. In a larger sense, Tartarus is the last stronghold of Juno and is the native territory of Allecto, of Tisiphone, and of the *Dira* attendant on the final actions of the poem. It may also be pertinent that Tartarus parallels Olympus. The point is not stressed, yet these walls are impregnable:

> porta adversa ingens solidoque adamante columnae,
> vis ut nulla virum, non ipsi exscindere bello
> caelicolae valeant.   (vi.552–54)

Opposite was an enormous gate, the columns of solid adamant, such that no human strength nor the gods themselves could destroy them.

The accounts of Titanomachy (580 f.), of the superhuman creatures who defied the reigning deities, of the human criminals—these reiterate the potential for disorder and anarchy, and the primacy of power. In solemn, sententious conclusion, the Sibyl proclaims that, even with a hundred mouths and a voice of iron, she could never describe all the shapes of crime or catalogue all the punishments in this place:

> 'non, mihi si linguae centum sint oraque centum,
> ferrea vox, omnis scelerum comprendere formas,
> omnia poenarum percurrere nomina possim.'   (VI.625–27)

The transition from Tartarus to the bright spaciousness of Elysium is accomplished by the depositing of the golden bough (628–36).

Though Elysium has its own sources of light, the expanse of sky is illusory. The reversal of time continues. Earlier episodes and places were marked by particular darkness, though it was day in the outer world; in Elysium, however, it seems to be bright day though, according to earthly times, night has begun to fall.

The residents of Elysium, like the residents of Tartarus, come from times both legendary and recent. They are, however, a different breed. There are the heroes of the Golden Age beginning with mythical Orpheus and the ancient ancestors of Troy:

> hic genus antiquum Teucri, pulcherrima proles,
> magnanimi heroes, nati melioribus annis,
> Ilusque Assaracusque et Troiae Dardanus auctor.   (VI.648–50)

Here is the ancient race of Teucer, a noble breed, great-hearted heroes, born in happier years, Ilus, Assaracus, and Dardanus, the founder of Troy.

(The first line parodies line 580, *hic genus antiquum Terrae, Titania pubes,* which introduced the damned in Tartarus.) Dardanus, Jove-begotten ancestor of Troy, enjoys a place of honor, but existence for these heroes is appropriately simple, honest, and joyful, as it is also for the other blessed ones, the patriots, priests, and poets, and others who benefited mankind. Their dwelling is idyllic—the green, pleasant fields, the groves of the fortunate shades, the abode of the blessed: "locos laetos et amoena virecta/ fortunatorum nemorum sedesque beatas" (VI.638–39).

But the travelers cannot dally. The Sibyl turns to Musaeus, son of Orpheus, who towers above all the others, and asks him where Anchises can be found. He answers:

> 'nulli certa domus; lucis habitamus opacis,
> riparumque toros et prata recentia rivis
> incolimus.'   (VI.673–75)

"None of us has a fixed abode: we dwell in shaded groves, and we lie on the soft riverbanks and the meadows kept fresh by the streams."

In the fields of peace and joy and permanence, this graphically contrasts with Aeneas's uprooted longing and his earthly search for a *certa domus*. The circumscribed condition of human life does not exist here. The shaded groves and riverbanks embody the spiritual Arcadia and its freedom, but to Aeneas groves and meadows and brooks have been only the wayside of his *iter*. Even the Sibyl is not quite comfortable in Musaeus's world; the way she phrases her question emphasizes stability of place: "quae regio Anchisen, quis habet locus?" [7]

They find Anchises deep in a *convalle virenti* ("in a green valley"), where he is telling the number of his offspring:

> omnemque suorum
> forte recensebat numerum, carosque nepotes
> fataque fortunasque virum moresque manusque.   (VI.681–83)

Just then he was counting over the full number of his descendants, his beloved offspring, and the fates and fortunes which would be theirs, their characters and their deeds.

The picture is quite different from that of Orpheus who "accompanies their measures on the seven strings of his lyre" ("obloquitur numeris septem discrimina vocum," 646). Nonlyrical numbers are appropriate to Anchises. His great desire is *"hanc prolem ... enumerare meorum"* (717), and even his waiting for Aeneas he describes as *"tempora dinumerans"* (691). There is a notable gap between the other idyllic regions of Elysium and the *seclusum nemus* of Anchises' dynasty, somewhat as there is in Book VIII between the austere peace of Evander's country and the golden revelations shown by Venus *in valle reducta* (VIII.609). Indeed, the similarities force themselves on us: father and son, mother and son; the grove by the river Lethe, the grove near a cold stream; the *innumerae gentes populique,* the *non enarrabile textum* of the Shield. In both scenes, Aeneas reacts in much the same way. Here Aeneas *horrescit visu* .../ *inscius* (710 f.: Aeneas, "bewildered, is startled by the sight"); in VIII, *rerumque ignarus imagine gaudet* (VIII. 730: "though ignorant of the events, he rejoices in the image").

Anchises greets his son warmly enough, but the tone of detached authority and expectation disquietingly recalls earlier scenes. The tone is there in *"venisti tandem"* (687) and in the repeated *equidem,* an intensive usually linked with *ego:*

'sic equidem ducebam animo rebarque futurum....'	(690)
'has equidem memorare tibi atque ostendere coram....'	(716)
'dicam equidem...'	(720)
'(credo equidem)....'	(848)

Like Anchises' own, Aeneas's words center on Anchises; in Aeneas, however, it is pure affection at first more than filial respect. But this informing humanity of Aeneas does not easily take to the other world; his progress toward his father is first described in the rough, almost stubborn words *tendentem adversum per gramina* .../ *Aenean* (684 f.). And Aeneas's spontaneous reaching out to his father is inevitably frustrated:

> 'da iungere dextram,
> da, genitor, teque amplexu ne subtrahe nostro'
>   . . . .
> ter conatus ibi collo dare bracchia circum;
> ter frustra comprensa manus effugit imago,
> par levibus ventis volucrique simillima somno.   (VI.697 f., 700–2)

"My father, let me take your hand—let me! Do not pull away from our embrace. . . ." Three times, then, he tried to put his arms around his father's neck; but three times his grasp was in vain, the shade slipped through his hands, like the light breezes or most like a fleeting dream.

The atmosphere of the nonhuman world remains too rarefied for Aeneas. Appeal and gesture recall the outcry to Venus, the apparition of Anchises in Sicily, and the meetings with Palinurus and Dido earlier, but most of all the final meeting with Creusa in Book II. Lines 700–2 here are repeated from II.792–94, in an altered context. At Troy, the attempted embrace occurred at the end of their meeting; she had come to him; she declared that her fate was to stay, apparently as priestess to Cybele, "*his oris*," that is, at Troy. In the underworld, the attempted embrace occurs at the beginning of their meeting; Aeneas has come to see Anchises; Anchises occupies a particular place right there, overseeing his family's future. By its very alterations, the context emphasizes the cyclical pattern.

After the unconsummated embrace, the narrative turns discreetly (*Interea,* 703) to the objects of Anchises' continuing attention, the *innumerae gentes* flitting around the river Lethe. They are like bees:

ac velut in pratis ubi apes aestate serena
floribus insidunt variis et candida circum
lili funduntur, strepit omnis murmure campus.   (VI.707–9)

Just so do bees in the meadows on a clear summer day settle on flowers of every kind and swarm around the gleaming lilies; and the whole field hums with their murmur.

The points of comparison are specifically the free flight of the souls around the river and their carefree buzzing. But the major elements in the simile invite attention: the vari-flowered *prata* about which the bees flit are remarkably like the abodes of the blessed as Musaeus definitively described them. *Floribus insidunt variis*—there is a total, unreflecting freedom essential to the picture. Singled out are the *lilia candida,* which may well look forward, rather than back, to the *lilia* for Marcellus dead (883). These seem the most reasonable referent for Anchises' words there, presumably to the shades: *manibus date lilia plenis.*[8]

When Aeneas, thunderstruck, asks what the sight means, *pater* Anchises [9] answers very briefly:

'animae, quibus altera fato
corpora debentur, Lethaei ad fluminis undam
securos latices et longa oblivia potant.'   (VI.713–15)

"These souls, who are destined to live in yet other bodies, now are drinking at Lethe's stream the waters that free men from care and provide long
release from memory."

Considering the novelty of all this, such brevity is intolerable. But
Anchises is not very interested in pursuing the matter. Rather,

'has equidem memorare tibi atque ostendere coram,
iampridem hanc problem cupio enumerare meorum,
quo magis Italia mecum laetere reperta.'   (VI.716–18)

"I myself have for a very long time desired to tell you about them and to
show them to you in person, to count out these descendants of mine, so
that you can rejoice with me even more in having found Italy."

Aeneas, however, does not share the urgency of this dynastic imperative; he returns to his question:

'o pater, anne aliquas ad caelum hinc ire putandum est
sublimis animas iterumque ad tarda reverti
corpora? quae lucis miseris tam dira cupido?'   (VI.719–21)

"O father, are we to believe that some souls leave here and soar up to the
outer world, to return to burdensome bodies? Why do these creatures suffer such an unholy lust for the light of earth?"

They talk at cross-purposes, almost like characters in Chekhov.
Aeneas cannot understand this desire to trade Elysium for earth. It is
for him a crucial question, in a sense the question he expected to be
answered in Hades. The meaning of Anchises' death and the meaning
of this *dira cupido* for life—these are closely related. Aeneas must
know whether life has meaning (though not necessarily what that
meaning is). The question is important not because he wants to die,
nor because he wants to remain in Elysium—there is no basis for
this view; nor is there basis for the notion that his morale is at its
lowest point. Aeneas's very maladjustment to the lower world belies

these notions; his most characteristic acts are his impulse of *dulcis amor* when he sees Dido and his attempt to embrace Anchises.

The spontaneous question, irrelevant to Anchises' promise of a pageant, reaches out to the peace and substance of reality here. The question arises for Aeneas's developing experience in his mission. Again and again, the gods and their ways have brought him to serious doubts about reality and its meaning; his faith is threatened, and that faith must be restored. The mission he has is not clearly relevant to his faith; to Aeneas the dimensions of that mission are far less important than the moral and ethical substance. But the gods and their agents persist in displaying his mission to him in terms of Fate and of history. These cannot answer his profoundest questions, any more than Jupiter's response to his prayer (in Book v) and the Sibyl's response can tell him what he most wants to know.

Good, just, honest, brave, humble, and harassed, Aeneas remains an outsider to this other world. Or, perhaps put more accurately, this other world remains outside Aeneas, away from him, elusive and incomprehensible. The Sibyl, constantly but unobtrusively in attendance, is but a weak link; Anchises is no link at all. So Aeneas, hearing the bland words about rebirth, asks what they mean; so, later, having seen the pageant, he asks about the melancholy figure of Marcellus.

Anchises responds to his question with the famous discourse on metempsychosis, presenting the doctrine as a kind of eclectic Stoicism with dashes of Platonism. The sources of existence, he says, are internal spirit (*"mens agitat molem"*), a fiery center of all reality (*"igneus ... vigor"*), but the *"corpora noxia ... terrenique ... artus moribundaque membra,"* since they are matter, imprison the spirit, and the purpose of reincarnation is continual purification so that the spirit may regain its pristine state.

The point of this discourse lies neither in the doctrine nor in its use as a device to lend verisimilitude to the pageant; other devices could as easily or more easily have been used. The point seems to lie rather in the cyclical view suggested. The world soul postulates the kind of unity that history is seen to be striving for. As Anchises explains, before these souls can return to the outer world, before they can even begin to desire to take on bodily life again, they must drink of the river Lethe. These spirits must forget the past in order to meet the unknown future:

> 'Lethaeum ad fluvium deus evocat agmine magno,
> scilicet immemores supera ut convexa revisant
> rursus, et incipiant in corpora velle reverti.'   (VI.749–51)

But past and future are not far apart: a ridge in Elysium divides Dardanus from Augustus Caesar.

The discourse answers Aeneas's question by denying its terms: these souls are not *miseri* nor is their intent a *dira cupido*. As it turns out, many of them are destined to be great in history, though Anchises never discusses the relationship of this greatness and metempsychosis. Not because of oversight; he is simply not interested.[10] The great thing is to display the *Dardaniam prolem* (756). He does—grandly and solemnly, his voice ringing with patriarchal pride. In the pageant, the point of view is that of Anchises. Whether or not Vergil shares it does not matter. In this display of power, Anchises, like the other nonhuman forces in the poem, is little concerned with the problems of power; no metaphysician in expounding the doctrine of reincarnation, he aptly shows himself no political or moral philosopher in expounding Dardanian history. He fastens on the figure of *Mavortius ... Romulus* and the splendid aura encompassing him: under his auspices,

> 'illa incluta Roma
> imperium terris, animos aequabit Olympo,
> septemque una sibi muro circumdabit arces,
> felix prole virum: qualis Berecyntia mater
> invehitur curru Phrygias turrita per urbes
> laeta deum partu, centum complexa nepotes,
> omnis caelicolas, omnis supera alta tenentis.'   (VI.781–87)

"That illustrious Rome will extend her kingdom worldwide and her spirit to the heights of Olympus; she will surround her seven citadels with a single wall and rejoice in her manly offspring: like the mother of Berecynthus [Cybele] when she is borne in her chariot wearing a towered crown, through the Phrygian cities, happy in her divine sons, embracing her numerous posterity, all of them dwellers in heaven on high."

Dynasty and empire: Anchises' hope for worthy descendants is more than fulfilled as his vision identifies his sons with the great city of the seven hills. In the simile, he glosses that vision: not only are Romulus and Rome one, they are one with Troy; Rome will replace Troy in history. This new Troy has as its focus the figure he displays next:

> 'Augustus Caesar, divi genus, aurea condet
> saecula qui rursus Latio regnata per arva
> Saturno quondam, super et Garamantas et Indos
> proferet imperium....'   (VI.792–95)

"Caesar Augustus, of divine lineage, will establish the golden age once more in Latium, in those very fields ruled of old by Saturn; he will extend his dominion far beyond the Garamantes and the Indians. . . ."

But ambiguities will not be so readily displaced. As the early kings parade by, Anchises reduces the meed of praise; about proud Brutus, who had his own sons executed, he says noncommittally that, whatever the future verdict, patriotism and desire for glory will prevail: "vincet amor patriae laudumque immensa cupido" (823). Admiring the stuff of the man, he evades moral assessment. Brutus and Torquatus, both with hands stained by filial blood, lead naturally to Pompey and Caesar, and to the wages of power. Faced with these, Anchises waxes eloquent but hardly profound; to these shades, he cries:

> 'ne, pueri, ne tanta animis adsuescite bella
> neu patriae validas in viscera vertite viris;
> tuque prior, tu parce, genus qui ducis Olympo,
> proice tela manu, sanguis meus!—'   (VI.832–35)

"O my sons, do not let your spirits become so used to terrible wars, do not turn the great strength of your country against her own heart! You be first, you relent, offspring of Olympus—throw away your weapons, you who are of my own blood!—"

The last line breaks off awkwardly; the dynastic imperative might yield when confronted with its eventual issue. But it does not. Anchises returns to earlier history and blandly recites glories without recognition of sides taken, of deep divisions in Roman polity, of the problems that troubled the sleep of some and drove others to violence and slaughter. In the final short passage (841–46), iron-booted militarists alternate with lawgivers and statesmen. The history of power, as Vergil well knew, is also a tale of madness and inhumanity.

For his part, Aeneas is not grandly inspired. Critics have assumed that he is, but the evidence is scant. At the first great climax, after a long and glowing tribute to Augustus Caesar (789–805), Anchises finds it necessary to give special stress to the moral for Aeneas's benefit:

> 'et dubitamus adhuc virtutem extendere factis,
> aut metus Ausonia prohibet consistere terra?'   (VI.806–7)

"Can we still hesitate, then, to assert our courage by our own deeds? or can fear keep us now from occupying Ausonia?"

At another point, Anchises lingers over Romans who will destroy Greeks (836 f.). The passage recalls the lines in Jupiter's prophecy, in Book I:

> 'veniet lustris labentibus aetas
> cum domus Assaraci Phthiam clarasque Mycenas
> servitio premet ac victis dominabitur Argis.'   (I.283–85)

In these lines, Jupiter is promising Venus that the time will come when the house of Assaracus will enslave Phthia (Achilles' land) and great Mycenae, and will rule over the conquered Greeks. Anchises' account takes particular relish in the details of that vegeance to be wrought by the new Troy on Greece. Mummius he characterizes as *"caesis insignis Achivis"* (837: "famous for the Greeks he has slaughtered"). Then he describes the exploits of Aemilius Paullus:

> 'eruet ille Argos Agamemnoniasque Mycenas
> ipsumque Aeaciden, genus armipotentis Achilli,
> ultus avos Troiae templa et temerata Minervae.'   (VI.838–40)

The details are deliberate and almost sadistic: Paullus will uproot not just Greece, but Argos, the Mycenae of Agamemnon; not just Greeks, but a descendant of Achilles. Thus will he avenge his ancestors and the defiled temples of Trojan Minerva.

All this is meant for Aeneas, of course, though one may wonder just how far he shares his father's feeling for the sweet uses of revenge. At Troy, he saw Pallas presiding from the citadel over the destruction of the city; on his wanderings, he made a kind of moral truce, if not peace, with the Greeks; and just before the descent, the Sibyl has told him to look to a Greek city for help in Italy. This outburst of Anchises has no more effect on Aeneas than did the Greeks he met earlier in the underworld.

Finally, Anchises' peroration, a resounding statement:

> 'excudent alii spirantia mollius aera
> (credo equidem), vivos ducent de marmore vultus,
> orabunt causas melius, caelique meatus
> describent radio et surgentia sidera dicent:
> tu regere imperio populos, Romane, memento
> (hae tibi erunt artes), pacique imponere morem,
> parcere subiectis et debellare superbos.'   (vi.847–53)

"Others, for so I can well believe, shall hammer forth more delicately a breathing likeness out of bronze, coax living faces from the marble, plead causes with more skill, plot with their gauge the movements in the sky, and tell the rising of the constellations. But you, Roman, must remember that you have to guide the nations by your authority, for this is to be your skill, to graft tradition onto peace, to shew mercy to the conquered, and to wage war until the haughty are brought low." (Tr. Knight) [11]

The last three lines, capturing and heightening the particular Roman genius, are justly famous; Anchises' farsighted declaration for peace gives some measure of profundity to his total concerns. Even so, the resonance of this passage can be too easily exaggerated by readers who wrench the lines out of context and impute the views, without qualification, to Vergil. The passage bears Anchises' stamp. He sees the competition as between alternative claims on glory, between what he conceives as Greek and Roman traits, not between total categories of reality.

This defiant peroration does not quite end the episode. Two figures approach, both named Marcellus. Noting the interest of Aeneas and

the Sibyl, Anchises singles out one Marcellus. He is, we note, the epitome of Anchises' prescription for greatness:

> 'aspice, ut insignis spoliis Marcellus opimis
> ingreditur victorque viros supereminet omnis.
> hic rem Romanam magno turbante tumultu
> sistet....'   (VI.855–58)

"See how Marcellus strides, illustrious with the supreme trophies, the conqueror who towers above all men. This man will restore the Roman
power when it is shaken by the great uprising. . . ."

It is, however, the other Marcellus who commands Aeneas's attention
and interest. Himself *pietate insignis et armis,* Aeneas is struck by
more than Anchises sees and asks who this figure is, and what manner of man:

> 'quantum instar in ipso!
> sed nox atra caput tristi circumvolat umbra!'   (VI.865–66)

"How noble is his presence! Yet black night circles about his head with
somber shadows."

The balance of these details parallels what Aeneas had perceived si-
multaneously (*egregium forma iuvenem ...| sed frons laeta parum.
... 861* f.). As before, Aeneas is almost irrelevant; as before, his
question arises out of a faltering interest in what Anchises found most
important.

Describing this other Marcellus, Anchises emphasizes the military
greatness the young man might have achieved. Even in the lines
about his untimely death and the mourning it caused (872 f.), the
presence of Mars cries war, and the *gemitus* and *funera* have double
meanings, as do *Iliaca* and *Romula* (875 f.). Anchises' panegyric nods
to *pietas,* while climbing to the heroic vision of an invincible right
arm, a mighty figure whom no enemy could have vanquished:

> 'heu pietas, heu prisca fides invictaque bello
> dextera! non illi se quisquqam impune tulisset
> obvius armato.'   (VI.878–80)

Pietas is limited here to patriotic prowess, while *invicta bello / dextera* is severely unequivocal. Anchises reveals why he singled out the successful Marcellus, saying of this one: [12]

> 'heu, miserande puer, si qua fata aspera rumpas!
> tu Marcellus eris.'   (VI.882–83)

"Alas, piteous boy, if only somehow you evade your harsh fates! A Marcellus you also will be."

The contemplation of such waste horrifies Anchises; his words are very pessimistic, out of tune with both his world-view and his stature in Elysium. As if present at the funeral, he gives full vent to his sense of futility (*"fungar inani / munere,"* 885 f.)

With the Sibyl, Aeneas leaves Hades by the mysterious ivory gate:

> Sunt geminae Somni portae, quarum altera fertur
> cornea, qua veris facilis datur exitus umbris,
> altera candenti perfecta nitens elephanto,
> sed falsa ad caelum mittunt insomnia manes.   (VI.893–96)

There are twin gates of Sleep. One of them is said to be made of horn, and by it an easy exit is provided for true shades. The other is made completely of white gleaming ivory. But it is false dreams that the spirits send to earth.

No one can say with confidence what these lines mean. The suggestions of illusion hover over them; the elusive details and deliberate vagueness argue that this final act of Book VI belongs with the dreamlike passage through the underworld and its changing patterns of reality. Past and future (one false, the other true?) have confronted Aeneas.

The lines also seem to epitomize the cyclical pattern of this underworld journey. The journey began in the "empty houses of Dis, the lifeless kingdom." In the center of that vestibule was the great elm tree with its multiple forms of illusion:

> In medio ramos annosaque bracchia pandit
> ulmus opaca, ingens, quam sedem Somnia vulgo
> vana tenere ferunt, foliisque sub omnibus haerent.   (VI. 282–84)

In the branches of this dark, ancient tree (so it is said) dwell False Dreams, clinging underneath its leaves. These *Somnia vana* are accompanied by hordes of *monstra*. Aeneas is frightened by them and draws his very tangible sword. But his knowledgeable guide reassures him: these things are bodiless, airy, flitting about under the empty semblance of a form—*tenuis sine corpore vitas / ... volitare cava sub imagine formae* (292 f.). In a word, they are perhaps the false dreams of the ivory gate.

Aeneas emerges from Hades and goes straight to his ships: *viam secat ad navis* (899). He is back where he began, continuing the journey to its next phase, a brief stop for the burial of Cajeta, his old nurse.

CHAPTER FIVE

ITALY

The mysteries of the underworld yield to domesticity and quiet as Book VII opens. No doubt the descent into Hades marked a turning point in Aeneas's enterprise, though it does not seem to be the dramatic climax or the point at which Aeneas becomes supremely confident of his glorious future. During the solemn journey, Aeneas received a display of favor: *"si te fata vocant."* His vision encompassed permanence and moral order, distilled in the happy fields of Elysium where the good and just men reside. This vision was necessary for the wanderer without roots; fate has not been so kind to him that he can accept unquestioningly its peremptory disposition of reality.

The temper of Aeneas emergent from Hades is suggested in the first act of Book VII, the touching but almost parenthetical burial of Cajeta, his aged nurse. She was the last personal tie to his old world of Troy; as he leaves the world of shades, she goes to it. The narration of the burial begins: *At pius exsequiis Aeneas ...* (VII.5). Without needing to separate name and epithet, Vergil does separate them, to emphasize the particular aspect of *pius* here—firmer, slightly colder, and specifically proper in the funeral rites. And then, the main action of the sentence, circumscribed by *At: tendit iter* (7). Perspective depends on the narrator's skeptical comment, *si qua est ea gloria* ("if there is any glory in becoming a legend"), which undercuts the etiological detail.

Aeneas acts, properly, ritually, and with cool dispatch; and he does not react. His assured command mirrors his detached understanding of what is emerging and his lack of sentimentality or self-pity. As we move through Book VII and Books VIII and IX, we realize that he is less active than at any other point in the poem; things are done to or for or apart from him, as if the stage is being set for his own definitive action, and as if, just now, few overt actions are called for from him.

The surprising quiet with which Book VII opens is imposed even on the weather—*aspirant aurae in noctem* ... (8 f.). Aeneas arrives in Latium, under the aegis of Neptune, amid a joyous dawn. The omen of the tables quickly follows. Hardly impressive, this episode shows Aeneas in confident command. What Ascanius considers a trifle, Aeneas quickly comprehends: this is what his *genitor Anchises* foretold. He is, Vergil emphasizes, *pater Aeneas* (119) here; the epithet is in marked contrast to *genitor* (122, 134). He is not worried now about the *Troiana fortuna:*

> 'salve fatis mihi debita tellus
> vosque' ait 'o fidi Troiae salvete penates:
> hic domus, haec patria est. genitor mihi talia namque
> (nunc repeto) Anchises fatorum arcana reliquit....'   (VII.120–23)

"Hail, land reserved for me by the fates!" he cries. "Hail, you Trojan gods, for you spoke true: here is our home, here is our fatherland. For I now recall that Anchises my father left me just these secrets of the fates. . . ."

He dispatches an embassy to King Latinus, wearing the olive branch of Pallas. They are to sue for peace; Aeneas meanwhile prepares for war:

> ipse humili designat moenia fossa
> moliturque locum, primasque in litore sedes
> castrorum in morem pinnis atque aggere cingit.   (VII.157–59)

Aeneas himself marks out his walls with a shallow trench and labors on the site; around their first home on this shore, he builds a rampart and battlements in the manner of a military camp.

This is the last we see of Aeneas himself until the opening of Book VIII.

Juno dominates the action of Book VII. The great queen of heaven also descends into Hades, but with a difference. In Tartarus, the re-

gion from which Aeneas was barred, Juno seeks the desperate last resources of her losing battle. In the end, Juno will win, even while losing; the effects of Tartarean intervention will harshly qualify both
the outcome itself and the nature of that outcome. But the fact that
the intervention is Tartarean and the cause for such upheaval is
firmly underlined: Juno is, here, *saeva Iovis coniunx* (286) in a particular way; what she feels is *"fatis contraria nostris/ fata Phry-
gum!"* (293 f.) and there is more truth than Juno likes in her ironic
observation, *"at, credo, mea numina tandem/ fessa iacent"* (297 f.:
"Must I admit that my divine powers are at last exhausted?"). She
broods on her own humiliation, capping it with the terrible decision:

> 'ast ego, magna Iovis coniunx, nil linquere inausum
> quae potui infelix, quae memet in omnia verti,
> vincor ab Aenea. quod si mea numina non sunt
> magna satis, dubitem haud equidem implorare quod usquam est:
> flectere si nequeo superos, Acheronta movebo.'   (VII.308–12)

"But I, the mighty consort of Jove, in my misery I have left nothing un-
tried, I have stooped to every expedient—I am beaten by Aeneas. But
if my divine powers are not great enough, surely I need not hesitate to
ask for help wherever it can be found. If I cannot bend the powers above,
then I will arouse Hell."

Freud saw in the final line an appropriate epigraph.

Juno's hysteria exposes the great difference between her venture
here and its parallel in Book I. Similar in many respects, the two episodes are sharply and significantly distinguished. There, she seduc-
tively cajoled Jove's officer, Aeolus, into releasing the forces of nature,
to prevent Aeneas from reaching Italy and so to avenge herself on the
Trojans. Her indignation was matched by her resolve to frustrate
Aeneas's destiny. In Book VII, no hope or clear purpose emerges. She
orders Allecto, a bat out of Hades, to churn up the passions of men
and women, to goad them to hatred and frenzy, and to create chaos.
Juno's hysteria is more divine than feminine. One with the older gods
in many respects, she fears displacement.

The stakes in this conflict must not be underestimated. When Juno
threatens to renew the misery of Troy (VII.318 f.), she is not indulg-

ing in an idle figure of speech. The imagery there, of firebrand, second
Paris, and wedding-torch, reflects what is involved. The story as a
whole turns on a love-death motif; Vergil suggests as much by invok-
ing Erato, Muse of Love, and by underscoring the place which Circe
has in the context.[1] But he goes further:

> maior rerum mihi nascitur ordo,
> maius opus moveo.   (VII.44–45)

A grander order of things arises before me, a grander theme I unfold.

In a general way, it may be said that this conflict goes beyond armies
and heroes. Juno's power is at stake, and so is the Saturnian heritage
and the world order in which power controls justice and morality, the
order of the chthonic gods brilliantly dramatized by Aeschylus in the
Oresteia. Aeneas represents the threat that mankind will transcend
these limited cycles (which are expressions of the gods' power and of
their triflings) and create a new world of justice and virtue. Juno's resistance informs the tragedy here; the compromise that must inevitably come will cloud the glory of that new world even at its birth. It
seems clear already that Aeneas's final victory will not be unqualified.
His participation in the war will hardly be the participation of the
hero in quest of glory and bounty; nor will it be the holy crusade of a
reborn and sanctified vessel of the gods. Like the journey, his action
and his victory will give each other their particular meaning.

Latinus receives the Trojans warmly, just as Dido did in Book I.
The similarities between the two scenes have been noted often: Ilioneus leads the Trojan band in each case; Latinus and Dido already
know something about the Trojans; each offers friendship. The differences are perhaps more important. Latinus's problems are of quite a
different dimension from Dido's. The visitors are not men shipwrecked on the shore; improvisation (Ilioneus's acting leadership in I,
the alliance of Juno and Venus, the interference of Mercury) gives
way to deliberate control; even the "knowledge" Latinus and Dido
have is various. Dido sees them as great warriors, almost legendary,
while Latinus identifies them as descendants of Dardanus.

These differences provide context for Latinus's crucial decision.
(The parallel between his situation and that of Evander in Book VIII
is highly suggestive.) *Sortes* and *monstra* forbid the marriage of his
daughter Lavinia to a man of her own race; in the Trojans, however,
Latinus sees the prophecies fulfilled:

> 'generos externis adfore ab oris,
> hoc Latio restare canunt, qui sanguine nostrum
> nomen in astra ferant. hunc illum poscere fata
> et reor et, si quid veri mens augurat, opto.'   (VII.270–73)

"The people into which she will marry are to come from foreign shores
—so they prophesy for Latium—and their blood shall exalt our name
to the stars. This man, then, is he whom the fates require: so I believe
and, if my spirit divines any truth, him do I choose."

On the face of it, everything points to such a conclusion; the circumstances of their arrival encourage such a view. The only jarring note
is Latinus's barely disguised irritation that Aeneas had not himself
come; he makes it a condition of peace that he and Aeneas shake
hands: "pars mihi pacis erit dextram tetigisse tyranni" (266).

But there are rumbles of discord. Vergil does not dwell on the reaction in Latinus's court; yet only the hasty reader could miss the emblems of passion already manifest, emblems emphasized by the Cir-
cean horses which Latinus sends *absenti Aeneae* (280 f.). Whether
Amata is present or not, we have good reason to know that she is enraged by this turn of events:

> femineae ardentem curaeque iraeque coquebant.   (345)

The line describes Amata as Allecto finds her; the words (*ardentem,
curae, irae*) are appropriate to the lady of frustrated passions. Earlier,
Amata was cast as the prime mover of the marriage of Turnus and
Lavinia:

> multi illam magno e Latio totaque petebant
> Ausonia; petit ante alios pulcherrimus omnis
> Turnus, avis atavisque potens, quem regia coniunx
> adiungi generum miro properabat amore.   (VII.54–57)

Many from all over Latium, from the whole of Ausonia, sought her hand; by far the handsomest of all the suitors was Turnus, a man who boasted great ancestry: the royal consort yearned, with a passion that was remarkable, to have him united to her as a son-in-law.

Regia coniunx would be merely periphrastic were the emphasis solely on maternal Amata; the echo of *Rex ... regebat* (45 f.) and the detail that Latinus was *iam senior* show otherwise. Amata's desire for Turnus is accented by the sound-echo of *coniunx / adiungi* and by *miro*, which defines her *amore* (57). The gap between Amata's urgency and the disposition of fate supports the suggestion of perversity: "sed variis portenta deum terroribus obstant" (58). While this may appear a harsh judgment on Amata, that is less relevant here than a clear understanding of the circumstances. For whatever reasons, Latinus believes that Aeneas is to marry the beautiful Lavinia who, like Helen and Dido, was sought after by many. The prime suitor is a noble prince who has the support of Queen Amata, who is herself attracted to him. Her attraction, however, contains elements of passion which overshadow the apparent problem. Amata's opposition to Aeneas, then, springs from sources deeper than maternal resentment against Latinus's choice.

That is the situation when Juno summons Allecto out of Hades. Latinus hopes that the Trojans "sanguine nostrum / nomen in astra ferant" (271 f.: "The new kindred shall add their strain to ours, and exalt our race to the stars."—tr. Knight). But, in malicious echo, Juno promises:

> 'sanguine Troiano et Rutulo dotabere, virgo,
> et Bellona manet te pronuba.'   (VII.318–19)

"Maiden, the blood of Trojans and Rutulians shall be your marriage portion, and Bellona, the goddess of war, awaits you as bridesmaid."

And to give *sanguine* its proper meaning, she dispatches Allecto with a mandate which is impressively ritualistic:

> 'fecundum concute pectus,
> disice compositam pacem, sere crimina belli;
> arma velit poscatque simul rapiatque iuventus.'   (VII.338–40)

"Stir up the fertile breast, shatter the compact of peace, sow the seeds of evil war; let them crave weapons, demand them and use them, all at once."

The structure calls attention to the correspondence between the first series of clauses and the second series, and to the richer correspondence between both series and the three episodes, of similar length, in which Allecto amply dispenses her poisons on Amata, Turnus, and Ascanius:

1. "fecundum concute pectus : arma velit [juventus]"—Allecto stirs up Amata, who inflames the Latin women, 341–405.
2. "disice compositam pacem : poscatque [arma juventus]"—Allecto rouses Turnus, who arms and declares war, 406–74.
3. "sere crimina belli : rapiatque juventus"—Allecto effects Ascanius's slaying of the royal deer, and fighting breaks out, 475–539.

The progression in all three cases is marked by passion, arms, and battle. The correspondence dramatizes distinctions in the three stages which might otherwise be lost: the aroused passion and outburst of enmity do not easily turn into actual fighting. By dramatizing the three stages, Vergil underscores the horror of war.

The activity and effect of Allecto vary from episode to episode, but their purpose remains single: chaos. On Amata, she casts a snake whose action at first goes unnoticed, as did the action of Amor on Dido in Book I. When Amata pleads with Latinus, there is the same sense of bare restraint that was present in Dido's first plea to Aeneas, and another unwitting echo in the appeal to patriotism and to earlier promises made so often to Turnus:

'quid cura antiqua tuorum
et consanguineo totiens data dextera Turno?'   (VII.365–66)

Amata presents a reasonable if casuistic brief for Turnus as the prophetically marked foreigner. But Latinus stands firm, and Allecto goads Amata on as she rages through the city and leads the women out. They abandon the city; Amata in frenzy brandishes a flaming torch, chanting an epithalamium and rolling her bloodshot eyes:

> ... ac natae Turnique canit hymenaeos
> sanguineam torquens aciem....   (VII.398–99)

Sanguineam aciem means, tropologically, her eye, but it suggests also
a battle line and echoes the various meanings of *sanguis*.[2]

Turnus reacts differently at first. To the old hag who claims to
come from *omnipotens Saturnia* (428), he answers curtly that the
Trojan fleet has not escaped his notice and that war and peace are
properly the business of men:

> 'bella viri pacemque gerent quis bella gerenda.'   (444)

There may be a hint here of his attitude toward Amata; certainly, the
words suggest the young hero's view of reality. But Allecto, stung by
the calm superiority, flings at him both a flaming torch and a sentence he will never be able to forget:

> 'adsum dirarum ab sede sororum,
> bella manu letumque gero.'   (VII.454–55)

"I am come from the abode of the Furies; in this hand, I bear war and
death."

The scornful echo in *"bella ... gero"* contradicts Turnus and dismisses his naïve hero's code that war is the business of strong men.
War, says Allecto, is neither business nor a matter of strength. And
now the *ira* associated with Juno and Allecto possesses Turnus:

> arma amens fremit, arma toro tectisque requirit:
> saevit amor ferri et scelerata insania belli,
> ira super.   (VII.460–62)

Madly he yells out for arms, arms he hunts by his bedside and all through
his house. Lust for the sword rages in him, and the accursed frenzy for
war, and fury above all.

It is important to realize that Turnus is less receptive to the demon
than Amata was; that his nobility, his aristocratic background, and
his prowess and *virtù* define him far more accurately than the mad

words he utters or his threats against Latinus; and that Allecto's job, as she understands it, is to create chaos, not just conflict. This is an understanding that Juno's words did not absolutely demand but that Juno's attitude justified. This understanding becomes indeed a revelation to Juno herself, so that when Allecto is through, Juno is shaken by what Allecto has done—shaken enough to reject Allecto's offer of further service (559 f.).

The fact that Allecto does not directly infiltrate the Trojans but rather guides the dogs and Ascanius's shot attests of course to the rightness of the Trojan cause in the Olympian economy. But the effect of Allecto's interference is again chaos. The similes in the three episodes bear this out. The first (378 f.) compares Amata to a spinning top; the second (462 f.) compares Turnus to a boiling kettle; the third (528 f.) compares the fighting between Trojan youth and Latin rustics to the churning, heaving sea. These similes apply uniformly to Allecto; they define the shape of her presence.

Allecto functions primarily to express the horror of war. The conflict between the farmers and the hunters which arises from the slaying of the royal deer is not in itself too small an incident to spark the conflict because the materials for conflict are patently there [3]— Amata's passion, Latinus's weakness, the noble prowess of Turnus, and the thoughtlessness of the Trojans. But Vergil preferred to symbolize unmistakably, in the horrific figure of Allecto, his and perhaps his generation's apprehension of war. For the third time in the poem, Ascanius's imitation of life is context to a critical action: in IV, in V, and here, Ascanius rides about on his horse. But this time Ascanius is himself involved. It is his arrow, guided by Allecto, that kills the deer.

The description of the deer, inserted in the middle of the episode (483 f.), has dramatic effect. Vergil could have put the passage first; instead, he shows us Allecto meddling in the hunt and only then describes the deer, in sharp contrast with both the *rabidae canes* (493 f.) and the eager youth. The pathos of this incident is enhanced by the first casualties. Almo, eldest son of the royal gamekeeper, is brought down by an arrow in the throat: *tenuemque inclusit sanguine vitam* (534). The adjective *tenuem* suggests the frailty of mankind's defenses against violence, passion, and Tartarean fury. Dead too is Galaesus,

an elderly nobleman, *iustissimus unus,* killed while trying to stop the
fighting—*dum paci medium se offert* (536).

The incensed Latins demand war:

> undique collecti coeunt Martemque fatigant.
> ilicet infandum cuncti contra omina bellum,
> contra fata deum perverso numine poscunt.   (VII.582–84)

Rushing together from all over, they clamored for war. Straightway, led by
some perverse power, they all demanded unspeakable war, against all the
omens and against the fates of the gods.

The repeated insistence on divine and human perversity is hardened
by the patterns of sound (especially the *c*'s) alternating with echoing
fate in each line. The passage also compresses the tumultuous scene at
the palace—the shouts, the arguments, the improvised counsels
back and forth. Latinus attempts to hold out, arguing that their desires are against the will of the gods, but his protests are futile. He
tries to impute blame to Turnus, but his collapse is, as it must be,
total, and he hides away in the palace: "saepsit se tectis rerumque re-
liquit habenas" (600).

With Latinus's abdication comes the collapse of all who resisted
Turnus, the shepherds, and the rest. Even then Latinus refuses to rat-
ify the decision; Juno herself must throw open the Gates of War.
Now the whole nation is committed and everywhere men take up
their arms (623 f.). The conversion to wartime Vergil describes in energetic lines as convincing and striking as anyone's; but he maintains
his own perspective:

> vomeris huc et falcis honos, huc omnis aratri
> cessit amor; recoquunt patrios fornacibus ensis.   (VII.635–36) [4]

To this has come all their pride in share and sickle, to this all their love
for the plough. In the furnaces, they retemper the weapons of their land.

This Vergilian perspective enlarges both the invocation and the catalogue which follow. In the midst of the invocation, the lines—

> quibus Itala iam tum
> floruerit terra alma viris, quibus arserit armis.   (VII.643–44)

—define the shape of the catalogue and epitomize the tragedy. There is genuine feeling for the dear, fertile land flowering with young manhood; the feeling has pervaded numerous passages about the good earth of Italy. But *terra alma* is also the subject of *arserit armis*, with its harsh sounds and terrible image of destruction. An analogous contrast informs the presentation of the first two figures in the catalogue, Mezentius and Lausus. Mezentius is the *asper contemptor divum* (647 f.), while Lausus, his son, is presented as the handsomest warrior apart from Turnus: *quo pulchrior alter / non fuit excepto Laurentis corpore Turni* (649 f.).

The figures of Turnus and Camilla climax and conclude the catalogue of Latin forces. Each unites the conflicting elements of *floruerit* and *arserit*, each is presented in an interplay of masculine and feminine details, each both attracts and somewhat repels the reader. Turnus is first described in terms of his vigorous, handsome manliness, evoking the description of Lausus. Dominant in Turnus's armor are the Chimaera and the figure of Io. The Chimaera embodies destructive energy:

> ... Aetnaeos efflantem faucibus ignis;
> tam magis illa fremens et tristibus effera flammis
> quam magis effuso crudescunt sanguine pugnae.   (VII.786–88)

. . . breathing from her jaws volcanic fires. The bloodier and gorier the battle became, the more she roared and spewed out wild flames.

Io, chosen perhaps because of Turnus's relationship with Inachus and Greece, suggests something else: the position of the victim of divine power, the human being who has been touched by the gods. It is a motif that shapes many sections of the poem—indeed, the story of Juturna later provides context for Turnus's last hours. The outlines of the tale of Io are barely suggested by Vergil, at one remove (*argumentum ingens:* though he described the Chimaera directly, he describes here the goldwork which presents Io). But he clearly expected his readers to understand meaning and tone.

Even more striking for the motif of duality is the Camilla section which climaxes the catalogue. The passage begins almost parenthetically—*Hos super....* But the figure of Camilla symbolizes both the Latin forces in general and the coming war. The warriors following her are described as *florentis aere:* the echo of *floruerit* from the invocation (644) is hardly accidental. Camilla is a *bellatrix* but she is also a *virgo:* the two nouns enclose lines 805–6 and give *virgo* the added meaning of *virago*. Not interested in ordinary female pursuits, Camilla is accustomed *proelia virgo / dura pati* (literally, accustomed, "a virgin, to endure harsh battles")—a choice and arrangement of words the ambivalence of which defies paraphrase.[5] The next four lines are justly famous:

> illa vel intactae segetis per summa volaret
> gramina nec teneras cursu laesisset aristas,
> vel mare per medium fluctu suspensa tumenti
> ferret iter celeris nec tingeret aequore plantas.   (VII.808–11)

> She could have skimmed along the blades of an unmown corn-crop
> Without so much as bruising their tender ears as she ran:
> She could have flitted over the waves of a swelling sea
> Without so much as wetting the quicksilver soles of her feet.
>
> (Tr. Day Lewis)

Image and sound embody Camilla's femininity and grace, and the peace-war, creation-destruction polarities suggested earlier. The contrast between land and sea, between the corn and the tender stalks on the one hand and the *fluctu tumenti* on the other, is harsh.

The final lines describe the *effusa iuventus* and the *turba matrum* (812 f.) who have come out to see Camilla and wonder at her (*miratur*). The two groups are natural enough choices—husbands and fathers are marching to war; but it is also significant that, in this sole glimpse of the onlookers, Vergil has chosen the two groups who in effect started the war. At any rate, the crowd *miratur ... et prospectat euntem.* The words convey their lingering gaze, the feelings with which they follow her progress (and by extension the progress of all the warriors)—the ambivalence of glory. In the following lines, as Conington points out acutely, Vergil compresses the babble of the onlookers. The details alternate between feminine and masculine, between ornaments and weapons:

> ut regius ostro
> velet honos levis umeros, ut fibula crinem

auro internectat, Lyciam ut gerat ipsa pharetram
et pastoralem praefixa cuspide myrtum.   (VII.814–17)

how the splendor of the royal purple covers her smooth shoulders and the
brooch entwines her hair with gold, and how she carries her Lycian
quiver and the shepherd's staff of myrtle tipped with steel.

The detail of the golden brooch foreshadows both her death and its
manner. The final image, enlarging this hint, epitomizes the tone and
texture of the catalogue—*pastoralem myrtum* enclosing *praefixa
cuspide*. This rich image, focusing the whole process of ploughshares-
into-swords, precariously unites the passage, the catalogue, and the
whole of Book VII.

The sequence of events and the structure of Book VII demand careful reflection. Various critics would have it that VII is generally a
"light" book, that it is less serious than VI or VIII, that it merely provides props for important actions to come. Such views are partial and
misleading, and ignore the rich symbolism and the ambiguities of VII.
The problems we are faced with here are not easily disentangled—
the relative merits of Trojans and Latins, the relative responsibility
of Aeneas and Turnus, the various forces producing the outbreak of
war. The Trojans are not prime culprits, but their role cannot be simply whitewashed. Turnus emerges a sympathetic character whom we
cannot dismiss as "the enemy." Whatever our judgment of Amata
and Allecto, the ultimate motives of Juno are not easily stated. Her
activity seems a kind of last-ditch malice, rather than a purposeful attempt to finish off Aeneas and the Trojans.

The structure is clearly whole; it is time to reject out-of-hand the
lingering notion that the first thirty-six lines provide a kind of orna-
mental-interlude-*cum*-transition. The similarities between Book VII
and Book I have been frequently noted, but too often without separat-
ing the incidental from the architectonic, the contingent from the
substantial. I have already remarked on the parallels between Dido
and Latinus, whose significance rests mainly on contrasts. Let us consider the parallels a little further.

Like Dido, Latinus is highly civilized; he sits on a throne in the
midst of a temple-palace; he welcomes Ilioneus calmly and cour-

teously; he has already heard of Troy and the Trojans; he asks the reasons for their coming, offers sympathy, and accepts them as guests. None of these similarities, however, can be considered compelling for the simple reason that none is unusual or surprising: they arise from a pattern of host-guest relationships well known in ancient poetry. They do, of course, contribute to an atmosphere in which other patterns from Books I and IV are more readily observed. But, as I argued earlier, we must recognize that the divergent modes of thought and action, the divergent motives and situations of Latinus and Dido are more important than the similarities.

Dido, for instance, impulsively offered her friendship; only later, tutored by Anna, did she see a possible boon for her people. Latinus, however, has a knotty domestic problem with perilous implications for his reign. On the one hand, he dare not undervalue the omens and portents and commands of his gods; on the other, he faces the strong resistance of his wife (*neque enim leve nomen Amatae,* 581, has larger meanings than the immediate context justifies)—a resistance reinforced by the fact that he promised Lavinia to Turnus. Amata is a strong, passionate, unstable woman; these traits are very prominent in the face of Latinus's indecision. Turnus, the great favorite of Amata and a formidable prince, has clearly not made any agreement with Latinus respecting the oracles and omens.

Yet, after one speech by Ilioneus, Latinus virtually hands over his kingdom to Aeneas—who was not even there. True, Latinus does hedge a bit. But the words are clear enough, so that the hedging is merely taking note of some technicalities. Surely, then, Latinus commits a blunder of major proportions. In effect, he is abandoning the interests of Turnus and Amata, and probably others, to these foreigners.

Under such circumstances, the reactions of both Amata and Turnus are not totally unreasonable or beyond comprehension. One might argue indeed that, by his unilateral action, Latinus provoked the conflict between Latins and Trojans. His hasty decision, which he then cannot enforce, shows him a wavering ruler whose power depends on factional politics. Clearly, the polity of Latium cannot be considered a matter involving only Latinus and Faunus. It might have been this, if Latinus were a strong king, with undisputed control over Amata and the nobles, and with no reason to believe Turnus would resist him. But he is not. And his speech to Ilioneus, combining petulant vanity with expediency, accurately forecasts his later course, when he washes his hands of everything even while insisting upon the authenticity of the omens (594 f.).

All of this illuminates the parallels between VII and I. When Ilioneus declares to Latinus that Italy will never regret having taken Troy to her bosom (*gremio excepisse*, 233), the metaphorical *gremio* evokes two key passages from Book I: Venus to Amor, "cum te gremio accipiet laetissima Dido" (1.685); and Dido fondling Amor-Ascanius, "et interdum gremio fovet inscia Dido ..." (718). So also, Ilioneus's later words to Latinus—

> 'sed nos fata deum vestras exquirere terras
> imperiis egere suis.'   (VII.239–40)

"Rather, the fates of the gods have forced us, by their commands, to seek out your land."

—evoke Aeneas's desperate words in Hades to Dido, themselves an echo of his hard defense in IV: "sed me iussa deum..../ imperiis egere suis" (VI.461 f.).

The motif of gifts also enters here, but explication necessarily becomes more tenuous. I distrust the easy assurance with which one critic explains the parallels: "It *follows* that, just as a Greek gift *spelt ruin* for Priam and Troy, and Trojan and Greek gifts *contributed to* the fall of Dido and Carthage, so the gifts here offered to Latinus conceal the destructive flames 'escaped' at Troy (and Carthage)." The trouble is not that the points are too neat; the trouble is this critic turns poetic motif, the workings of association, into contributory causes. The importance of the gifts-motif throughout the *Aeneid* lies in overtones and associations, beginning with the archetypal gift of the Wooden Horse.[6]

At times, the gifts are associated with their source, as in Laocoon's acute refusal to trust the Greeks bearing gifts. But even with respect to the Wooden Horse, the associations connected with it— particularly religious and mythic associations—are more significant. When Juno promises to reward Aeolus with nymphs, she does so to goad him on to violence, in a context in which her own *sexual* superiority is seen as questioned (her jealousy of Venus and her frustration at Pallas's successes as compared to her own failures); in that whole episode the association between sex and violence is unmistakable. The gifts Aeneas gives Dido exist in the aura of Paris and Helen; the *monimenta amoris* (in v.572, Ascanius's horse) are intimately connected with *amor* and violence.

As a motif, then, gifts acquire body from the contexts to which they belong and the overtones they carry from context to context— the interpenetration of feeling, action, and motive which they suggest. Latinus's gifts to Aeneas include horses,

> semine ab aetherio spirantis naribus ignem,
> illorum de gente patri quos daedala Circe
> supposita de matre nothos furata creavit.   (VII.281–83)

of divine pedigree and breathing fire from their nostrils. They were from that stock of bastard horses which the cunning Circe had bred when she crossed a mare with the stallions she had stolen from her father the Sun.

While not in the same category as the *ornatus Argivae Helenae* (I.650), these gifts are noteworthy, particularly for the mythic details, the forebodings of violence, and the fact that this is the third appearance of Circe in Book VII.

Circe seems to function as part of a larger pattern of women-fiends in Book VII. Dominant in this pattern are, of course, Juno and Amata; those two, brooding on the Trojan War, its mythic cause, and its impending reenactment, permeate it with their own violent sexuality. At the close of her furious monologue, Juno decrees a reordering of history. If Lavinia and Aeneas must eventually marry and join the two races, it will be at frightful cost—mutual bloodletting for a dowry, Bellona goddess of war for bridesmaid. In Juno's frenzied vision, marriage torches become funeral torches; Hecuba's living nightmare, that she had conceived a firebrand, must be repeated, complete with a second Paris (this time the son of Venus) and a second Troy for him to bring to ruin:

> 'hac gener atque socer coeant mercede suorum:
> sanguine Troiano et Rutulo dotabere, virgo,

et Bellona manet te pronuba. nec face tantum
Cisseis praegnas ignis enixa iugalis;
quin idem Veneri partus suus et Paris alter,
funestaeque iterum recidiva in Pergama taedae.'   (VII.317–22)

As for Amata, even before she is completely controlled by Allecto, she
reflects Juno's vision. So, pleading with Latinus on behalf of Turnus,
she summons up the figure of Paris penetrating Sparta, Paris carrying
off Helen of Troy:

'at non sic Phrygius penetrat Lacedaemona pastor,
Ledaeamque Helenam Troianas vexit ad urbes?'   (VII.363–64)

In these examples, such refraction of the mythic Troy responds strikingly to the gifts which Aeneas sent to Latinus, the relics saved from
the ashes of Troy: *reliquias Troia ex ardente receptas* (VII.244).

Some critics have attempted to explain the relevance of the Trojan
war as model for the Italian war. But it seems to me that the role of
the Trojan war must be connotative, not allegorical; that, at the
point we have reached, the antagonists are not yet sharply distinguished; and that, in any event, the outcome would have to be very
strained to achieve any satisfactory parallel with the end of the Trojan war.

Furthermore, Vergil has whittled away the distinctions Aeneas felt
about Trojans and Greeks. In II, friends and enemies were sharply set
off; even in the context of fate, Aeneas regarded the Greeks as a
collective monstrosity. His view became less simplistic as his history
developed. During the wanderings, there was the revenge wrought on
Pyrrhus by Orestes; there were Achaemenides and the figure of Ulysses, *infelix*. At Cumae, Aeneas received the paradoxical prophecy that
he would find salvation from a Greek city. Shortly, he will meet
Evander the Greek, while the Latins are refused the aid they expected
from Diomedes, the Greek whom the Trojans most feared and hated.

To understand what relevance past Troy has in the later books of
the *Aeneid,* we must keep such changes in mind. The epic is more
than a lengthy sum of its parts; the tones and overtones of Book VII,
elusive as they are, will become both more complex and more mean-
ingful as the poem proceeds.

CHAPTER SIX

WAR IN ITALY

The prelude of Book VIII (1–17) may seem slightly apart from its main matter, Aeneas's visit to Evander. The book, however, is no mere interlude. While the purpose of Aeneas's actions is manifestly to recruit allies for the war and while a major event is his gaining divine armor, accomplishment outdoes purpose. Much else happens, including the visit to the site of Rome and the pageantry of the Shield, of course, though in some readings these have been divorced from context.

The first seventeen lines deal with the gathering Latin forces and the mission to Diomedes. Some lines seem distinctly summary:

> ductores primi Messapus et Vfens
> contemptorque deum Mezentius undique cogunt
> auxilia et latos vastant cultoribus agros.   (VIII.6–8)

Their commanders Messapus and Ufens and Mezentius, who scorned the gods, were the first to muster troops from all around, despoiling the fields far and wide of their laborers.

Here are recalled the uprising and mustering of forces, and the canonical description of the leaders of Book VII; beyond these, the tone of that book lingers in the echoing image of line 8, the leaders plundering fields of their *cultoribus,* a word which means both "tillers" and "devotees." More than summary is the verbal hint in the final line (17), part of the message to Diomedes: *Turno regi aut regi ... Latino.* The roughness of sound and the repetition draw our attention to the internecine strife that the words suggest. So does the phrase *Talia per Latium* (18: "so things went throughout Latium"). Involving much of Italy, the war will be marked by confusion of frontier and confusion of scope. While the scene of battle is Latium proper, the scope is enlarged early to include several kinds of civil strife, cutting across many tribal limits, so that the war mirrors the Italian troubles in Vergil's own century.

But, as in Book VII, these opening lines are closely attached to the movement and tone of the whole book in which they appear. There is no structural weakness, no vagueness or diffusion. Suggesting the wholesale resistance to Aeneas, the muster provides context for the appeal to Evander, the alliances, and the Shield. Aeneas's appeal to Evander wins him not just Arcadian forces but others as well and involves him in a larger conflict. Furthermore, the mission to Diomedes is counterpointed with Aeneas's mission to Evander—the fulfillment of the Sibyl's paradoxical promise of help from a Greek city. Finally, the opening lines provide a point of departure for Book IX, which opens with a reminder that the events of IX occur at the same time as the events of VIII. Neither Book VIII nor Book IX, then, can be considered *in vacuo.* The strands of each parallel the other. Each book is totally coherent within itself (*pace* the critics who consider the Nisus and Euryalus episode as digressive as the Hercules-Cacus episode) and totally congruent with the other.[1] Different in character and movement, these parallel strands join in Book X, at the crucial point when Aeneas's fleet arrives and the figure of Aeneas the Destroyer is seen by Latins and Trojans.

Even before Aeneas's bargain with Evander, it is evident that the war cannot remain limited. Mezentius and Pallas, Tarchon and Diomedes, Messapus and Ufens are all involved. Allecto's madness cannot remain localized or confined to one side. There is also the confusion of battle lines. Allusion and statement evoke the archetype of Troy, but in the end (Book XI) Greek rejects Latin, and Greek joins arms with Trojan; a foreign prince leads the Latin troops, an ejected tyrant is pursued by his people who are themselves following another foreign prince, while the Latin elders press for peace. Trojans and Latins work together in the forests, gathering wood for the funerals (XI. 133 f.), and later try to kill each other. Considering Books

VII–XII in general, if we look to the Trojan war for a paradigm, there is no pattern, even in inverse terms. The larger theme that suggests context and pattern is, rather, the theme dominating the earlier books—Dardanian Aeneas's journey home. The fulfillment of the Sibyl's paradoxical prophecy of aid from a Greek city is that even the notion of *natural* enemies fades away.

Some of the intertwined causes are eventually resolved—by the death of Mezentius, for instance; but Vergil does not draw our attention to such resolutions. In the deliberate turmoil stirred up by Books VII and VIII, the point of the enlarged war is the tone, not the details. It is the tone that pervades the deaths of Lausus and Pallas and the fatal adventure of Camilla. The whole impact of the Arcadian-Etruscan-Trojan alliance gradually dissolves and the focus of the war shifts. When Mezentius dies, he dies not so much as the Etruscan tyrant but as a stand-in for Turnus and as the father of Lausus. When Camilla dies, she dies not as Latin ally but as the comrade of Turnus. The whole point becomes the personal struggle between Aeneas and Turnus. As we shall see later, the carnage of Book X is significant precisely as carnage, not as critical battles in a mounting conflict. There seems to me only one critical battle in Books X and XI—the attempted ambush, during which Camilla happens to be killed. After it, the only possible development is the face-to-face encounter of Aeneas and Turnus. Earlier battles, including the sortie of Book IX and Turnus's stupendous fighting, have but limited relevance to long-range or short-range strategy. Especially in Book IX, but not only there, strategy itself becomes a comment on much of the fighting.

With these generalities in mind, we can look briefly at Evander's commission to Aeneas to lead the Etruscans against their tyrant Mezentius. A prophecy, not unlike that tendered Latinus, has ruled out Italian leadership; the Etruscans are to seek a foreign commander:

> ' "nulli fas Italo tantam subiungere gentem:
> externos optate duces." '   (VIII.502–3)

Though a foreigner, Evander himself could not accept the role because of his age and weakness (*"tarda gelu saeclisque effeta senectus,"*

508). Nor could the younger Pallas, because he was born of an Italian mother. Thus, Evander turns to Aeneas, providentially sent to Italy at this juncture:

> 'tu, cuius et annis
> et generi fata indulgent, quem numina poscunt,
> ingredere, o Teucrum atque Italum fortissime ductor.'   (VIII.511–13)

"To you the fates have been generous, both in your age and in your race; you are the one whom the divine powers summon: go, then, most valiant leader of Trojans and of Italians."

Over and above this, Evander entrusts to Aeneas the budding career of Pallas. Even though he sought Evander's help (at the suggestion of the god Tiber), Aeneas is troubled by the commission; with his eyes downcast, *Aeneas Anchisiades* reflects sadly on what lies ahead (*multaque dura...*, 522). Some critics have—irrelevantly —seen this as wavering. But the salient point is that Aeneas does not need more burdens to carry: this, rather than a premonition of Pallas's doom, is the significance of the epithet *Anchisiades,* with its evocation of his dynasty-minded father. In the developing action, the death of Pallas leads to the death of Mezentius, and indirectly to the death of Turnus; it leads also to a wholesale carnage that defiles Aeneas's quest for home and peace. Willy-nilly, the conflict grows out of all proportion, to a size Aeneas surely did not imagine when he laid out his stockade.

His gloomy thoughts are interrupted: Venus flashes a sign through the clear sky:

> namque improviso vibratus ab aethere fulgor
> cum sonitu venit et ruere omnia visa repente
>
>   . . . .
>
> arma inter nubem caeli in regione serena
> per sudum rutilare vident et pulsa tonare.   (VIII.524–29)

Suddenly the heavens shook with a flash of lightning and thunder crashed, and everything appeared to be suddenly falling into ruin. . . . Amid a cloud they saw arms, gleaming red in the clear sky and clashing thunderously.

With its connotations of energy and power, the sign is both reassuring and harsh. Whatever Aeneas might have expected before, the outlook now is for a great and bloody war, running with rivers of blood. Aeneas takes on an aspect that becomes tragically familiar:

> 'heu quantae miseris caedes Laurentibus instant!
> quas poenas mihi, Turne, dabis! quam multa sub undas
> Scuta virum galeasque et fortia corpora volves,
> Thybri pater!'   (VIII.537—40)

"Oh what horrible slaughter awaits the Laurentians! What a price you will pay me, Turnus! How many shields and helmets and corpses of brave men you will roll beneath your waves, father Tiber!"

The echo of his first words in the poem (I. 99–101) is vengeful and hard; the tone of these lines is far different from his confident reply to the Sibyl, "I am ready for the fight in Italy." Now Aeneas the Destroyer, he begins by spilling blood—*laetus adit*—at the altar of Hercules. Then he says no more until Book X, where he utters a prayer.

Two points may be added here to clarify context and interpretation. First, the notion that Aeneas has a premonition of Pallas's death, that this prompts his sadness, as a father himself and as one who remembers his own aged father—this notion has a curious artificiality about it. There is no hint of it in anything Aeneas says here, and there is plenty of evidence against it. Actually, the premonition of Pallas's death pervades Evander's farewell speech, a profoundly moving speech set against the great war impending: *"maior Martis iam apparet imago"* (557). Within that frame, Evander's parental grief is both singular and universal. He dwells on the weariness and impotence of age, he embraces Pallas long and tearfully; like despairing Anchises, he longs for death to spare him from the envisioned catastrophe. By word and tone, he conjures up the spectre of Fate; and then, having taken leave of his son, he faints.

Texture and statement are loaded; it suffices to point out merely *genitor* and *supremo* in lines 583–84:

> haec genitor digressu dicta supremo
> fundebat: famuli conlapsum in tecta ferebant.

These words the father poured out at this final parting; he collapsed, and his servants carried him into the house.

But Vergil discreetly says nothing about Aeneas's reaction. In X, Pallas's safety is not a dominant concern of Aeneas as the fleet lands and in the strategy used in the beachhead battle. Thus, the fact that his immediate reaction to the news of Pallas's death is a barbaric rampage must be weighed carefully in interpretation. For the moment, suffice it to say that there are no grounds for assuming that Aeneas regards Pallas paternally or with special affection, or that the safety of Pallas is his primary concern.

The second point is a corollary of the first. Critics have been reluctant to admit that Aeneas becomes excessively destructive in the course of the war.[2] Thus, unless they ignore it, they must explain away the latter half of Book X, usually in terms of the Pallas theme, but such explanation combines sentimentality and rationalization. They must also ignore or explain away the fact that at times in Books X and XI and XII it would be impossible to distinguish between Aeneas and Turnus as each destroys his enemies, were not clear identification given. Adjectives and adverbs, tone of voice, manner, similes—these describe a murderous butcher. Indeed, in one long passage in Book XII, Vergil deliberately pairs Aeneas and Turnus; it begins, *inque vicem nunc Turnus agit, nunc Troius heros* (XII. 502). It has a startling double simile, comparing Aeneas and Turnus to fires raging through forests and rivers pounding their way to sea, *quisque suum populatus iter* (521 f.). It presents first one, then the other, in symmetrical alternation, each methodically going about his business. Gradually, the passage moves out from the microcosm to the broader macrocosm—*omnesque Latini,/ omnes Dardanidae*—conluding with universal, unceasing slaughter: *nec mora nec requies, vasto certamine tendunt* (553). I will return to this passage again in discussing Book XII, but at least one aspect of it is perfectly clear: Vergil is far less reluctant than his critics to look honestly and unflinchingly at the war and its implications.

A pastoral atmosphere pervades the first half of Book VIII. The mood is suggested even before Aeneas reaches Arcadia. The river-god,

Tiber, who sends Aeneas to Evander, describes himself as lapping the banks and flowing through fertile fields:

> 'stringentem ripas et pinguia culta secantem,
> caeruleus Thybris, caelo gratissimus amnis.'   (VIII.63–64)

As the ships sail, Vergil emphasizes the pastoral, personifying waves and woods amid verdant words and sounds:

> mirantur et undae,
> miratur nemus insuetum fulgentia longe
> scuta virum fluvio pictasque innare carinas.   (VIII.91–93)

The very waves wonder and the woods, unused to the spectacle, wonder at the flashing shields of warriors and the brightly painted ships floating on the stream.

As if the first ships ever to sail on that silent stream, the Trojan boats cut through the green reflections of the woods in the peaceful water (*viridisque secant placido aequore silvas,* 96).

The story of Hercules and Cacus belongs to the conventional mythology of the pastoral world. The story celebrates simple virtues; the issues are sharply defined; it ends with poetic justice. The interest in the story derives both from the story itself and from the clear distinction between right and wrong in it. Cacus is prehistoric evil, Hercules a prehistoric knight-errant. In the praises sung of him, Hercules is the doer of deeds in a world apart. The ritual is detached and complete: the song includes Hercules' strangling of the snakes sent by Juno, his descent into Hell, and his destruction of Troy. The apparent connections with the *Aeneid* seem startling—even to the fact that Juno's enmity caused his labors. But these apparent connections remain distinct from the ongoing reality.

It is appropriate, then, that the Arcadian visit should climax in a vision of the Golden Age, and that the vision should encompass the story of Saturn's flight from Olympus, fleeing Jove's arms, an exile from his throne:

> 'primus ab aetherio venit Saturnus Olympo
> arma Iovis fugiens et regnis exsul ademptis.'   (VIII.319–20)

We may well suspend judgment here, as well as disbelief, for, as Evander says, these woods were once the abode of native Fauns and Nymphs, and of a race of men sprung from trees:

> 'haec nemora indigenae Fauni Nymphaeque tenebant
> gensque virum truncis et duro robore nata.'   (VIII.314–15)

The tour of the site of Rome is of a piece with the other Arcadian events. It has been dubbed "Aeneas in Wonderland," with partial accuracy. We note that Aeneas *miratur;* we should also note that he is taken, enchanted (*capiturque locis et laetus...*, 311) and that he is very much concerned with *virum monimenta priorum* (312) and *veterum monimenta virorum* (356)—"the relics of earlier generations." This emphasis on the distant past is restated at beginning and end of the tour. The imagery of woodlands and the etymological play on *Latium* (because Saturn *latuisset*), emphasizing the hidden, are both significant. The woodland remains the abode of the innocent and the inexperienced; the etymological device reminds us forcefully of the double meaning in *condere*—to found and to hide (*conditor*, 313). All of this causes a shock, properly, to the historical-minded reader when he notes the parenthetical place given the two "important" lines referring to the Nymph Carmenta,

> vatis fatidicae, cecinit quae prima futuros
> Aeneadas magnos et nobile Pallanteum   (VIII.340–41)

the prophetic seeress, who was the first to sing that Aeneas's sons would be great and Pallanteum noble.

Certainly important, this detail is hardly the point of the whole episode. The moral is the moral of Arcadia, where the Golden Age can almost be felt, where that lingering dream operates both as nostalgia for imagined past and as measure for waiting present:

> 'aurea quae perhibent illo sub rege fuere
> saecula: sic placida populos in pace regebat,
> deterior donec paulatim ac decolor aetas
> et belli rabies et amor successit habendi.'   (VIII.324–27)

"Under his [Saturn's] reign passed those ages which men called Golden, so gently and peacefully did he rule; until little by little an inferior and tarnished age replaced it, with the madness of war and the lust to possess."

On this particular tour, indeed, the pastoral scene is complete with a local Presence and an enchanted wood:

> 'hoc nemus, hunc' inquit 'frondoso vertice collem
> (quis deus incertum est) habitat deus....   (VIII.351–52)

That night, Aeneas sleeps in Evander's hut, the hut Hercules himself had once occupied. Evander invites him in with lines which have become so famous (364–65) that context, meaning, and function are overlooked:

> 'aude, hospes, contemnere opes et te quoque dignum
> finge deo, rebusque veni non asper egenis.'
> dixit, et angusti subter fastigia tecti
> ingentem Aenean duxit stratisque locavit
> effultum foliis et pelle Libystidis ursae.   (VIII.364–68)

"My guest, have the courage to scorn riches and so mold yourself that you too may be worthy of the god: do not despise our poverty." So saying, he led great Aeneas under the roof of his simple dwelling, and showed him his bed, a couch of strewn leaves and the skin of a Libyan bear.

The juxtaposition of the great Aeneas and the tiny hut, the live hero and the mythic figure, overshadows the seemingly Homeric cast of the details. Evander is plainly asking more than a special kind of momentary humility; he is assigning Aeneas a role, bringing him fully into their Arcadian life. It comes as no surprise then to read that, in the morning, Evander is called from his hut by the warm comforting light and the morning song of birds under the eaves:

> Euandrum ex humili tecto lux suscitat alma
> et matutini volucrum sub culmine cantus.   (VIII.455–56)

The pastoral atmosphere that lingers in the wake of the Venus-Vulcan episode pervades even the locale chosen for the presentation

of the armor—as if no place in this rustic land is untouched by it.
Bringing the armor, Venus sees Aeneas in a large grove near the cool
stream of Caere, a place traditionally regarded as sacred:

> religione patrum late sacer; undique colles
> inclusere cavi et nigra nemus abiete cingunt.   (VIII.598–99)

Enclosed by curving hills and encircled with dark fir trees, the grove
is devoted to Silvanus, god of fields and flocks: *arvorum pecorisque
deo* (601).

These pastoral elements are not digressive. The contrast between
Arcadia and the war to be waged is immeasurably heightened in
these passages. If they afford a sort of respite, in which we can contemplate the ferocity of Juno and the destruction of Troy as elements
in the Hercules myth, this is the calm before the storm. The reality
will press upon us in Book IX, the most "heroic" book in the poem,
but that pressing reality is present here too. Venus comes to Aeneas
in a lonely valley by the cool stream,

> natumque in valle reducta
> ut procul egelido secretum flumine vidit...,   (VIII.609–10)

and the Arcadian mythology fades into the golden past. The emergent polarity is harsh. The heart might long for Arcadia and its
Golden Age, but the more brittle gold of the Shield, gilding Rome
and Augustus, inexorably involves Janus and Saturn, Vulcan and
Venus. The episode of Venus in the brutal arms of Vulcan is facilely
dismissed by some as "easily traceable to . . . Homeric sources" (Conington). But it won't be put aside that easily.

Although some details in this episode seem to share Arcadian pastoral characteristics (even to the similarity between the dialogue of
Venus and Vulcan, and the litany of Hercules), the Arcadian tone begins to fade from the very first line:

> nox ruit et fuscis tellurem amplectitur alis.   (VIII.369) [3]

Night fell and embraced the earth in her dark wings.

The image of embrace, *amplectitur,* is echoed in *cunctantem amplexu molli fovet* (388) and in:

> optatos dedit amplexus placidumque petivit
> coniugis infusus gremio per membra soporem.   (VIII.405–6)

He gave her the desired embrace; and then, relaxing upon the breast of his wife, he let the sleep of pleasure steal over his limbs. (Tr. Knight)

But the larger content is not; rather, *fuscis alis* evokes II.360 (*nox atra cava circumvolat umbra*) and VI.866, where Aeneas felt dread as he saw the somber cloud of night fluttering about the head of Marcellus.

The Homeric source is also ambiguous. Actually, Vergil used at least two sources, *Iliad* XIV.159–351 and XVIII.369–467. The latter episode—Thetis approaching Hephaistos to request armor for her son—is dignified and moving; both the hero's mother and the maker of the Shield are fully in tune with the whole situation (remarkably, in view of the comic way Hephaistos is often treated). From this episode, Vergil took only the barest outline. He drew mainly on the Hera-Zeus episode of *Iliad* XIV, both for attendant details and for its deliberate sexuality. And even here he has made some striking and fundamental changes. Like Hera, Venus is determined to trade on sex; like Zeus, Vulcan is boastful and self-assured. But Venus has also been vulgarized and Vulcan made both foolish and violent. The wit and beauty of *Iliad* XIV Vergil has deliberately written out of his episode.

Both this episode and the final passage of VIII, the Shield, are marked by the abrupt *at Venus....* Less diagrammatic than in IV (*At regina.....*), the formula collides with narrative both times in VIII. In the final scene, Aeneas and his men have dismounted and are relaxing in the grove near the river Caere when Venus comes; here we are made to understand that Venus's maternal heart is alarmed, with good reason:

> at Venus haud animo nequiquam exterrita mater....   (370)

Venus has intervened before on Aeneas's behalf, with what results we have already seen. Perhaps suggesting these earlier incidents, the word *mater* is interesting both in content and in position; its full force will be realized shortly.

Her first words to Vulcan seem bland enough, uttered on the "golden bed" (*thalamo aureo,* 372). But unlike the allusion to Laomedontian Troy in the Hercules litany, her recital of Troy's unhappy history is devious prologue. Embedded in her words are curious paradoxes, such as the verbal clash between the doom of Troy and her obligations to Priam's people (*debita,* 372; *deberem plurima,* 379), and the parallels between

> 'non arma rogavi/... carissime coniunx'   (376 f.),

"I did not then ask you for arms, my dearest spouse,"

and

> 'sanctum mihi numen/arma rogo, genetrix nato.'   (382 f.)

"I ask the deity whom I reverence for arms, a mother on behalf of her son."

All in all, her request to Vulcan is astonishing. However, the emphasis on Aeneas by name (380) and on the adultery which begot him, the contrast of conjugal ties and freewheeling creative activity—these do not trouble Venus. They are easily overshadowed, she knows, by her repeated appeal to Vulcan's peculiar function, *arma.* Commentators have considered the passage indelicate and embarrassing (even without noting the erotic play in the final lines, e.g., in *coeant populi* and *clausis/ferrum acuant portis,* 385 f.). But Vergil knows what he is about. Vulcan is conquered both by the frank sexuality of his wife and by his own vision of her son. To his Cyclopes, he says later:

> 'arma acri facienda viro. nunc viribus usus....'   (441)

"Now arms must be made for a hot-blooded hero. Now there is need for your power. . . ."

Viribus pointedly echoes his earlier words to Venus (404) and *acri* tells us as much about himself as it does about Aeneas.[4] At the same time, Vulcan sees Aeneas as a proper reflection of himself, a chip off the old block, as it were.

The quality of his connection with Venus is drawn in detail; Venus ends her surprising speech, and

> niveis hinc atque hinc diva lacertis
> cunctantem amplexu molli fovet. ille repente
> accepit solitam flammam, notusque medullas
> intravit calor et labefacta per ossa cucurrit,
> non secus atque olim tonitru cum rupta corusco
> ignea rima micans percurrit lumine nimbos.   (VIII.387–92)

Her snowy-white arms encircling him, the goddess fondled him— though he hesitated—with a warm embrace. Immediately, he caught the flame, as always; the familiar glow penetrated to his very marrow and coursed through his body, melting him; just as, often, a flash of lightning darts, sparkling and dazzling, through storm clouds burst by the flaming thunder.

The crowding words for fire and flame in both narrative and simile convey what Venus has in her favor: not just the charms of Hera in *Iliad* XIV, potent as they are, but the limitless source of power, Jupiter, the hurler of thunderbolts. That is one implication of this simile, as it subsumes the imagery of serpent and flame. Thus the lines convey erotic movements, the anticipated activity in the forges, and some of the larger meanings; and wifely Venus can be pleased with her cleverness, her beauty, and her extensive success:

> sensit laeta dolis et formae conscia coniunx.   (393)

Vulcan may hesitate and hold back (*cunctantem,* 388), but he is enchained by eternal love: *aeterno devinctus amore* (394). The phrase may well be drawn from Lucretius, describing Mars as *aeterno devictus vulnere amoris* (*De rerum natura,* 1.34). If so, Vergil's use only strengthens the ironic allusion to the whole episode in *Odyssey* VIII, where comic Hephaistos traps his wife Aphrodite and her lover Ares in an iron net and so chains them together.

Vulcan's response (395 f.) to Venus unwittingly elaborates some of the implications in her speech. He loudly dismisses the notion that his power would have been ineffectual at Troy. If she had been as warm to him then as she is now (*similis si cura* ..., 396), Jove himself and even the Fates would not have brought Troy down. He is, naturally, speaking nonsense, but what he says is less important than what he does. In words erotically charged, he promises full satisfaction this time—the utmost that iron and molten alloys can produce ("quod fieri ferro liquidove potest electro," 403). Then he gives the *optatos amplexus* (405); interestingly enough, *optatos* is translated and glossed variously by various commentators—as the desires of Venus and as the desires of Vulcan. More discreetly, some leave the word ambiguous—as it should be.

The simile that follows provides transition from conjugal chamber to Cyclopes' cavern:

> Inde ubi prima quies medio iam noctis abactae
> curriculo expulerat somnum, cum femina primum,
> cui tolerare colo vitam tenuique Minerva
> impositum, cinerem et sopitos suscitat ignis
> noctem addens operi, famulasque ad lumina longo
> exercet penso, castum ut servare cubile
> coniugis et possit parvos educere natos:
> haud secus ignipotens....   (VIII.407–14)

Then, as soon as first repose had dispelled sleep, at the midpoint of the declining night hours—the time when the housewife stirs up the embers that are slumbering in the ashes and adds the nighttime to her working day—for her burden is to endure life dependent on her loom and Minerva's humble toil: so she keeps her maids toiling by lamplight at their lengthy task; and thus she strives to keep her marriage-bed chaste and to provide for her little children; just then did the Fire-lord. . . .

Vulcan is compared to a frugal housewife who works late at night: the domestic note jars the reader, cools off the passions that have been called up, and casts an ironic light on Venus's trading in sex, Vulcan's lusty violence, and the harshness of all this intrigue. Vergil's excuse for this simile is slim: the point of comparison is simply the nighttime. But by focusing on the virtues and motives in the life of the obscure, but very real, housewife, he effects a sharp contrast with the erotic glamour of power politics. The smallest details are telling—

for example, the symbolic *cinerem et sopitos ignis* and the precarious *castum cubile* are quite alien to Vulcan's ready lust (*solitam flammam, notusque calor*) and the *thalamo aureo* on which Venus could confidently depend. Notable too is the contrast between the wife's attempt to keep her husband from straying and Vulcan's past failure to keep Venus chaste. Perhaps the most oblique simile in the poem, this is also one of the most successful.

This whole episode is neither "indelicate" nor a matter of the "irrelevant" amours of Venus. By his poetic strategy here, Vergil has brought to bear on the making of the Shield a context of brutal sex-and-violence. In so doing, he has linked the multiple erotic implications of this entire scene, including the activity in the forges, to the larger pattern sketched earlier, that including Juno, Amata, and the foreign-marriage motif of Book VII. He has set his episode a world away, morally, from Homer's Hephaistos and Thetis (deliberately alluded to in 383 f.) and called our attention to the complex problems of power. The violence of reality is moving in on Arcadia.

As everyone knows, the famous passage describing the Shield (626–728) differs from Homer's in its concentration on history against Homer's depiction of scenes from the world of peace. The segments of Roman history designed by the *Ignipotens* (628) are polarized by creation and destruction. The glory of the descendants of Ascanius is set against a background of violence, even from the beginning: the founders of Rome were suckled by a wolf in Mars' green cave (*viridi Mavortis in antro,* 630 f.). The image suggests how precarious is the union of the pastoral and the violent.

Achievement depends on violence; the whole enterprise *somehow* leading to Augustus and to the final scene of his triumph is perfused by the necessity of violence. The movement seems to be from the pair rent by primeval fratricide to the final act of cumulative civil strife, the defeat of Antony and Cleopatra. There is undeniable Roman grandeur in

> hinc Augustus agens Italos in proelia Caesar
> cum patribus populoque, penatibus et magnis dis,
> stans celsa in puppi, geminas cui tempora flammas
> laeta vomunt patriumque aperitur vertice sidus.   (VIII.678–81)

On one side was Augustus Caesar leading the Italians into the battle, and with him the senate and the people, the home-gods and the great gods. He stood high on the stern; his joyous brow poured forth twin flames and on his head dawned his father's Julian star.

The echo in line 679 of III.12, where Aeneas sets out on his uncertain journey *"cum sociis natoque penatibus et magnis dis,"* may remind us that this grandeur is only part of the story. Just as in Book VI, this showpiece passage must not be divorced from context and function. The Shield deals with war specifically, lacking many of the larger themes that enriched the Hades pageant. What Aeneas sees encourages him, though he does not understand it. But none of it applies directly to the burden he has carried since Troy. Thus that *nefas* Cleopatra epitomizes the madness of war and suggests the difficulties of his enterprise only obliquely. Here are the heavy lines describing the battle of Actium:

> saevit medio in certamine Mavors
> caelatus ferro, tristesque ex aethere Dirae,
> et scissa gaudens vadit Discordia palla,
> quam cum sanguineo sequitur Bellona flagello.   (VIII.700–3)

Mars raged in the thick of the battle, his figure wrought in iron, and from the sky the grim Furies descend. Here Discord strides exultant in her torn mantle, followed by Bellona with her bloody scourge.

The two middle lines, weighed down with spondees, convey the divine displeasure. But line 703, vividly evoking Juno and Allecto from Book VII, emphasizes the relevance of the trail of blood, the figure of Bellona, and perhaps also the foreign-marriage motif, to Aeneas's own subsequent experience. The helmet he will wear has been described as spouting flames and with terror in its crests, and his breastplate as blood-colored and vast:

> terribilem cristis galeam flammasque vomentem,
>   ...loricam ex aere rigentem,
> sanguineam, ingentem....   (VIII.620–22)

While *sanguineam* belongs to the symbolic pattern from Book VII, these details are echoed when he is first seen in Book X, by friend and foe alike, a bearer of death and destruction (X. 270 f.).

The final image of Book VIII joins the burden to hope:

> Talia per clipeum Volcani, dona parentis,
> miratur rerumque ignarus imagine gaudet
> attollens umero famamque et fata nepotum.   (VIII.729–31)

He stared in wonderment at such scenes on Vulcan's shield, and on his mother's gifts. Though he did not understand the events, he took pleasure in the portrayal, as he lifted onto his shoulders the glory and the fates of his descendants.

Architecturally, the image distinctly evokes the end of II, Aeneas bearing his father on his shoulders to the mountains. Here, as there, Aeneas is profoundly *ignarus,* a point made also by the contrast with Vulcan (who is neither *vatum ignarus* nor *venturi inscius aevi,* 627). The exact meaning of Aeneas's ignorance, in both VIII and II, is elusive; the reader is easily prone to confuse what he himself knows with what Aeneas knows, and so to postulate a kind of supreme confidence that is hardly justifiable. Aeneas's determination, his general readiness of mind and spirit, are clear enough. What is surely less than clear, however, is his certainty of immediate success or of the glorious long-term validity of that success.

Just as at Troy, Aeneas lifts up a burden and a responsibility. He is neither Augustus nor an allegory for Augustus (though there is a profound moral here for the Augustans). Seeing him simply as Aeneas, we can say this much: he is not craving to wage war; he is physically and psychologically ready to do battle against Turnus and the Latins within the context of the clear divine will that Italy is to be his new-old home. More broadly, he is the instrument of larger powers shaping a history he helps to make; but he does not enjoy the luxury of understanding that history. He has, in fact, become an agent of destruction.

Encompassing world history from the Golden Age of Saturn through successive ages of war and the climactic battle of Actium to the Augustan age thereafter, Book VIII defines the present while celebrating the future. The clash of these elements, expressed mainly in the Arcadian setting and the destructive aura about Aeneas, is epitomized in the concluding symbol of Aeneas bearing burden and glory. Just as generally, we may say that Book IX defines the present while celebrating the past.

Book IX is often considered unsatisfactory for one or more reasons. The book is said to lack over-all unity—for example, the Nisus-Euryalus episode is easily detached, as is the episode of Trojan-ships-into-nymphs and its explanation. Turnus's fiery speech is sometimes called anticlimactic because it does not lead directly to fighting. The battles themselves seem generally perfunctory, as if marking time. Duckworth and others describe IX as an "interlude." [5] Now, though these judgments are sound enough within narrow limits, they miss the main theme of Book IX and ignore its fundamental unity.

As noted earlier, IX in many ways parallels VIII. The opening lines recall the beginning of VIII and indicate also that the action of both books is largely simultaneous. While Aeneas, gathering allies and inspecting divine armor, receives his commission to a larger war (sanctioned by Venus who flashes in a clear sky), Iris moves Turnus to precipitate the battle and, by a coup, end the war. Anticipating such action, Aeneas (*optimus armis,* 40) earlier sternly ordered the Trojans not to engage the Latins in open combat. To this end, he left Mnestheus and Serestus in charge (171 f.). The Trojans chafe at this order—"conferre manum pudor iraque monstrat" (44)—but they obey.[6] The strategy is important: the Trojans cannot afford to do battle with the now-superior forces of the Latins.

Strategy plays a major role in Book IX. As one plan fails, another is devised. Turnus's first gambit is to draw the Trojans out from behind their walls, so he attacks the ships with fire. That night, Nisus and Euryalus attempt to bring Aeneas word of the Latin attack and hasten the relief. Next day, Turnus attacks the tower, and his brother-in-law taunts the Trojans on the walls. Finally, when Pandarus and Bitias open the gates Turnus has his great chance—but instead of exploiting it, he fights himself into a corner and has to escape by the river. These attempts at large strategy stand out both because they fail and because of the way they fail.

The first of these attempts, Turnus's attack on the ships, is foiled by divine intervention. He succeeds in burning the ships but not in luring out the Trojans; the marvelous transformation of the ships into nymphs strikes fear on almost all sides. At this point, Vergil halts the narrative to explain the origin of this marvel. The digression brings the headlong action to a standstill, with the antagonists left openmouthed as it were, while the author takes us back to Troy and the period when Aeneas was building his fleet. But despite its strangeness, this passage has at least two notable features. In returning the tale briefly to Troyland, it prepares for Turnus's speech. Secondly, it highlights Aeneas's mortality and the chanciness of his whole enterprise. At one point, Jupiter rebuked his mother Cybele (*"quo fata vocas?"*) and drew a sharp line around Aeneas:

> 'certusque incerta pericula lustret
> Aeneas? cui tanta deo permissa potestas?'   (IX.96–97)

"Would you have Aeneas pass with certainty through all the uncertain dangers? What god is permitted such power?"

The oxymoron *certusque incerta* underscores the element of doubt; nowhere else does Jupiter qualify destiny as he does here.

While the phenomenon frightens everyone else, it only provokes Turnus to make a bold and rousing speech:

> at non audaci Turno fiducia cessit;
> ultro animos tollit dictis atque increpat ultro.   (IX.126–27)

His easy exegesis is effective beyond measure. His speech, beginning with dubious logic, evolves into a blistering attack that yokes racial pride, heroic spirit, and deliberate policy. When Turnus cries, *"nil me fatalia terrent"* (133), his tone rings true. Such frivolous deities seem to him hardly formidable. More to the point: *"sat fatis Venerique datum"* (135): the claims of Venus and the Fates have been satisfied, that is, in the fact that the Trojans have reached Italy. Turnus identifies the protective strengths on the Trojan side with Venus, that goddess whom he can scorn with bravado. His words powerfully echo Hector's in Book II—*"sat patriae Priamoque datum"* (II.291)—

which marked the end of an era. His gist is clear enough: the Trojans are in for a repetition of Troy:

> 'sunt et mea contra
> fata mihi, ferro sceleratam exscindere gentem
> coniuge praerepta; nec solos tangit Atridas
> iste dolor, solisque licet capere arma Mycenis.'   (IX.136–39)

"Against that, I have my own destiny—to root out, with my sword, this cursed race which has stolen my bride from me. The sons of Atreus are not alone in suffering that agony, nor was it permitted to Mycenae alone to take up arms."

There is nothing spurious here. Heroic spirit responding to opaque oracles—this is characteristic of Turnus. He rejects the allegation that the Trojans have suffered enough, countering sarcastically that one rape of Helen should also have been enough:

> ' "sed periisse semel satis est": peccare fuisset
> ante satis....'   (IX.140–41)

The words evoke perjured Laomedon or Anchises despairing on his bed. Point after point goes home, with blunt force or unwitting irony. Thus the detail—

> 'at non viderunt moenia Troiae
> Neptuni fabricata manu considere in ignis?'   (IX.144–45)

"But have they not seen the walls of Troy—built by Neptune's own hand—collapse in flames?"

—reminds us of the irony of Book II, Neptune destroying the city he had built, even while the destructive fire symbolizes Turnus.[7]

Later on, Turnus's points are amplified and somewhat distorted by his brother-in-law Remulus (598 f.). Cruder than Turnus, Remulus spills out *digna atque indigna relatu*, assaulting the Trojans as *"bis capti Phryges"* (599) and *"vere Phrygiae, neque enim Phryges"* (617). Remulus boasts of the Spartan life his people lead:

'at patiens operum parvoque adsueta iuventus
aut rastris terram domat aut quatit oppida bello....'   (IX.607–8)

"Our young men endure hard work and a frugal life; they conquer the
land with their hoes or shatter towns in warfare. . . ."

This he contrasts mockingly with Phrygian softness—

'vobis picta croco et fulgenti murice vestis,
desidiae cordi, iuvat indulgere choreis,
et tunicae manicas et habent redimicula mitrae.'   (IX.614–16)

"As for you, you wear dresses embroidered in saffron and shining purple;
you love to loaf or to dance, and your tunics have frilled sleeves and your
bonnets have long ribbons."

—commending them to Mother Berecyntia and admonishing them
not to play with fire. In the torrent of harsh sounds, the sarcastic dac-
tyls of line 616 are virtually spit out.

For his pains, Remulus is brought down by an arrow from the bow
of Ascanius, the boy who was wont to terrify fleeing beasts (*fugacis,*
591), now having his moment of glory. For all the Roman symbolism
attendant on Ascanius here and later, and emphasized by Apollo himself, Remulus's taunts must not be dismissed. Whatever pride-before-
a-fall there may be here, his tactic was to get the Trojans out where
they could fight man to man; the response is an arrow through the
head, as if attesting the accuracy of his indictment.

The differences of temperament, style, and intent between Turnus
and Remulus are less important than they appear. And in one important point the two agree: they reject the Greek way of conquering the
Trojans. Remulus says:

'non hic Atridae nec fandi fictor Vlixes.'   (602)

"Here there are no Atridae, no deceitful Ulysses."

And Turnus, earlier:

'tenebras et inertia furta
Palladii caesis summae custodibus arcis
ne timeant, nec equi caeca condemur in alvo:
luce palam certum est igni circumdare muros.
haud sibi cum Danais rem faxo et pube Pelasga
esse ferant, decimum quos distulit Hector in annum.'   (IX.150–55)

"They need not worry about any cowardly thefts, in the darkness, of the
Palladium, with the sentries of the high citadel butchered; nor will we
conceal ourselves in the horse's blind belly. By day, openly, I am resolved
to encircle their walls with fire. I will force them to admit that they are
not dealing with Danaans or with the young warriors of Greece, whom
Hector fought off till the tenth year."

Ironically, and tragically, Turnus's disclaimers are right in several
ways. But more important, Turnus's speech—with some amplifica-
tion from Remulus's—provides for the current action some of the
context of old Troy.[8] The significance of this context will be seen
shortly.

The Nisus-Euryalus episode is the longest in Book IX. At the outset,
the motives of Nisus and Euryalus seem compounded of restlessness,
impetuosity, and heroic instinct. Outlining his plan, Nisus says:

'dine hunc ardorem mentibus addunt,
Euryale, an sua cuique deus fit dira cupido?
aut pugnam aut aliquid iamdudum invadere magnum
mens agitat mihi, nec placida contenta quiete est.'   (IX.184–87)

"Euryalus, is it the gods who are inflaming our hearts for battle? or is our
own unholy desire becoming itself a god for us? For a long time, I have
been yearning to fight or do something great; I am not content with this
peaceful quiet."

To his *"nam mihi facti / fama sat est"* (194 f.), Euryalus responds ar-
dently:

'est hic, est animus lucis contemptor et istum
qui vita bene credat emi, quo tendis, honorem.'   (IX.205–6)

"Here, too, is a spirit that scorns life and that would think it a good bargain to exchange my life for that glory which you desire."

The purpose of their sortie is defined by Nisus: to bring Aeneas word of the Latin assaults and thus hasten his return with the allies. Together they go to the council of the Trojan leaders, where Nisus presents his plan and asserts his hope of success in fairly persuasive terms. But the meeting of the council disintegrates into fantasy. Aged Aletes (246 f.), burbling with joy that there are Trojans willing to risk their lives, totally ignores the patent ambiguities. Ascanius outdoes Aletes in unrestrained promises of rewards. Nobody raises the crucial questions of precisely *what* and *how;* in the next sixty lines or so, the plan itself is engulfed in an emotional orgy.

Ascanius's long speeches deal exclusively with rewards and gifts. Wth an exaggerated self-importance, Ascanius promises them twelve maids of rare beauty (*"bis sex ... lectissima matrum/ corpora"*) and more (272 f.). He promises them Latinus's estates (274). (He even promises, a little surprisingly, one of the gifts from Dido— "cratera antiquum quem dat Sidionia Dido" [266]: Ascanius retains a casual notion of the Carthage episode.) Ascanius prudently includes Euryalus's mother as beneficiary of his largesse (301 f.). The detail is important because it shows how impossible Ascanius's promises are. In Book XII, Aeneas's arrangements with Latinus totally ignore the commitments made here. Aeneas may have been, probably was, unaware of them.

When the two young men at last get under way, the Trojan leaders and Ascanius accompany them to the gates with encouragement and counsel:

> nec non et pulcher Iulus,
> ante annos animumque gerens curamque virilem,
> multa patri mandata dabat portanda; sed aurae
> omnia discerpunt et nubibus inrita donant.   (IX.310–13)

For his part, handsome Ascanius, exhibiting a spirit and manly concern beyond his years, gave them many messages to take to his father. But the breezes scatter all these things and make them a worthless gift to the clouds.

It is as if Ascanius suddenly sees everything in perspective—and it is too late. What exactly the *aurae* whirl aloft and disperse is not clear; *omnia* may refer simply to Ascanius's final words after the departing figures, or to all these *vota* and *mandata*. Most probably, it includes these and more: the last word, *donant,* epitomizing the *praemia* and *dona* promised, reflects ironically on the whole sortie and includes in *omnia* all the promised rewards and gifts.

The actual sortie lives up to the confusion of the council scene. Full of confidence, Nisus and Euryalus set out through the dark night:

> castra inimica petunt, multis tamen ante futuri
> exitio.   (IX.315–16)

They seek the fatal camp, but first they themselves will bring death to many.

Inimica, while foreshadowing their doom, bristles with ambiguity (as does *petunt*), but the word *tamen* is the giveaway—"first," or "nevertheless," or "despite their specific object." For though they could have accomplished the mission even after the carnage, the carnage itself quickly becomes their main concern: *nunc ipsa vocat res* (320). They butcher sleeping guards and soldiers; Nisus rages

> impastus ceu plena leo per ovilia turbans
> (suadet enim vesana fames) manditque trahitque
> molle pecus mutumque metu, fremit ore cruento.   (IX.339–41)

like a starving lion running amuck in the sheepfolds, driven by his maddening hunger; he mangles and mauls the meek sheep, dumb with fear, and foams bloody at the mouth.[9]

This kind of simile belongs to the open battlefield, not to the secret mission. For his part Euryalus, *incensus et ipse / perfurit* (342 f.). At length, Nisus realizes how far they have gone: *nimia caede atque cupidine* (354, with an echo of *dira cupido,* 185).

It is already too late. Captured by a Rutulian patrol, Euryalus is slain by Volcens; Nisus takes revenge on the slayer, and himself dies:

> tum super exanimum sese proiecit amicum
> confossus, placidaque ibi demum morte quievit.   (IX.444–45)

Pierced through, he flung himself across the lifeless body of his friend and there at last found quiet in the peace of death.

The echo of line 187—*"nec placida contenta quiete est"*—is poignant and ironic; their first impetuosity, inflamed by the contagious impetuosity of Ascanius, climaxes here in a *quies* neither had quite foreseen.

Like the pathetic simile at Euryalus's death, Vergil's apostrophe is well known, but it has rarely been examined with care:

> Fortunati ambo! si quid mea carmina possunt,
> nulla dies umquam memori vos eximet aevo,
> dum domus Aeneae Capitoli immobile saxum
> accolet imperiumque pater Romanus habebit.   (IX.446–49)

> Ah, fortunate pair! if my poetry has any influence,
> Time in its passing shall never obliterate your memory,
> As long as the house of Aeneas dwell by the Capitol's moveless
> Rock, and the head of the Roman family keeps his power.
>   (Tr. Day Lewis)

The patriotic force here is undeniable. But, considering the portrayal Vergil has forged, with its rashness and impetuosity, the highlighted gift-motif, and the confusion pervading the episode, we must ask what precisely *Fortunati* means and what their fame is. *"Mihi facti/ fama sat est,"* Nisus declared: but the *factum* was the mission itself, the attempt to get through to Aeneas. They did not achieve this; in fact, they completely lost sight of it. The damage they wrought, the plunder they gained—these were not only irrelevant, they were directly damaging to the mission. What was a properly heroic motive gradually became utter rashness; *immemorem* in lines 373 f.—

> et galea Euryalum sublustri noctis in umbra
> prodidit immemorem radiisque adversa refulsit.

And the helmet betrayed Euryalus as it reflected light in the night's glimmering shadows—he had forgotten that.

—suggests how far they have forgotten, not only in excessive slaughter and plunder, but in Euryalus's donning the captured helmet as one might on the battlefield.[10] Lost in the dark woods, loaded down by his plunder,

> Euryalum tenebrae ramorum onerosaque praeda
> impediunt,   (IX.384–85)

—Euryalus is easily caught. Nisus goes round and round looking for him:

> rursus perplexum iter omne revolvens
> fallacis silvae simul et vestigia retro
> observata legit dumisque silentibus errat.   (IX.391–93)

Again he retraces the tangled path through the deceptive wood, and at the same time looks carefully for his own tracks, and gropes about in the silent thickets.

Describing confusion and dismay, the passage symbolizes their blindness, their retrogression into the past, their inadequacy. The verbal echoes of Book II—Aeneas's mad dash back into Troy, the futile search for Creusa—clarify meaning: what these heroic youths seek no longer exists.

Their fame, then, and their *fortuna* (the word recurs significantly, e.g., 214, 240, 260, 282) is that they acquitted themselves well within their limits. They were so devoted to each other that Nisus joined Euryalus in death when he might have escaped—a conclusion Aeneas himself had sought in Book II, but was not granted. (The fact remains, of course, that had Nisus escaped, he might still have carried out the original mission.) Both the pathos and the irony are everywhere apparent, in such touches as *nequiquam*—

> haec [dona] ... umeris nequiquam fortibus aptat.   (364)

These treasures Euryalus fitted on to his own strong shoulders—in vain.

—and in the first line of the succeeding passage, where the irony is two-edged:

Victores praeda Rutuli spoliisque potiti....   (IX.450)

Now the victorious Rutulians, masters of new plunder and spoils....

Certainly these remarks do not aim to debunk the standard view of this episode, of the sympathy Vergil makes us feel for his youthful heroes, of the sadness in their untimely death, or of the pity of war. But the whole episode belongs in a larger perspective. That is the perspective of the past, of old Troy, of the kind of heroism and the kind of individualism that might have been appropriate before but now carry their own irony. In this perspective, Vergil never permits us a wholly partisan feeling; the deaths of the sleeping Rutulians are part of the brutality, part of the horror—as much so as the misery and grief that drive the enemy to affix the heads of Nisus and Euryalus on spears and parade them before the Trojan walls, and the wails and outcries the sight produces in the Trojan camp itself.

As the Latins attack the Trojan camp in force, Vergil again invokes the Muses, preluding the *aristeiai* of Turnus. We have already noted the brief incident in which Ascanius brings down Remulus, who was attempting to draw out the Trojans. Shortly before this, the tower crashed in flames, exposing a few Trojan heroes; immediately following is the intervention by Apollo. While the Trojans wildly cheer Ascanius, Apollo praises him and prophesies his future greatness; then in the guise of aged Butes, Apollo counsels him to withdraw from the fighting: from now on, boy, stay out of the war: *"cetera parce, puer, bello"* (656). And he vanishes in mid-word, *in tenuem ... auram* (658). Left in the wake of these two comments, which balance each other, Ascanius does not reappear in the poem until briefly in Book XII.

Ascanius's success boosts Trojan morale but does not foster prudence. Shortly, the gates are daringly thrown open, not as part of a design, but simply as an act of exuberance, in the swell of battle. The warriors responsible are Pandarus and Bitias, huge fighters the size of giant oak trees. A first success, and the Trojans grow bolder, forgetting completely Aeneas's order that they stay in camp:

tum magis increscunt animis discordibus irae,
et iam collecti Troes glomerantur eodem
et conferre manum et procurrere longius audent.   (IX.688–90)

But the success is short-lived. Turnus brings down Bitias, not with
an ordinary *iaculum* but by catapulting a *phalarica* (a huge spear
with a head of heavy iron) like a thunderbolt—*fulminis acta modo*
(706); for Turnus here strikes like mighty Jove himself, with a power
normally beyond human strength. Now Pandarus shuts the gates—
again recklessly, for Trojans are locked outside, at the mercy of the
mounting Rutulian forces, and Turnus is inside:

> demens, qui Rutulum in medio non agmine regem
> viderit inrumpentem ultroque incluserit urbi,
> immanem veluti pecora inter inertia tigrim.   (IX.728–30)

Fool, for he did not see the Rutulian prince right there in their midst,
breaking through; and he freely locked him in there—like a monstrous
tiger among the helpless flocks.

The simile is apt: the Trojans are without a *pastor*. Throughout these
fast-moving lines, Vergil registers the changes in Trojan spirit—
exuberant after Ascanius's arrow, confused after the gates are open,
exuberant as they regroup and drive back a few of the enemy, confused and dispirited at Bitias's death. Manifestly, Apollo's injunction
of prudence was meant not only for Ascanius but for the Trojans generally.

As Turnus kills Pandarus, the Trojans seem on the verge of utter
destruction; Turnus's taunt recalls Pyrrhus in Book II (574 f.):

> 'hic etiam inventum Priamo narrabis Achillem.'   (IX.742)

"You can tell Priam that here too you found Achilles."

Victory is within his reach, but Turnus himself, raging individualist
here like Achilles, shows no more strategic sense than the Trojans
have:

Diffugiunt versi trepida formidine Troes.
et si continuo victorem ea cura subisset,
rumpere claustra manu sociosque immittere portis,
ultimus ille dies bello gentique fuisset.
sed furor ardentem caedisque insana cupido
egit in adversos.   (IX.756–61)

In wild panic, the Trojans turned and ran; and, if at that moment the
conquering Turnus had had the desire to smash the bolts and let in his
comrades through the gates, that day would have been the last day of the
war and of the Trojan race. But blazing fury and the violence of his
bloodlust drove him headlong against the enemy.

When Pandarus and Bitias threw open the gate, Turnus had what he
wanted—a direct confrontation with the Trojans. Earlier events were
either abortive attempts at this or irrelevant distractions. In slaying
Bitias and Pandarus, the heroic defenders, Turnus cleared the last
large obstacle to the kind of fight his strategy called for. But now, he
utterly forgets his original strategy. He ignores the closed gate, which
is keeping out the Latin army as well as some hapless Trojans. His
cura is to butcher and to destroy. The quoted lines properly indict
Turnus's tactical failure.

But the indictment is not partisan. The whole passage is part of the
dramatic movement of this episode and of all Book IX. In line 759,
the sense turns both ways: that day would have been the last for the
Trojans because of *their own* rashness and strategic failures. While
Turnus's flashing sword acts out his stupendous blunder, the scene remains an epitome of Trojans and their rout, of the collapse of order
and discipline—the kind of collapse anticipated in the frenetic council scene, shown in the hapless sortie of Nisus and Euryalus, and cli-
maxed in the opening of the gate. In full perspective, the heroic
struggle of Turnus in the Trojan camp embodies the forces of waste
and disorder, and graphically illustrates the madness of war; *furor*
and *insana cupido* characterize much of this book; *egit* well expresses
the blind driving force of war. The ambivalent ending to the scene
and to Book IX is poetically logical.

On the Trojan side, disorder is anatomized in:

> Tandem ductores audita caede suorum
> conveniunt Teucri, Mnestheus acerque Serestus,
> palantisque vident socios hostemque receptum.   (IX.778–80)

At length, hearing the slaughter of their men, the Trojan commanders Mnestheus and fierce Serestus arrived, and saw their comrades scattered and the enemy within their gates.

In charge during Aeneas's absence, Mnestheus and Serestus were no-where in sight during the fighting at the gate. The spondaic rhythm of line 778, marching heavily and dully, conveys the distressing meaning: "At long last, finally"—the word *tandem* seems to ask, where were they? *Ductores* highlights their reprehensible absence, as does *suorum*—in the double sense that these men, their Trojans, were explicitly entrusted to them by Aeneas. And the fact that they *hear* the carnage (*audita caede*) is pointed up by *vident* in line 780. Without pushing further—every word is indictment here—we may finally note the ordinary meaning of *conveniunt* (779): they assemble, they gather, they meet, without any apparent sense of urgency.

These few lines are quite as damning as the earlier passage quoted. The angry words with which Mnestheus rallies the Trojans and saves them from total disgrace cannot disguise this fact. Even at that, the rallying is late. Turnus has already cut a broad swath through the camp and has reached the river—and Iris, who started these two days of chaotic and fruitless fighting, comes again, this time to Juno, bringing Jupiter's warning to get Turnus out of the Trojan camp.

Book IX closes with Turnus leaping into the river; the traditional epic act becomes ritualistic:

> tum demum praeceps saltu sese omnibus armis
> in fluvium dedit. ille suo cum gurgite flavo
> accepit venientem ac mollibus extulit undis
> et laetum sociis abluta caede remisit.   (IX.815–18)

Then at last he plunged headlong down, armor and all, hurling himself into the river. The river received him on its yellow stream and carried him on its gentle wave, washing away the blood of slaughter; and it carried him back, in high spirit, to his comrades.

The cleansing waters (of the Tiber—so partial to *Aeneas* at the beginning of Book VIII!) are juxtaposed with the dirty, sticky stream of sweat choking Turnus (*piceum flumen*), in an image that suggests rebirth even as it brings Book IX to a quiet close. The shift in tempo, the reduction of frenzy are accomplished by ritual, and by sound and rhythm; significant also is the return to the peaceful, natural world in which Book IX opened, the wood where Turnus sat, consecrated to his ancestor Pilumnus:

> luco tum forte parentis
> Pilumni Turnus sacrata valle sedebat.   (IX.3–4)

The world of nature throughout the Italian books of the *Aeneid,* beginning at least with Tiber in its *fluvio amoeno* (VII.30), is a peculiarly hallowed world, resisting the incursions of violence and thrusting always back toward its rustic innocence.

All in all, Book IX is highly effective. The events, far from being detachable, are wrought into a coherent whole. The tempo increases steadily as incident follows incident in a pattern of anachronistic heroism. The Nisus-Euryalus sortie is no less outmoded than the *aristeiai* of Turnus; the effusions of Ascanius and the elders contribute to the texture of the Nisus-Euryalus episode. The breakdowns of strategy are paradigmatic, for the whole book is a vision of war as it can no longer be.

The rhythm of Book IX is Iliadic in a special sense: the allusions to Hector casting fire on the Greek ships, or to Dolon's escapade, or to Achilles and the river Scamander—these all cooperate in the expanding theme of the fall of Troy, the old heroic days that are no more. It is the theme broadcast and almost defined by Turnus's speech, and developed in such details as the images of those great oaks, Bitias and Pandarus, crashing to earth.[11]

Vergil has, in short, built Book IX around the old-fashioned type of heroism—the kind that Aeneas gave himself over to again and again in Book II, the kind he was called *from* to his new though undefined mode of life. Tactic after tactic fails in IX because it is diverted—by the heroic stance, the quest for glory, the lust for blood, the sheer instinct to fight. Strategy is abandoned or neglected or simply overlooked; the Trojans and their appointed leaders are disorganized and routed, and almost defeated—but not quite, because strategy fails totally and the fighting is to no end. Death is not grand here; it is futile and wasteful. In Book IX, the poet takes us from the pleasant grove to the cleansing river via the heaps of carnage piled up by the "heroic" spirit. Focusing a harsh light on prowess, Book IX shows it to be in part sheer stupidity.

What readers have called Vergil's distaste for combat is not that at all. It is rather the profound discontent we inevitably feel about such *pointless* butchery. Vergil's so-called lack of gusto would be irrelevant here, even if it could be demonstrated. In his poetic strategy, he nourishes our discontent because it is the only effect relevant to what must happen. In Book II, Vergil brilliantly dramatized warfare from the viewpoint of the defeated; here in IX, though less brilliantly, he has dramatized warfare in its most irrelevant mode.

CHAPTER SEVEN

PIUS AENEAS AND THE WAGES OF WAR

In Book X, Aeneas enters the battle proper. In the preceding three books, we have seen various themes and motifs: the polarization of love and hate, sex and violence; the recurring cycle of Troy and of antique heroism and rampant individualism; the extension of the war to most of "Italy" (though as the war develops it becomes a conflict between Aeneas and Turnus, and the stand-ins for Turnus); the problems of the nature of war itself and its objectives; and, in the broadest sense, the question of what it is that Aeneas is doing.

This last is most important. Ever since Hades, the figure of Aeneas has been somewhat blurred. He appears only briefly in VII; in VIII, the Arcadian background and the problematic Shield render him less distinct. The facts are indisputable—his orders to the Trojans, for instance, or the imposing confidence he displays in directing the whole enterprise when the company first reaches Latium. But neither such facts, nor judgments on them, can justify the common generalizations—for example, that Aeneas has changed (without qualification) from an uncertain instrument of destiny into the confident proto-Roman; that he is now quite certain of his glorious destiny; that he is model for Augustus—or modeled after Augustus. None of these easy generalizations will do, for the best of reasons. Whatever the deficiencies, Vergil has created a rich and profound complexity in Aeneas. While Aeneas is not diffident about the war, neither does he look forward to it with "gusto"; while Aeneas surely has some clear ideas about where he is going, the clarity of these ideas diminishes in proportion as "where" is defined in terms of fate or Rome or Augustus. His clearest notion, in fact, remains much what it was when he first left Troy—the goal is a home, a *sedes,* a dwelling place safe from the uncertainties of the seas or of the gods or of the future itself.

The details of prophecy or patriotism in the poem must not be overstressed. Jupiter prophesies to Venus, but Aeneas has the immediate reality of lost ships, scattered men, and a strange land; Anchises passes Roman heroes, famous and infamous, in review, but Aeneas has the immediate reality that Elysium is for him a momentary respite before the war in Italy; Venus and her spouse delight on a golden bed and in the brittle gold of Roman history, but Aeneas has the immediate reality of a war whose scope is getting out of hand. What nexus is there between Aeneas and these other things? Tentatively, we can say that the prophecies and the pageants reflect on the nature of Aeneas's mission, that they suggest some of the implications; such observations must always depend upon our realization of what Aeneas himself knows and does and is. I hope I do not seem to be relegating these grand passages to a very peripheral place; still, whatever that risk, it is crucial that such passages be kept in proper perspective.

Books IX, X, and XI are each marked by a council scene—the hectic Trojan meeting that dispatches Nisus and Euryalus; the council of the gods; and the council of the Latins. In Book XII, two episodes, while not full-dress councils, have the formality of such sessions: the solemn covenant between Aeneas, speaking for the Trojans and their allies, and Latinus, speaking for the Latins and their allies; and the solemn dialogue between Jupiter and Juno. In this list, one may suspect a distinct progression in order, maturity, and achievement.

The structure of the council scene opening Book X is symmetrical:

1–5	processional (solemn)
6–15	Jove's measured address
18–62	Venus's sarcastic tirade
62–95	Juno's furious response
96–99	murmuring among the gods
100–3	composure and control of Jove
104–13	Jove's measured address
113–17	solemn oath and recessional

This outline describes Jove's short speeches as "measured." At least, that quality is what they seem to attempt.

The scene opens in solemn rhythms:

> Panditur interea domus omnipotentis Olympi
> conciliumque vocat divum pater atque hominum rex.   (x.1–2)

Meanwhile the palace of omnipotent Olympus was thrown open and the father of the gods and king of men called a council.

Jupiter rebukes the gods harshly for interfering despite his prohibition (*"quae contra vetitum discordia?"*) but throws a sop to their blood-lust, their penchant for rapine and slaughter, by promising full play to their hatreds in the future Punic Wars:

> 'adveniet iustum pugnae, ne arcessite, tempus,
> cum fera Karthago Romanis arcibus olim
> exitium magnum atque Alpis immittet apertas:
> tum certare odiis, tum res rapuisse licebit.'   (x.11–14)

Iustum tempus and *licebit* are broadly ironic, but Venus ignores the thrust and turns the imputations of bloodlust and injustice against Juno. She does not, however, appeal to Justice; she appeals rather to Power:

> 'o pater, o hominum rerumque aeterna potestas
> (namque aliud quid sit quod iam implorare queamus?)'
>   (x.18–19)

"O father, O eternal power over men and their affairs—for what else is there that we can now call upon?"

She sets Troy's fate against Troy's destiny. Ironically, she invokes his tender clemency to relieve the Trojans from this second disaster, take them back to Troy, and let them die there—in disgrace but at home. In the constant harping on Troy and the Trojans, her argument is that, while Jupiter's power was originally pledged to their destiny (including the destruction of Troy and a glorious future), Juno's violence has clearly prevented him. "All right, then, let your Power be flouted. But spare me little Ascanius."

Aurea Venus is answered by *regia Juno / acta furore gravi* (62 f.). Brittle taunts and furious responses turn the solemn council into a brawl. Juno lashes out with wild accusations, bold-faced lies, and telling points—the last for example, in 65 f.:

> 'Aenean hominum quisquam divumque subegit?
>
> . . . .
>
> Italiam petiit fatis auctoribus (esto)
> Cassandrae impulsus furiis....
>
> . . . .
>
> quid soceros legere et gremiis abducere pactas,
> pacem orare manu, praefigere puppibus arma?
>
> . . . .
>
> me duce Dardanius Spartam expugnavit adulter,
> aut ego tela dedi fovive Cupidine bella?'

"What mortal or what god forced Aeneas? . . . 'The Fates bade him to seek Italy': all right—but he was moved by the ravings of Cassandra. . . . What of the fact that they choose whose daughters they will marry and seduce betrothed girls from their lovers' breasts? and that they cry peace while arraying their ships with weapons? . . . Was I the guide when the Dardanian adulterer broke into Sparta? Did I provide the weapons or use Amor to kindle a war?"

The implications of Juno's counterattack are not lost on Jupiter. In the stern repetition of his command to keep hands off, Jupiter professes solemn impartiality, but his words recognize the hopeless discord that he is restraining. Certainly he knows what the outcome will be, so there is some irony in his statement, *'fata viam invenient':* "the Fates will find a way" (113). Yet, considering the problems the gods themselves have been creating, the outcome is not the point. The point is the relationship between power and justice. And Jove emerges as the god of power, not of justice. Indeed, justice barely affects his administration of Fate.

The partisan workings of Venus and Juno are identified with their power and the uses of it. From the first appearance of each in the poem, this has been a constant theme. Juno works her will by usurping the particular province of power under Aeolus's control; Venus counteracts with protective measures for Aeneas—first by appeal to Jove, then by exercising her power via Amor, her son. In the power play that destroys Dido and nearly wrecks Aeneas, both goddesses triumph, for that exercise, like the others, involves primarily their chthonic characteristics, characteristics that need have no regard for moral relationships or moral problems.

Venus and Juno are portrayed by Vergil as subordinate to Jove both in the range of their authority and in its nature. Less primitive than Aeschylus's Furies, they are not so far from Homer's chthonic deities. In moral terms, there simply is no comparison between these goddesses and the human hero. Aeneas acts in a continuing attempt to achieve and maintain moral equilibrium, or justice; many of his obstacles are created by the past and by these two goddesses who belong essentially to that past.

The centrality of Troy in the goddesses' ongoing brawl confirms this last observation. The *tantae ... irae* of I.11, explicitly applied to Juno (*saevae memorem Junonis ob iram*), belong to Venus too. Her charter for Aeneas's destiny is Anchises' writ large: a re-creation of old Troy, an avenging of the injuries done her. In pursuit of these, she uses Aeneas just as Anchises used him. For Aeneas, Troy is a symbol of the past he wants buried and forgotten; to these goddesses, Troy is a fixation. Sometimes like a throbbing toothache (*"mea vulnera restant,"* says Venus, x.29), it is the central fact of their existence here. Venus sees Aeneas's venture in terms of Troy reborn, an extension of the old power and the old history that includes Paris, Anchises, and Phrygian domination.[1] Like Anchises, she expects and looks for the same anew.

Jove succeeds at least in limiting the goddesses' activities. The issue, he maintains, rests on the antagonists, whom he will treat impartially ("Tros Rutulusne fuat, nullo discrimine habebo," 108). Each man, he declares, will freely determine his own fortune, good or bad; Jupiter is king over all alike. At the same time, the Fates will find a way:

> 'sua cuique exorsa laborem
> fortunamque ferent. rex Iuppiter omnibus idem.
> fata viam invenient.'   (x.111–13)

This noninterference he stipulates, for what it is worth, is the noninterference of Power, which remains divorced from Justice. In taking the goddesses out of the war, he is attempting to remedy the malady of the war itself. It was a war he had specifically forbidden (x.8), but if it must go on, let it at least have boundaries. These it could not have if Juno and Venus continue to stir up trouble.

How dangerous Juno's and Venus's outbursts are appears in the mixed reaction of the other gods described by a simile:

> ceu flamina prima
> cum deprensa fremunt silvis et caeca volutant
> murmura venturos nautis prodentia ventos.   (x.97–99)

As when the rising blasts of a storm, caught in a forest, moan and rumble, and (though muffled) warn sailors of gales to come.

The simile clashes with the calm forcefully imposed when the *pater omnipotens, rerum cui prima potestas* (100) speaks—a calm demonstrating his ultimate control over the very forces of nature which, in the simile, portend disaster for *men.* A later simile, describing the battle on the beach, curiously parallels this one:

> magno discordes aethere venti
> proelia ceu tollunt animis et viribus aequis;
> non ipsi inter se, non nubila, non mare cedit;
> anceps pugna diu, stant obnixa omnia contra:
> haud aliter Troianae acies aciesque Latinae
> concurrunt, haeret pede pes densusque viro vir.   (x.356–61)

So, high up in the heavens the opposing winds do battle with each other, equally matched in spirit and strength: none yields before the other, nor do the clouds or the sea yield, so that the struggle goes on, with the issue doubtful, and all are locked in the great fight. Just so did the ranks of Troy clash with the ranks of Latium, foot locked to foot, man pressed against man.

Like the winds of heaven, each side devastates the other, but neither makes headway. For the moment, one feels that the Trojan-war cycle is being repeated.[2]

Aeneas's arrival is marked by a meteorological simile, but of quite a different order. As the fleet lands, shortly after the break of day, Aeneas raises his blazing shield—*clipeum ardentem* (261 f.). It is seen by both armies:

> ardet apex capiti cristisque a vertice flamma
> funditur et vastos umbo vomit aureus ignis:
> non secus ac liquida si quando nocte cometae
> sanguinei lugubre rubent, aut Sirius ardor
> ille sitim morbosque ferens mortalibus aegris
> nascitur et laevo contristat lumine caelum.   (x.270–75)

The crest of his helmet blazed, flame poured from its plumes, and the golden boss of the shield spouted floods of fire. Just so, in the clear night, comets glow, blood-red and sinister; just so the fiery Dog Star—that star which brings drought and pestilence to suffering humanity—rises and saddens the sky with its baneful glare.

Like the simile of the migrating cranes immediately preceding in the text, this double simile deals partly with a time of year. The difference is otherwise enormous. On one level, the comets and the Dog Star portend horror for the Latins, relief for the Trojans. But few of Vergil's similes are so simple in structure or meaning. The pairing of the two terms—comets and Sirius—is important. The comets may suggest the omen toward the end of Book II, seen there at night; these comets, however, are bloody. The rising of the Dog Star, with its portents of baneful effects for men in general, is described as *nascitur,* echoing *nascentis Troiae* (x.27) and *Troiam nascentem* (x.74 f.). *Ardor* is a key word, echoing *ardet* in 270 and *ardentem* in 262. The implications are inescapable: the Dog Star does not discriminate in its choice of victims. Neither does war.

The immediate victims of the enlarged battle are indiscriminately Latin and Trojan, as both sides fight furiously. Gradually the focus narrows to Pallas and Lausus, the doomed youths for whom Book x is in part an anthem. Pallas comes into prominence as he rallies his faltering trops. His words, suited to his actions, ring heroic:

> 'numina nulla premunt, mortali urgemur ab hoste
> mortales; totidem nobis animaeque manusque.'   (x.375–76)

"These are not gods pressing upon us; we are men, hard pressed by enemies who are also men. We have as many lives and hands as they do."

He spreads destruction, becoming more and more the fiery warrior. So does his opposite number, young Lausus, son of Mezentius. Unafraid,

Lausus shows himself a tower of strength (427, *pars ingens belli*). He does not let his troops panic before Pallas. He brings down Abas, who had been holding back the Latins (428, *pugnae nodumque moramque*), then begins killing Arcadians and Etruscans, and even Trojans who had escaped the Greek slaughter at Troy:

> sternitur Arcadiae proles, sternuntur Etrusci
> et vos, o Grais imperdita corpora, Teucri.   (x.429–30)

Vergil deliberately balances the two heroes:

>   hinc Pallas instat et urget,
> hinc contra Lausus, nec multum discrepat aetas,
> egregii forma, sed quis Fortuna negarat
> in patriam reditus.   (x.433–36)

Pallas and Lausus are matched in prowess and strength, in age, in physical beauty, and finally in their doom: Fortune has denied both of them a return to their homelands. Then Vergil adds the curious detail:

>   ipsos concurrere passus
> haud tamen inter se magni regnator Olympi;
> mox illos sua fata manent maiore sub hoste.   (x.436–38)

The sovereign of great Olympus would not allow these two to confront each other; their fates await them, soon, from a mightier enemy.

Why does Jupiter keep them apart? Is one to infer that they were so evenly matched that any fight would be a standoff? Or does the over-all pattern of fate demand that their deaths occur at the hands of Turnus and Aeneas? Certainly both of these suggestions might be taken into account. However, considering story-line alone for the moment, Turnus's killing of Pallas affords a kind of "logical" explanation for the final scene of the poem. But this hardly accounts for the deliberate parallels between the death of Lausus and the death of Pallas. Also, the relationship which Vergil develops between Pallas and Aeneas is simply not strong enough to serve as major motivation in the final scene.

We should note that Turnus provides a properly heroic death for Pallas—death at a great hand—just as Aeneas does for Lausus. In whatever mode the pattern of fate works here, there is also human truth: Pallas and Lausus were both marked for death by character and circumstance. Both are too eager, too impulsive, too heroic. Both die specifically heroic deaths, in contexts adapted from Homer. The incidents immediately preceding Pallas's fight with Turnus (his prayer to Hercules and Jupiter's response) recall Zeus and Sarpedon in *Iliad* XVI. To these, Vergil adds other echoes and enriches the whole with his own insight.

Jupiter's words to Hercules are famous:

> 'stat sua cuique dies, breve et inreparabile tempus
> omnibus est vitae; sed famam extendere factis,
> hoc virtutis opus. Troiae sub moenibus altis
> tot nati cecidere deum, quin occidit una
> Sarpedon, mea progenies: etiam sua Turnum
> fata vocant metasque dati pervenit ad aevi.'   (x.467–72)

"For each man his day stands fixed. For all mankind the days of life are few, and not to be restored. But to prolong fame by deeds, that is valour's task. Under Troy's high ramparts fell all those many sons of gods; yes, and with them fell my own son, Sarpedon. Turnus also has his doom calling him; he too has reached the goal of his allotted years." (Tr. Knight)

The words are comforting to Hercules; he understands them well. Thus is Pallas inducted formally into the ranks of heroes. While the shape of heroism seems simple—individual glory can triumph over time—the whole passage has a melancholy and ambivalent tone, hinted at in Homer. Jupiter sanctions individualistic heroism with the example specifically of Sarpedon; the sanction extends to Turnus, about whose imminent doom Jupiter speaks without overt hostility, and with a solemn echo of Turnus's own words: "sunt et mea contra/ fata mihi" (IX.136 f.: "And I, too, have my own fates"). Later on, as Turnus recognizes just how his *fata* stand toward him, he recognizes also another dimension in his own career and in the whole struggle. He knows that Aeneas will soon win over him, but he fears not Aeneas but the gods:

'non me tua fervida terrent
dicta, ferox; di me terrent et Iuppiter hostis.'   (XII.894–95)

In the actual portrayal of Pallas's death, Vergil seems almost to obliterate the line between victory and defeat. He apostrophizes Pallas:

haec te prima dies bello dedit, haec eadem aufert,
cum tamen ingentis Rutulorum linquis acervos!   (X.508–9)

This day introduced you to war, this day carries you off; even so, you leave behind great heaps of dead Rutulians.

Echoing lines 436–38 (quoted above), these words heighten the ambiguity in the description of Pallas falling:

una eademque via sanguis animusque sequuntur.
corruit in vulnus (sonitum super arma dedere)
et terram hostilem moriens petit ore cruento.   (X.487–89)

By the same route poured his blood and his life. He fell prone on the wound, his armor clanging above him, and as he died, he sought the hostile earth with bleeding mouth.

Via is broadly symbolic. The image of action in the last line combines with *moriens* for a specific life-death contrast.

The death of Lausus is commemorated warmly by the poet. Like Pallas, Lausus fights heroically and selflessly, but also rashly; like Pallas, he is cut down by a superior opponent who kills him in a fury of exultation. Both leave grieving fathers. Prototype of both heroes, Turnus will come to a similar end.

The anthem for doomed youth is drowned out through much of Book X by the stormy rages of Turnus and Aeneas. Bold and confident, Turnus is not visibly upset by Aeneas's appearance; rather, he is provoked, as he was in Book IX at the phenomenon of the ships turning into nymphs. Without hesitating, he calls out to his troops and taunts them (*ultro animos tollit dictis atque increpat ultro*, 278: the line is repeated from IX.127). Here is your big chance, he cries, if you can act like men, like husbands and fathers, like worthy inheritors of your ancestral fame:

> 'in manibus Mars ipse viri. nunc coniugis esto
> quisque suae tectique memor, nunc magna referte
> facta, patrum laudes. ultro occurramus ad undam....'   (x.280–82)

The recurrent *ultro* bears out his cry, *"audentis Fortuna iuvat"* (284). He throws all his forces against the disembarking enemy, but even so suffers reverses from the hot swords of Aeneas on one flank, Pallas on the other.

When he comes to the relief of Lausus's Etruscans, Turnus singles out Pallas as his opponent and claims him as victim:

> 'solus ego in Pallanta feror, soli mihi Pallas
> debetur; cuperem ipse parens spectator adesset.'   (x.442–43)

The harsh line—"I only wish his father were here to watch"— recalls the Pyrrhus episode in Book II and reintroduces a theme that will weave through Book X and build to an intricate climax, the theme of fathers and sons. Slaying Pallas, Turnus bids the Arcadians to return his body to his father Evander with this message:

> 'qualem meruit, Pallanta remitto.
> quisquis honos tumuli, quidquid solamen humandi est,
> largior.'   (x.492–94)

"I am sending back his Pallas, as he deserved him. Whatever honor there is in a tomb, whatever comfort in burial, that I freely grant."

Pity is intermingled with scorn, and a measure of heroic magnanimity: *largior.*

But Turnus's next action has both immediate impact and broader significance. Having spoken (*fatus*), he tears off Pallas's sword-belt, described as *immania pondera baltei*—heavy, massive, but also monstrous, as the following lines elaborate:

> impressumque nefas: una sub nocte iugali
> caesa manus iuvenum foede thalamique cruenti,
> quae Clonus Eurytides multo caelaverat auro.   (x.497–99)

The scene which Clonus engraved in thick gold on the belt is characterized as a *nefas*—the murder of the fifty sons of Aegyptus by the
Danaids on their wedding night. The moment is profoundly impressive. The symbolism of the belt is not easily defined. Brooks Otis var-
ies the standard, gratuitous view when he says the belt is "fitting
booty for the breaker of a marriage treaty!" But Turnus has some
claim to be considered the aggrieved party. In any event, both the
belt and the battle represent an inversion of the expected order:
slaughter and hatred where marriage and love were expected.

Over-all, the context echoes *fatum* (note lines 451, 459, 466, 472,
480, and 501); in that context, the burden of symbolism is rich and
complex. For the moment, Turnus's unreflecting joy as he takes the
belt turns that *fatum* on himself:

> quo nunc Turnus ovat spolio gaudetque potitus.
> nescia mens hominum fati sortisque futurae
> et servare modum rebus sublata secundis!
> Turno tempus erit magno cum optaverit emptum
> intactum Pallanta, et cum spolia ista diemque
> oderit.   (x.500–5)

Turnus rejoiced and exulted in the spoils he had won. How blind men are
to fate and the future, how imprudent when favored by success! For Turnus, the time will come when he would willingly pay any price to have
kept Pallas unharmed, and when he will loathe this day and these spoils.

But like many passages of this kind, this one should be read less as
auctorial intrusion than as dramatizing the meaning of action. The
lines prophesy Turnus's death and suggest an apparent reason for that
death. But there is more involved. The comment, first general then
specific, heightens the effect of this moment and this action; we are
forced to reflect on it in much larger terms. Just so, elsewhere, Vergil
uses a comment less to intrude on his narrative than to heighten the
effect and meaning of a crucial action. Thus, in Book IV, when Dido
sought justification in expiatory rituals, we read:

> heu, vatum ignarae mentes! quid vota furentem,
> quid delubra iuvant? est mollis flamma medullas
> interea et tacitum vivit sub pectore vulnus.   (IV.65–67)

How little the seers know! What help can prayers or shrines be to an impassioned woman? All the while, the fire consumes her soft marrow and the hidden wound of love throbs in her breast.

The lines dramatically express the extremities of Dido's state, highlighting the void between superficial act and inner meaning. The validity and force of the observation depend not on its *sententia* but on the fullness with which it is borne out in image and incident, in the very fabric of the poem. In the comment, Turnus is identified as a marked man (not for the first time). But the action and the comment, rather than serving as cause of his condition, are symbol and symptom of that condition—specifically, the anachronistic heroism he lives by. The view of myth provided in the emblem on Pallas's belt is itself a commentary on the dying world in which Turnus and Troy, and to some extent Aeneas, are struggling.

There is a difference between the Turnus of Book x and the Turnus of Book IX. In IX, he was operating in a world he understood spontaneously; the failures of strategy were, in fact, inconsequential. He was the hero, defined by the heroic code appropriate to the cycle of Troy. The leaderless Trojans also operated in that kind of world. In the absence of Aeneas, they almost lose and Turnus almost wins— almost but not quite, paradoxically because of the code to which Trojans and Turnus alike subscribe. Glory and instinct supersede strategy and high purpose.

In Book x, the irrelevance of the old rules becomes clearer to the reader. Even Juno seems to have a vague awareness of this. When Turnus almost precipitates the end by his recklessness, Juno removes him. But she does so in a way particularly hers. While *summissa* (611), she does not abase herself before omnipotent Jove. To his genial condescension, she responds with broad contempt. Sarcastically, she calls him *pulcherrime coniunx* and reminds him that he did not always have the upper hand:

> 'si mihi, quae quondam fuerat quamque esse decebat,
> vis in amore foret....'   (x.613–14)

"If my love had the kind of power which it once, properly, had. . . ."

Such as, for instance, the power Venus exercised over Vulcan. But Jupiter grants her request. Her way now is to trick Turnus by providing a *tenuem umbram / in faciem Aeneae* (636).

The wraith is compared to the phantoms that flit about after death or the images that delude men in dreams (*quae sopitos deludunt somnia sensus,* 642). To Turnus, however, the key fact is that this figure of Aeneas is in flight. He flings taunts after it, taunts which vanish as did Ascanius's words to Nisus and Euryalus, on the winds: *nec ferre videt sua gaudia ventos* (652). Only when the *trepida imago* disappears does Turnus realize what has been done to him:

> tum levis haud ultra latebras iam quaerit imago,
> sed sublime volans nubi se immiscuit atrae.   (x.663–64)

Then the airy wraith sought no more for the shadows, but soaring into the air, it blended into a dark cloud.

This shifting reality, expressed by elusive syntax and diction as well as detail, is beyond Turnus. Unable to cope with it, he feels himself disgraced. Juno acted out of an *amor* that mimicked Venus, but he answers by trying alternately to kill himself and to return to the battlefield. Despite three mighty attempts, he is restrained by Juno:

> ter conatus utramque viam, ter maxima Iuno
> continuit iuvenemque animi miserata repressit.   (x.685–86)

Though it takes all her power, Juno finally gets him home: *et patris antiquam Dauni defertur ad urbem* (688). The slack passive and the unwanted security of his father's city close the passage.

This episode, with its shadows and phantoms and dreams mocking Turnus's spontaneous heroism, anticipates the final episode of the poem in important ways. There, at the last, Turnus is faced with the fullness of what he cannot understand; buffeted like a man in a nightmare, he goes down before it.

Meanwhile, fiery Mezentius, prompted by Jupiter, replaces Turnus in the battle:

> At Iovis interea monitis Mezentius ardens
> succedit pugnae Teucrosque invadit ovantis.   (x.689–90)

Fierce but brave, he will die for Turnus. The rhythm of *Mezentius ardens* (689) is quasi-formulaic in a way unusual in Vergil; recurring noticeably throughout this entire episode, it certifies Mezentius as heroic:

haud aliter, iustae quibus est Mezentius irae....	(714)
sic ruit in densos alacer Mezentius hostis.	(729)
ad quae subridens mixta Mezentius ira.	(742)
at vero ingentem quatiens Mezentius hastam....	(762)
talis se vastis infert Mezentius armis.	(768)

It is surely no accident that the similes in this episode are heavily Homeric. In quick succession, Mezentius is compared to a great sea-beaten rock (693 f.), a frightening boar (707 f.), and a famished lion (723 f.).

Mezentius is the specific target of the Etruscans—*omnibus uni,/ uni odiisque viro telisque frequentibus instant* (691 f.)— but, for all the spears they hurl at him, neither their bravery nor their skill is proportionate to their hatred. Holding them off, Mezentius is compared to a rock, beaten by furious winds and waves, enduring all the force and violence of sea and sky: [3]

> obvia ventorum furiis expostaque ponto,
> vim cunctam ataque minas perfert caelique marisque
> ipsa immota manens....   (x.694–96)

"Yet it stands unmoved." The point here is simply that there is no real contest between the unmoved rock and the battering winds and waves. They slap at it, then draw back. So too the simile comparing Mezentius to a boar reflects on the Etruscans; they are like the hunters,

> nec cuiquam irasci propiusque accedere virtus,
> sed iaculis tutisque procul clamoribus instant.   (x.712–13)

None of them has the courage to show his anger and come closer; from a safe distance they harass it with yells and javelin-casts.

The Etruscans carry on their fight long-distance, hurling missiles and shouts (*missilibus et vasto clamore*, 716). Perhaps a trapped boar, Mezentius remains *impavidus* before these hunters.

Mezentius's prowess is related to his view of the gods. His response to Orodes (described in a simile as *fugax*) combines irony and fatalism:

> 'nunc morere. ast de me divum pater atque hominum rex
> viderit.'   (x.743–44)

"Now die. Let the father of gods and king of men worry about my fate."

The words are less contemptuous than factual. As has been observed, Mezentius is probably not an atheist, but rather, in Henry's words, an "under-rater" of the gods.

The gods themselves watch Mezentius in the battle:

> Iam gravis aequabat luctus et mutua Mavors
> funera; caedebant pariter pariterque ruebant
> victores victique, neque his fuga nota neque illis.
> di Iovis in tectis iram miserantur inanem
> amborum et tantos mortalibus esse labores;
> hinc Venus, hinc contra spectat Saturnia Iuno.
> pallida Tisiphone media inter milia saevit.   (x.755–61)

Now the heavy hand of Mars was dealing out agony and death impartially; both sides killed and were killed, conquerors and conquered alike, nor did any of them think of falling back. In the halls of Jove, the gods felt pity for the pointless fury of both sides, grieving that mortal men should suffer such ordeals. Here Venus, there, opposite, Saturnian Juno watched; right in the midst of the armies pale Tisiphone raged.

Mirroring the conflict, the heavy pairings in these lines convey not so much the sorrows of the gods as the futility of the war. Both sides in the mortal warfare are equally victimized, so that the real conflict seems to be between the human opponents and Mars and Tisiphone. The gods themselves are various. Bloody Mars and pallid Tisiphone circumscribe the group who feel some compassion, while Venus and Juno maintain ambiguous neutrality—they are described as spectators but separated by *contra* with its two meanings of location and mood. The brief shift to the halls of Jove maintains perspective. Then Vergil continues, *at vero*—nevertheless, even so; that is, Mezentius remains the fierce hero, now moving to another sector of the battle-field, where he will encounter Aeneas.

He shows no hesitation, no fear. With a mock prayer, he casts his spear, but the spear, deflected by Aeneas's shield, ricochets an enor-mous distance and pierces a warrior named Antores (778). Antores was a Greek who settled in Italy and attached himself to Evander; thus he happens to be in this strange war. Vergil exploits the circum-stances: *infelix* Antores, felled by a wound not properly his (*alieno vulnere*, 781), dies looking up at the sky and remembering his dear Argos. *Alieno* here indicates the blow intended for another; it suggests also "foreign" as that applies specifically to Antores and his dying memory of native sky.

Not merely pathetic, the circumstance enlarges context. We recall that Aeneas himself had no quarrel with Mezentius; he reluctantly accepted the expanded scope of the war. All three—Antores, Me-zentius, Aeneas—are foreigners to the soil they fight on, as is Tur-nus. Minor as such circumstances may be, they contribute a particular tone and a particular irony to the whole sequence of events. To grasp this, it is necessary to backtrack briefly and sketch the career of the warrior Aeneas in Book x.

Aeneas's prowess manifests itself immediately upon landing (287 f.); Latins go down one after the other—Theron and Lychas (*tibi, Phoebe, sacrum,* 316) and the brothers Gyas and Cisseus (who derived no more benefit from their connection with Hercules than did Pallas, 319 f.). Aeneas's martial feats equal those of Turnus in Book ix; but, after the death of Pallas, Aeneas outdoes Turnus. *Ardens,* he cuts a broad swath before him as he attempts to get to Turnus. Bar-barically, Aeneas marks eight young prisoners for immolation: [4]

> viventis rapit, inferias quos immolet umbris
> captivoque rogi perfundat sanguine flammas.   (x.519–20)

He took them alive, intending to sacrifice them to the shades and then pour the captive blood over the flames of the pyre.

His slaughter of Magus (521–36) vividly recalls Achilles slaying Lycaon (*Iliad* XXI.64 f.). With bloody sword he savagely kills the son of Haemon, then Caeculus, Anxur and Tarquitus, Lucagus and Liger, and others. He is compared to Aegaeon, the legendary giant of a hundred hands, who breathed out fire from fifty mouths and fifty chests—*quinquaginta oribus ignem / pectoribus arsisse* (566 f.). If the details recall the simile of the Dog Star (272 f.), the narrative underscores the connection:

> sic toto Aeneas desaevit in aequore victor
> ut semel intepuit mucro.   (x.569–70)

Just so did Aeneas rampage over the whole battlefield, irresistible once his sword grew warm.

Most of his victims are little more than faceless names, but they share with Lausus and Pallas the horror of the butcher's inhumanity. Turnus scornfully cried before his fight with Pallas: "cuperem ipse parens spectator adesset" ("I only wish his father were here to watch," 443); variations upon this cruel theme inform Aeneas's ferocity. Magus cries for mercy, taking hold of Aeneas's knees and begging him, by the shade of his father and the rising hopes of his son, to spare him for his own son and father:

> et genua amplectens effatur talia supplex:
> 'per patrios manis et spes surgentis Iuli
> te precor, hanc animam serves natoque patrique.'   (x.523–25)

To this appeal of a suppliant, Aeneas retorts brutally:

> 'hoc patris Anchisae manes, hoc sentit Iulus.'   (534)

"This is the judgment of my father Anchises' spirit, this of my son, Ascanius."

Thus imputing bloodlust to father and son, he kills Magus:

> sic fatus galeam laeva tenet atque reflexa
> cervice orantis capulo tenus applicat ensem.   (x.535–36)

As he spoke, he gripped Magus's helmet in his left hand, bent his neck back, and, even as he pleaded, drove the sword home up to the hilt.

In context, the act recalls distinctly Aeneas's own description of Pyrrhus killing Priam:

> 'traxit et in multo lapsantem sanguine nati,
> implicuitque comam laeva, dextraque coruscum
> extulit ac lateri capulo tenus abdidit ensem.'   (II.551–53)

"Pyrrhus dragged him [Priam], slipping in the pool of his own son's blood; in his left hand he twisted Priam's hair, while with his right he drew the flashing sword and buried it to the hilt in his side."

The next victim, identified only as son of Haemon, is *Phoebi Triviaeque sacerdos* (537). Like Panthus, priest of Apollo at Troy, his special status cannot save him.[5] In one of the more horrible passages, Aeneas decapitates Tarquitus:

> tum caput orantis nequiquam et multa parantis
> dicere deturbat terrae, truncumque tepentem
> provolvens super haec inimico pectore fatur:
> 'istic nunc, metuende, iace. non te optima mater
> condet humi patrioque onerabit membra sepulcro.'   (x.554–58)

> Then, as he begged for mercy, uselessly babbling, Aeneas
> Struck off his head, sent it rolling, and pushing away the still warm
> Trunk of the man, stood above it, saying these pitiless words:—
> "Lie there, you terrible warrior! Your lady mother shall never
> Inter you, commit your remains to the tomb of your ancestors."
>   (Tr. Day Lewis)

After all this, one could hardly expect that the two brothers Lucagus and Liger will be spared. Liger hurls brave words which, like those of Remulus, evoke Troy:

> 'non Diomedis equos nec currum cernis Achilli
> aut Phrygiae campos: nunc belli finis et aevi
> his dabitur terris.'   (x.581–83)

"Here you see no horses of Diomedes or chariot of Achilles or the fields of Phyrgia. This hour and this land will be the end of the war and of your life."

Aeneas kills Lucagus first, then goes after Liger, the unarmed charioteer, who holds out helpless hands (*inertis palmas*) in supplication:

> 'per te, per qui te talem genuere parentes,
> vir Troiane, sine hanc animam et miserere precantis.'   (x.597–98)

"O hero of Troy, by your own self and by the parents who begot so great a man—spare this life, have pity on one who pleads with you."

But Aeneas, again echoing Pyrrhus (ii.547 f.), retorts:

> 'morere et fratrem ne desere frater.'   (600)

"Die. As a brother, you cannot desert your brother!"

I quote in such detail because these passages are so easily overlooked. They form a very definite pattern, leading up to the deaths of Lausus and Mezentius. Let us return now to the death of Antores and the final episodes of Book x.

> sternitur infelix alieno vulnere, caelumque
> aspicit et dulcis moriens reminiscitur Argos.
> tum pius Aeneas hastam iacit....
>
>   . . . .
>
>   imaque sedit
> inguine, sed viris haud pertulit. ocius ensem
> Aeneas viso Tyrrheni sanguine laetus
> eripit a femine et trepidanti fervidus instat.
> ingemuit cari graviter genitoris amore,
> ut vidit, Lausus, lacrimaeque per ora volutae.   (x.781–90)

Unlucky Antores, felled by a wound meant for Aeneas, lay gazing at the sky and, as he died, recalled his dear Argos. Then pious Aeneas hurled his spear. . . . It lodged low in the groin [of Mezentius], though it failed to drive home its full power. Aeneas, rejoicing at the sight of Etruscan blood, swiftly drew his sword from his side and rushed furiously on the dazed Mezentius. Seeing this, Lausus cried aloud in pain, out of love for his dear father, and the tears rolled down his face.

There are many significant aspects of this passage. Apparently, Aeneas does not even notice the futile death of Antores. The epithet *pius* is striking. Considering it in the terms defined by most scholars and critics, we can see it as suggesting the differences between Aeneas and the *contemptor divum,* Mezentius. But context demands more. The only earlier use of the epithet in Book x occurred when Aeneas taunted his dying victim Lucagus: *quem pius Aeneas dictis adfatur amaris* (591). Clearly ironic then, *pius* appears to be ironic in the present passage also. There is a significant contrast between *pius Aeneas . . . sanguine laetus* and the youth Lausus. Aeneas exults, but Lausus is conscious only of his filial feeling toward Mezentius: the phrase *cari . . . genitoris amore* (789) calls up others, such as *cari genitoris imago* (II.560), and both are evoked again a few lines later, as the epithet *pius* is applied to Aeneas for the third time in Book x.

To underline the contrast, Vergil halts the action in mid-career, Aeneas rushing forward, Mezentius dazed, Lausus weeping— creating a kind of tableau for us to contemplate while he apostrophizes Lausus:

> Hic mortis durae casum tuaque optima facta,
> si qua fidem tanto est operi latura vetustas,
> non equidem nec, te, iuvenis memorande, silebo.   (x.791–93)

And now, I promise you that, if antiquity can win any belief for so great an act, I shall never pass over in silence your hard death and your heroic deeds, and your own self, so worthy of fame.

The apostrophe is remarkable, in part because it is unique: it is the only such apostrophe that *precedes* the event. Striking too is the almost pathetic quarrel between the warm words and the crabbed syntax.

As the action is resumed, many of the Latins rush up to help Lausus defend the wounded Mezentius and cover his retreat. But Aeneas deliberately ignores the others and singles out Lausus. He taunts the

youth with ridicule ("Why rush to your death by daring something
beyond your powers?") and with gratuitous brutality ("Your *pietas*
has made you reckless"):

> Lausum increpitat Lausoque minatur:
> 'quo moriture ruis maioraque viribus audes?
> fallit te incautum pietas tua.'   (x.810–12)

Of course, Aeneas is addressing an enemy and is whipping up his own
furies, in standard fashion. But the pattern highlighted by *pietas*
forces us to recognize his viciousness here.

Vergil does not at any point explicitly call Aeneas barbaric; the
closest he seems to come is in line 802, *furit Aeneas,* and even the
simile which follows avoids overt indictment. But that is as it should
be (and a clear warning not to accept his "portrayal" of Turnus at
face value: statement is one of the least acceptable modes of poetic
saying). Aeneas's barbarism emerges dramatically, from the action itself. In this long day of carnage, as we have seen, Aeneas has disre-
garded various canons; his plan to immolate the eight young men (all
of them defined as sons) was an act that Vergil's own time considered
barbarous and abhorrent.

The emotional climax, both of this episode and of the whole of
Book x, is reached at Lausus's death:

> at vero ut vultum vidit morientis et ora,
> ora modis Anchisiades pallentia miris,
> ingemuit miserans graviter dextramque tetendit,
> et mentem patriae subiit pietatis imago.
> 'quid tibi nunc, miserande puer, pro laudibus istis,
> quid pius Aeneas tanta dabit indole dignum?
> arma, quibus laetatus, habe tua; teque parentum
> manibus et cineri, si qua est ea cura, remitto.
> hoc tamen infelix miseram solabere mortem:
> Aeneae magni dextra cadis.'   (x.821–30)

But when Anchises' son looked upon the dying youth's face and features
—features suddenly become so pallid in such strange ways—he
groaned deeply in pity and stretched out his right hand; the image of
filial affection touched his spirit. "O piteous boy, what can the pious
Aeneas give you that is proper to your great glory, or worthy of your nobility? Those arms you rejoiced in, keep them; and—if this can matter

to you—I release you, to join the shades and the ashes of your fathers. Still, poor boy, you can have some solace in your miserable death, in this fact: you fell by the right hand of mighty Aeneas."

Anchisiades is not elegant variation; we have seen how insistently Aeneas's name is repeated. The epithet here defines Aeneas's sudden realization of what he has been about. He did not see this shortly before, killing Lucagus and Liger, sending brother to join brother; nor in the rest of his death-dealing. Now, he feels piercingly the relevance of *pietas*—as he felt it on another occasion when he had been swept away by madness: *subiit cari genitoris imago* (II.560). Echoed in line 824, these words are from the Fall of Troy, specifically from the moments just after Aeneas witnessed the deaths of Polites and Priam, son and father, at the hands of Pyrrhus. The force of this complex allusion is overwhelming.

Deeply shaken, he addresses Lausus, calling him *"miserande puer,"* the words applied (by Anchises) to Marcellus (VI.882). Aeneas speaks sadly, echoing yet again an earlier *si qua est ea gloria* (VII.4)—for death remains ambiguous: does heroism or the immortality of a name have real meaning? In effect, Aeneas is saying, "What shall I give you to replace the praises due such bravery and such filial devotion? What can Aeneas, who claims to be *pius,* do that is worthy of such a spirit?" The conventional things seem neither relevant nor satisfactory, so he adds this: *"tamen . . . Aeneae magni dextra cadis."* The words are self-mocking. Aeneas sees himself, for the moment, stripped down to the bare warrior-hero.

This passage illuminates the final episode, the death of Mezentius. After receiving his son's corpse with great dignity, Mezentius expresses a sincere if late repentance. He feels that his worst crime is a failure of *pietas:* he has let Lausus die in his place and has defiled him with his own guilt—"idem ego, nate, tuum maculavi crimine nomen" (851). Returning to the battlefield, he finds Aeneas and responds to his challenge with a simplicity that is noble: "quid me erepto, saevissime, nato / terres?" ("Now that you have taken my son, brutal foe, do you think you can frighten me?" 878 f.). He has come to die ("nec mortem horremus") but would take Aeneas with him if he can.

The manner in which Mezentius dies befits his consistently heroic character. Aeneas taunts him—"ubi nunc Mezentius acer?"—but Mezentius brushes this off:

> contra Tyrrhenus, ut auras
> suspiciens hausit caelum mentemque recepit:
> 'hostis amare, quid increpitas mortemque minaris?
> nullum in caede nefas, nec sic ad proelia veni,
> nec tecum meus haec pepigit mihi foedera Lausus.
> unum hoc per si qua est victis venia hostibus oro:
> corpus humo patiare tegi. scio acerba meorum
> circumstare odia: hunc, ore, defende furorem
> et me consortem nati concede sepulcro.'
> haec loquitur, iuguloque haud inscius accipit ensem
> undantique animam diffundit in arma cruore.   (x.898–908)

But the Etruscan looked up at the sky and drank in the air; and recovering consciousness, said: "Harsh enemy, why all this scorn, all these threats? There's nothing wrong with killing; I did not make war on any such terms, and my Lausus made no such bond for me with you. But, if the vanquished may seek any favors, I ask only one thing: allow my body to be covered with earth. I know how bitterly my people hate me; I ask you to protect this corpse from their fury and let me share a sepulchre with my son." So he spoke, and then deliberately offered his throat to the sword, pouring out his life in waves of blood over his armor.

In this final hour, Mezentius achieves a stature that transcends the old guilt. Unafraid of either life or death, unconcerned even now with the gods, he seeks an end proper to the heroic code. He wishes to be reconciled with his people (the word *Tyrrhenus,* 898, crystallizes that feeling), to share a grave with his heroic son. The *contemptor divum* rises above the chosen of the gods.

In praising Vergil's superb handling of Mezentius, critics often overplay their hand:

What poet, except Virgil, would have lavished such pity on a character like Mezentius? For pity him we do with all our heart. As the book closes and the echoes of war die away, Aeneas is almost forgotten. We find ourselves hoping against hope that this father has at long last found peace by the side of the son he loved so tenderly.[6]

But to "forget" Aeneas here is to take Mezentius and Lausus out of context and to diminish them. Vergil's art deserves better. Mezentius and Lausus climax the developing father-son motif in Book x. As metaphor for *pietas,* the motif enlarges the dimensions of the poem.

In his moment of grief before dead Lausus, Aeneas refers to himself in the third person as *pius Aeneas* (826). This *pietas* includes more than his relationship to Anchises and to Ascanius. It includes also the relationship of Priam and Polites, of Pyrrhus and his own father, of the enemies Aeneas has been slaughtering, and of Mezentius and Lausus.[7] More, it is the focal point of human justice and human morality. Here, Aeneas uses the word *pius* in a normative rather than descriptive sense: "Aeneas is supposed to be *pius.*"

The lines to Lausus conclude with another reference to himself in the third person: *"Aeneae magni dextra cadis"* (830). This is the other half of the recurrent phrase, used both *of* Aeneas and *by* Aeneas himself, *pietate insignis et armis.* Few critics have considered the phrase much more than an elegant variation on the opening words, *Arma virumque.* Yet there lies the precise problem: in this context, the oblique references polarize *pietas* and *arma.* The very recurrence of the formula or its variations must suggest that the two terms are hardly coequal or coexistent. They can seem so only in narrowly legalistic ways. Thus: Aeneas is pious because, in war, he does what is necessary for him as founder of the Roman people to do. Or: Aeneas, having shown himself *insignis* in *armis,* can now show himself as *pietate insignis* also, by being humane toward Lausus. As if *pietas* and *arma* can be neatly pigeonholed! No. The figure of Aeneas holding up Lausus's head and yielding the corpse to his Etruscan friends provides emphatic comment.

The implicit question in the poem is which of these, *pietas* and *arma,* will prevail in their interaction and counteraction. Vergil offers little hope that they can have completely equal terms or easily coexist. The visions of history presented to us have, in fact, shown the uneasy truce between *arma* and *virum.* Book x, the bloodiest day in the war, dramatizes the uneasiness. In the contrast between Aeneas and Mezentius as the book closes, we have yet another victory of *arma* over *pietas.*

There cannot of course be any quarrel with Aeneas's act of killing

Mezentius. As the last words of Book x suggest, Mezentius's death embodies the limitations of *arma*. Furthermore, Aeneas's moment of shame before the dying Lausus argues that he is fundamentally superior to Turnus, the slayer of Pallas. Yet even so, the whole tone is wrong, deliberately. In the end our sympathies are with Mezentius, because Vergil has made us feel the force of old clichés: blood begets blood, war is irreconcilable with humanity. And as for Aeneas, only a great effort of will can offset this catastrophic reality and invest his enterprise with the justice and humanity he seeks. We may hope that Aeneas will achieve some measure of that justice and humanity. But by the same token we cannot evade the harsh facts here.

Book x opened with the ascendancy of power over justice. It closes now with the ascendancy of *arma* over *pietas* and, thus, *virum*. The fragile balance of creation and destruction is almost shattered by this book. If the war in Italy is Vergil's *maius opus,* that is because it confronts squarely the profoundest questions of Vergil's time, and of ours—peace and war, justice and power, creation and destruction, *pietas* and *arma.*

CHAPTER EIGHT

AENEAS AND TURNUS

With the death of Mezentius, a major phase of Books VII–XII virtually ends. The musterings and alignments of VII and VIII have faded in importance; the chaotic and often futile carnage of IX and X is halted. In Book XI, a great deal of effort is expended in revaluation and assessment of what has been happening. This effort is manifest in dialogue and in action.

Book XI begins—unlike any other book in the poem—with daybreak; it ends with nightfall. Between, there is a seesaw rhythm of uncertainty and inconclusiveness. In the opening lines, day breaks upon internal disquiet and orderly, deliberate ritual:

> Oceanum interea surgens Aurora reliquit:
> Aeneas, quamquam et sociis dare tempus humandis
> praecipitant curae turbataque funere mens est,
> vota deum primo victor solvebat Eoo.   (XI.1–4)

And Aurora rose up, leaving Ocean. Although he felt impelled to turn immediately to the burial of his comrades and was deeply distressed by the carnage, the victor Aeneas started at daybreak to fulfill his vows to the gods.

The break of day permits a shift from the vengeful butcher of X to a more recognizable Aeneas.

The poet does not tell us explicitly that Aeneas acceded to Mezentius's dying wish, but the change of tone suggests that he did. *Surgens Aurora* reminds us that this is the morning after, not the morning before. But at that time, too, Aeneas was described as profoundly concerned: *magnus ... Aeneas secumque volutat / eventus belli varios* (x.159)—*varios* suggesting the possibilities and implications that kept him sleepless through the night (*neque enim membris dat cura quietem,* x.217). Now he is the *victor,* faced with the burial of the dead, an act of humane *pietas.* His impulse is to bury the dead first, but the ritual calls for immediate sacrifice to the gods. Troubled by the wholesale slaughter in which he had such a large role, he takes refuge in the canonical order of ritual.

The uncertainty suggested by the seesaw rhythm of xi comes directly from the action. Between rising Aurora and declining Phoebus at the end—

> roseus fessos iam gurgite Phoebus Hibero
> tingat equos noctemque die labente reducat.   (xi.913–14)

—there are large, well-defined scenes. The divisions of xi are few and well-articulated: the funerals, the council, the renewal of the war. But within these large divisions, the amount and kind of movement is remarkable: the funeral party sent to Evander, and sent back; the Latin envoys sent to Aeneas, and sent back; the return of the envoys from Diomedes; the dispatching of the dead warriors to Hades. In smaller ways, the same kind of motion is seen: in the details of the plan of ambush, for instance; in the closing of the gates at the end; even in the similes.

Nothing conclusive happens in xi. While the episodes flow easily from each other, there are other possible choices. Just when the council is on the verge of reaching a decision to act, Aeneas's army invades, following a plan alternative to the single combat Aeneas had defined for the Latin envoys. Just when the ambush is about to succeed, the news of Camilla's death disperses it. Just when Aeneas and Turnus meet, night falls and postpones their combat.

The detail is appropriate. The duel between Aeneas and Turnus would be impossible at the end of xi. Indeed, something like this seems the point of the inconclusiveness running through the whole book. It recalls Book ix in some general ways (e.g., the irrelevance of the talk in council), but the main point of Book xi lies in the futile

attempts on both sides to redefine meaning, to take firm hold of
events.

On the Trojan side, attempts at revaluation are made by Evander
and Aeneas. Evander sees Pallas's death as *"sors ista senectae / debita
... nostrae"* ("the lot destined for my old age," 165) and persists in
speaking of Aeneas as *"pius"* (170). Such tragedy is the price of war.
But it has poignant immediacy for Evander, which it did not have for
Aeneas. Even though Aeneas took the blame upon himself, his act
was an impulse of hindsight.

Evander needs no such hindsight. He foresaw Pallas's death and
now he unconsciously adapts it to the pattern of antique heroism. His
outpouring of grief is balanced, if not solaced, by the paradigm of
youth, bravery, and glory. The death of Pallas calls for more death,
his own and Turnus's. At the climax of his lament, he enunciates specific *mandata* to be conveyed to Aeneas:

> 'quod vitam moror invisam Pallante perempto
> dextera causa tua est, Turnum natoque patrique
> quam debere vides. meritis vacat hic tibi solus
> fortunaeque locus. non vitae gaudia quaero,
> nec fas, sed nato manis perferre sub imos.'   (XI.177–81)

> "Tell him I linger on, though I care not for life now Pallas
> Is gone, to receive the debt which he knows is owing to father
> And son—vengeance on Turnus: it's the sole task that remains for
> His courage and luck to accomplish. I ask it, not to gladden
> My life—that were wrong—but to bring the good news to my
> son in the Underworld."   (Tr. Day Lewis)

The difficult syntax here does not diminish the recurrent echo in
debere of Turnus's *"soli mihi Pallas / debetur"* (x.442), nor the echo
in line 181 of Pyrrhus's brutal words to Priam as he killed him: *"referes
ergo haec et nuntius ibis / Pelidae genitori"* (II.547). In these inter-
woven echoes, the parallelism shown in the previous chapter is made full.
Turnus's killing of Pallas and Aeneas's killing of Lausus are closely
linked in this last, unwittingly ironic, outcry of Evander. But it is
neither *merita* nor *fortuna* that brings death to Turnus. Rather, at
this one point in the pattern Turnus and Aeneas are different. Aeneas

saw in Lausus's death a reproach and a warning; Turnus exulted in the death of Pallas and in the *balteus* he took. That *balteus* will be his downfall.

For Aeneas, the victory has been ashes. In his address to the troops at the beginning of XI, there is a noteworthy inversion; he stipulates a definite course of action, a march on Latinus and Latium ("nunc iter ad regem nobis murosque Latinos," 17), then almost negates it by calling for funerals and for a cortege to accompany the body of Pallas to Arcadia. Later, he seems to reverse himself again by specifying (to the envoys) his desire to meet Turnus in single combat.

The funerals begin on a curious note:

> Aurora interea miseris mortalibus almam
> extulerat lucem referens opera atque labores   (XI.182–83)

And now Aurora had lifted her strengthening light for suffering humanity, recalling them to their labor and their burdens.

The repetition of Aurora (XI.1) reinforces the verbal texture. During twelve days of truce, Trojans and Latins fraternize freely and easily:

> per silvas Teucri mixtique impune Latini
> erravere iugis.   (XI.134–35)

It belongs to their condition that they were recently slaughtering each other, soon will be slaughtering each other again, and eventually will be compatriots. As *victor Aeneas* well knows, there are other tears yet to be shed; the fates of war still call:

> 'nos alias hinc ad lacrimas eadem horrida belli
> fata vocant....'   (XI.96–97)

This is the reflective, compassionate Aeneas; yet these *belli fata* cannot be ignored. His next act is broadly symbolic—he returns to the fortifications of his camp:

> nec plura effatus ad altos
> tendebat muros gressumque in castra ferebat.   (XI.98–99)

On the Latin side, the pause for reflection is even more painful. The Latin envoys are received by Aeneas with both pity and harshness. Their statements center mainly on their dead, but Aeneas puts it to them that the living are also involved: "equidem pacem et vivis concedere vellem" (111). Aeneas reminds them that the *fata* have brought him here and claims that he did not start the war and that Turnus could have brought it to an end. Drances seizes on this and on Aeneas's imputation of total guilt to Turnus and proposes complete capitulation, even to the extent of building their destined city for the Trojans:

> 'quin et fatalis murorum attollere moles
> saxaque subvectare umeris Troiana iuvabit.'   (XI.130–31)

But Drances cannot really propose anything. His grandiloquent flattery of Aeneas (*"o fama ingens, ingentior armis,"* etc.) betrays him: he is a man of words, intrigue, expediency. He can offer only a general hope, spiced by a hint of palace-guard politics: "If Fortune makes it at all possible, we will unite you to King Latinus. Let Turnus seek out other allies."

> '... te, si qua viam dederit Fortuna, Latino
> iungemus regi. quaerat sibi foedera Turnus.'   (XI.128–29)

He has long hated Turnus, the old man using all his talents to protect his vested power against the young upstart—

> ... senior semperque odiis et crimine Drances
> infensus iuveni Turno....   (XI.122–23)

—because Turnus's nobility and prowess represent a serious threat to him and to those who stand with him. Now, if he can arouse the Latins against Turnus, he may be able to salvage some power and regain his old place. However, as events show, he has underestimated Turnus. The Latins, grieving as they bury their dead, condemn the war and Turnus—*dirum exsecrantur bellum Turnique hymenaeos* (217)—but there is a solid pro-Turnus faction. This is partly because of the queen's outspoken support for him (*magnum reginae nomen obumbrat*, 223: the image in *obumbrat* suggests also Amata's possessiveness, her way of seeing Turnus), and partly because of his own heroic character, his reputation and his great deeds:

> multa virum meritis sustentat fama tropaeis.   (224)

The message which the envoys bring back from Diomedes dramatizes the Latin dilemma and augments it. In rejecting their overtures, Diomedes warns them unequivocally not to fight Aeneas. In the council scene, Latinus exploits this warning in an attempt to reassert his power. He casts himself as conciliator. To his own, he offers surrender with honor:

> 'nec quemquam incuso: potuit quae plurima virtus
> esse, fuit; toto certatum est corpore regni.'   (XI.312–13)

"I would not blame anyone. Whatever utmost valor could do, it has done: we have fought with all the strength of our kingdom."

To the Trojans, he would offer compromise—but in terms that bear small relevance to the whole war: a choice of land (now cultivated by Rutulians) or a fleet to sail away in.

But Drances supports Latinus. Goaded by the unbearable fact of Turnus's glory, he shows himself in full character (*lingua melior...*, *seditione potens*) and shrewdly supplies what Latinus had omitted:

> 'unum etiam donis istis, quae plurima mitti
> Dardanidis dicique iubes, unum, optime regum,
> adicias, nec te ullius violentia vincat
> quin natam egregio genero dignisque hymenaeis
> des, pater, et pacem hanc aeterno foedere firmes.'   (IX.352–56)

"Most excellent of kings, add but one more gift to all those which you so generously bid us take or promise to the Dardanians—just one; and let no man's violence prevent you, her father, from giving your daughter to a splendid suitor in an honorable marriage. Thus will you confirm this peace in an eternal covenant."

Despite the unctuous flattery, Drances employs powerful rhetoric. The devious lines smoothly hit many points: that Latinus still is king, that the Trojans are descendants of Dardanus, that as father Latinus has the final word on who shall marry his daughter, that a Latin-Trojan compact would be far more valuable than one between Latinus and Turnus; and much more. Another thread can also be seen: Drances is trying to divide and conquer the supporters of Turnus. He builds up the attack on Turnus to a crescendo, making him out to be the enemy of Latium and the cause of all its misery. Then elaborately and with obvious reference to Turnus's unexplained absence during the battle (in x), he challenges Turnus either to leave or to redeem himself by facing Aeneas in single combat.

The Latinus-Drances faction stands firmly against Turnus. They have made a strong case, but they have not allowed for two crucial facts. First, the issue has been drawn more sharply than ever between the older and the younger. Second, in accepting Diomedes' estimate, they have missed the whole burden of Diomedes' message. (So, indeed, has Turnus.)

No one is allowed to forget that Diomedes was the conqueror of Troy. As the legates put it, "We shook the hand that wiped out Ilium" (*"contigimusque manum qua concidit Ilia tellus,"* 245). But this conqueror weighs his words carefully. Diomedes characterizes the Latin operation as *ignota bella* (254); he reveals the Greeks' own phantasmagoric fate:

> ' "quicumque Iliacos ferro violavimus agros
> (mitto ea quae muris bellando exhausta sub altis,
> quos Simois premat ille viros) infanda per orbem
> supplicia et scelerum poenas expendimus omnes,
> vel Priamo miseranda manus...." '   (XI.255–59)

" 'All of us who profaned the land of Ilium with the sword—I say nothing about the miseries of the war under Troy's great walls, or the heroes swallowed up by the Simois—all of us have suffered unutterable punishments for our guilt throughout the whole world, and have become a band whom Priam himself might pity. . . .' "

Most of his message describes the catastrophes of their journey home; we are reminded again and again of Aeschylus's *Agamemnon.* When, finally, he comments on his old enemies, Aeneas and Hector, the comments derive their substance from this context, that in such wars there are no victors, there is only the terrible hand of the gods: *"nec veterum memini laetorve malorum"* (280).

Though the message is powerfully framed, no account is taken of it in the council. Latinus and Drances understand only the refusal, without comprehending Diomedes' excursions into nightmare or the inferences he draws so plainly. Latinus even speaks of the Trojans as "undefeated," either in supreme misunderstanding or in deliberate distortion. Obviously, Drances and Latinus prefer the way of power politics and intrigue. They fasten on Turnus as a scapegoat, thus skirting all responsibility for the war or its significance.

In his response, Turnus effectively beats down both Latinus's proposals and Drances' assault. Their way is the way of dishonor and cowardice, and while he skittishly avoids Drances' charge of flight during battle, he hammers out realistic proposals that are relevant, climaxing in his fervent acceptance of single combat. But Turnus has not, for his part, understood Diomedes' message either. The reason appears in the tone and assumptions of his speech. Allowing the feasibility of Latinus's proposal that they sue for peace, he adds a bitter lament for the demise of antique valor: *"quamquam o si solitae quicquam virtutis adesset!"* (415). The thought of limp sword-hands *(dextras inertis,* 414) he finds repugnant. As long as their forces are intact, why not continue the war? He invokes the warrior's credo, the quasi-mystical certainty that somehow time and change improve things, that Fortune mocks men only to turn about and smile on them:

> 'multa dies variique labor mutabilis aevi
> rettulit in melius, multos alterna revisens
> lusit et in solido rursus Fortuna locavit.'   (xi.425–27)

He argues that they are still strong enough. Yet if, nonetheless, it is to be single combat, Turnus declares himself ready, in solemn tones: [1]

> 'vobis animam hanc soceroque Latino
> Turnus ego, haud ulli veterum virtute secundus,
> devovi.'   (xi.440–42)

"I, Turnus, second in courage to none of the heroes of old, devote my life
to all of you and to Latinus, the father of my bride."

All these lines ring with the spirit of heroic virtue. This is Turnus's
glory—and his disastrous limitation. In its gusto, the whole speech
may conceal some natural measure of fear. Furthermore, whatever the
motivation of Drances, Latinus surely has been moved by the great
cost of blood—a matter that is meaningless to Turnus.

But Turnus has made his point. When Aeneas's approach is announced, the young men raise the war cry, but the older men weep:

> arma manu trepidi poscunt, fremit arma iuventus,
> flent maesti mussantque patres.   (XI.453–54)

Turnus's whole speech was a defense of honor; by it, he retained the
moral initiative. While Latinus in his vacillation and Drances with
his grandiloquence appeal to the fickle mob (only yesterday stirred
by the slogan, "Aeneas the Adulterer"), Turnus preserves a kind of
heroic integrity. *Exarsit ... violentia Turnus* (376): the very words
become attached to Turnus, as if to characterize this heroism and this
integrity. He is right, morally, to insist upon his honor, but the *violentia* and the *ardor* which are the stuff of such honor no longer
have relevance.

Clearly, neither Latins nor Trojans have profited from their revaluation. The aborted debate leads to the Camilla episode and the last
great Latin effort; when this fails, the war is virtually over. Camilla's
whole adventure springs from the kind of instinctive heroism embodied by Turnus. It may be that, in renewing the war, Turnus has deliberately (some would say, out of cowardice) evaded the chance to meet
Aeneas in single combat. The sequence of events is open to such a
reading but hardly demands it. At any rate, the fact remains that
Aeneas's march on the city takes them all by surprise. The debate has
not yet foreclosed the possibility of renewing the war (*dubiis de rebus
agebant,* 445) when Aeneas's army approaches. The arguments for
peaceful settlement depended heavily on the continuation of the good
will Aeneas had earlier shown. His march in force dissipates this; the
act contradicts Latinus's and Drances' positions, much as Aeneas's for-

tifying his first camp in Latium contradicted the legation of peace he had sent to Latinus.

Thus it all seems to be beginning again. Juno's impassioned desire to delay the outcome is being fulfilled. It is almost as if the course of war has made Allecto's ministrations unnecessary, as if men will deliberately make for themselves a destiny of doom. Latinus has been warned again that his encounter is both fated and fatal (*fatalem Aenean,* 232); the burden of Diomedes' message to the Latins is that the *vis superum* (whose abiding presence is felt throughout these books) affects both victors and vanquished. Even so, the actions of both Latins and Trojans seem designed to intensify their difficulties and to distort the blurred shape of destiny even more. *Fata viam invenient* (X.113): no doubt the fates will find a way, but the way need not be easy or just.

Splendid and tragic, the Camilla episode is widely praised as superb narrative but dismissed for its "episodic" character. But it has a specific function in the rhythm of the whole *Aeneid.* The ambush-strategy is a last stand ("vocat labor ultimus omnis," 476); when Camilla is dead, there will no no place left to hide. From another point of view, the episode delays further the confrontation between Aeneas and Turnus while providing a special kind of setting for that duel, a setting far different from Homer's. Vergil's entire strategy becomes quite non-Homeric: witness the ambush, the cavalry action, the Trojan march on the city.

The *aristeiai* of Camilla are carried out in the midst of renewed carnage:

> funditur ater ubique cruor; dant funera ferro
> certantes pulchramque petunt per vulnera mortem.
>   At medias inter caedes exsultat Amazon
> unum exserta latus pugnae, pharetrata Camilla.   (XI.646–49)

Everywhere the dark blood streams; the combatants deal out doom with the sword and strive for a glorious death in battle.

Right in the midst of the slaughter, an Amazon with one breast bared for the fray, armed with her quiver, Camilla exults.

Camilla is described as an Amazon, with numerous details distinctly evoking the figure of Penthesilea that anticipated Dido in Book I. At the same time, the twanging of the golden bow, Diana's weapon— "aureus ex umero sonat arcus et arma Dianae" (652)—connects Camilla with the important pair of similes linking Aeneas to Apollo (IV.143 f.) and Dido to Diana (I.498 f.).

For Camilla and her warriors, Vergil uses a simile that reflects the tension of primitive heroism and barbaric frenzy, the naïve pleasure of the huntress in a sunny dell and the ferocity of her violence:

> quales Threiciae cum flumina Thermodontis
> pulsant et pictis bellantur Amazones armis,
> seu circum Hippolyten seu cum se Martia curru
> Penthesilea refert, magnoque ululante tumultu
> feminea exsultant lunatis agmina peltis.   (XI.659–63)

They were like the Amazons of Thrace when they go to war in their brilliant armor and make Thermodon's streams resound with hoof beats as they escort Queen Hippolyta, or when martial Penthesilea returns in her chariot and the women warriors, shrieking wild battle-cries, exult and wave their crescent shields.

Threiciae (*pace* Conington and Page) obviously refers to the land where Mars is honored by barbarism and martial lust; the reference is underscored by *Martia ... Penthesilea.*[2] *Pictis armis,* while expressing the brightness and freshness of Camilla (like *florentis,* VII.804), also suggests the exotic and the grotesque. In *magnoque ululante tumultu, ululante* is feminine in association, as distinct from *magno turbante tumultu,* describing triumphant warriors (see VI.857). *Exsultant* echoes *exsultat Amazon* (648), while the final phrase, *lunatis agmina peltis,* derives directly from the Penthesilea passage (I.490).

Camilla's deeds are remarkable by any heroic measure. She brings down Ornytus, the Etruscan (667), and Orsilochus and Butes, who are like Pandarus and Bitias, *duo maxima Teucrum / corpora* (690). By her successes, she antagonizes male Jupiter, who stirs up Tarchon. Rebuking the fearful Etruscans, Tarchon sarcastically contrasts their cowardice with their prowess against women at other times: "at non

in Venerem segnes nocturnaque bella...." (736). But when Camilla is killed, it is not by a warrior worthy of her; it is by cowardly
Arruns.

Arruns dogs Camilla, looking for a safe target. By chance, Camilla
is taken with the shining armor of Chloreus, formerly a priest of Cybele, who is decked out in bronze and gold and purple, and has a
golden bow and a golden helmet. Perhaps she hoped to affix that re-
splendent Trojan armor to a temple wall, or perhaps she had visions
of herself triumphant in golden booty:

> sive ut templis praefigeret arma
> Troia, captivo sive ut se ferret in auro.   (XI.778–79)

At any rate, Camilla stalks him, blind to everything else (*caeca*) and
reckless to danger in her girlish passion for this booty:

> femineo praedae et spoliorum ardebat amore.   (782)

This is her downfall; she never even hears the spear that brings her
down (*nihil ipsa nec aurae / nec sonitus memor ...*, 801 f.).

Camilla's single-minded pursuit of Chloreus looks like female irra-
tionality, but Vergil has tactfully qualified the incident with a mixture
of motives. Camilla remains both warrior and woman at once and
loses none of her tragic heroism. Cupidity for shining armor belongs
to the heroic world as such; Euryalus (IX.364 f.) perished because of
it even more distinctly than Camilla.

Camilla's death, described briefly but movingly, leaves her forces in
disarray. Before the growing Trojan onslaught, the Latins panic. In a
confusion ominously like that during the Night of Troy, the gates of
Laurentum are shut and Latins are slaughtered helplessly: *limine in
ipso .../ oriturque miserrima caedes* (881 f.; see II.411, 531). Turnus, meanwhile, informed of Camilla's death and the peril to the city,
abandons his ambush—just as Aeneas was about to fall into the
trap. The two leaders meet near the city:

> ac simul Aeneas fumantis pulvere campos
> prospexit longe Laurentiaque agmina vidit,
> et saevum Aenean agnovit Turnus in armis
> adventumque pedum flatusque audivit equorum.   (XI.908–11)

At the same moment, Aeneas looked far across the plain smoking with dust and saw the Laurentian columns, and Turnus recognized Aeneas, deadly in his armor, and he heard the march of the troops and the snorting of the horses.

By the very structure of the lines Vergil suggests the confrontation that ought to take place and at the same time defers it. Nightfall provides a convenient excuse for the delay, but it is not the ultimate reason. Dramatically and thematically, such a confrontation is not feasible here. Camilla's catastrophe is too fresh in the reader's mind; like Mezentius, she succeeds, by her heroism and her death, in enhancing the stature of Turnus. At the same time, Aeneas has not yet repaired the moral damage of his rampage in Book x.

Book XII opens on a note of certainty.[3] Turnus, ready for single combat, rejects the entreaties of king and queen. He heaps scorn on Aeneas and thus defines his measure of the war: that man who should have perished at Troy ("*desertorem Asiae*") epitomizes the Phrygian tradition. But if he should win, then "*cedat Lavinia coniunx*" (17). The rhythm of this phrase dominates the scene; Turnus echoes it in his concluding line:

'illo quaeratur coniunx Lavinia campo.'   (XII.80)

"Upon that field let Lavinia's hand be won."

At the very end, in Turnus's final words to Aeneas, the rhythm recurs:

'tua est Lavinia coniunx'   (XII.937)

"Lavinia's hand is yours."

Turnus's certainty rests on his heroic spirit, his fatalism, and his love for Lavinia. But distraught Latinus misreads the young hero. Fatuously, he reminds Turnus that there are other girls around; attempting to regain his grip, he changes his tone and speaks hard (but just) words, asserting the inevitability of this marriage, even referring to

Aeneas as *"genero"* (31). At the end he collapses into incoherent pleas.

His words and Turnus's brief response intensify Amata's fears. She cries out that Turnus will die and that Turnus will go away. The insane argument is a naked plea to Turnus to stay alive *somehow,* and *somehow,* without fighting, to prevent Aeneas from taking Lavinia. But there is method in her madness: *ardentem generum moritura tenebat* (55). Her pathetic clinging to Turnus, as much as her words, rejects Latinus's decision that Aeneas is to be his son-in-law; for Amata, the husband of Lavinia will be more than son-in-law, he will be the male in the household. Like Dido, she is *moritura*—both destined to die and willing to die for her passion. She cries out to Turnus,

> 'in te omnis domus inclinata recumbit
>
> . . . .
>
> qui te cumque manent isto certamine casus,
> et me, Turne, manent.'   (XII.59, 61–62)

"On you rests our whole collapsing household. . . . Whatever perils await you in this combat, O Turnus, they await me also."

Though decency demands periphrasis, her meaning is clear enough (if there has ever been any doubt). Lavinia blushes deeply—out of modesty, or fear, or perhaps because of Amata's tone? Vergil does not say. The *amor*—Lavinia's certainly, but perhaps also Amata's— disturbs Turnus. He answers Amata simply but formally, calling her *"o mater"* and disposing of her passion in three short lines. The last of these has puzzled scholars:

> 'neque enim Turno mora libera mortis.'   (74)

Servius called it one of the twelve insoluble passages in Vergil, while offering an explication based somehow on Fate. But the meaning seems tolerably clear: "nor would, for Turnus, a delay be a reprieve from death." The words deliberately echo Turnus's opening line (XII.11: "nulla mora in Turno"); now he understands that both Latinus and Amata are urging a cowardly compromise, itself a form of death to his heroic spirit.

The unpleasant implications in the speeches of both Latinus and Amata have not been missed by Turnus. Amata's glaring passion embarrasses him; he fixes his attention on Lavinia (*figit,* 70). Latinus's suggestions are astounding, however just his strictures. Implying that the king has clearly missed both the character and the spirit of his proposals, Turnus rejects, courteously but firmly, any offer of escape, any inference that he might be no match for Aeneas: "letumque sinas pro laude pacisci" (49). Convinced of the essential criminality of the Phrygians and trusting only the ethic of valor, he can see but one divine force behind his enemy, that of Venus, and but one standard for himself to live by: "Let me trade my life for glory" (49).

So he arms himself, brandishing a sword tempered in the Styx; but the volcanic fire that tempered the metal seems transferred to Turnus himself:

> his agitur furiis, totoque ardentis ab ore
> scintillae absistunt, oculis micat acribus ignis.   (XII.101–2)

By such furies is he driven; fiery sparks shoot from his face and his eyes blaze with searing flames.

We can ignore neither the heroism nor the patent damnation. Turnus is marked by destiny and outlawed by it; his defect is the quality essential to all such heroes—*vis,* which can become *violentia* like that which moved Aeneas to carnage in Book X.

This dualism has been emerging from the very beginning of Book XII. Showing us Turnus ready for single combat (*ultro implacabilis ardet*), Vergil compares him to a wounded lion striking back:

> Poenorum qualis in arvis
> saucius ille gravi venantum vulnere pectus
> tum demum movet arma leo, gaudetque comantis
> excutiens cervice toros fixumque latronis
> impavidus frangit telum et fremit ore cruento:
> haud secus accenso gliscit violentia Turno.   (XII.4–9)

Just as in the fields of Carthage a lion, gravely wounded in the breast by the hunters, at last moves to the attack; joyfully shaking his shaggy mane, he snaps off, fearlessly, the spear which the invader planted in him and roars with bloodstained mouth: so did the violence swell in the enraged soul of Turnus.

The simile glosses *violentia,* a word several times associated with Turnus. It means instinctive heroism, the desire for noble and honorable battle; it means also the appetite for danger, an appetite expressing confident measures of himself. Not simply irrational, *violentia* includes the impulse to extend oneself, to expose oneself to danger at whatever cost.

The simile should make the reader pause and recall the tragedy of Dido at Carthage. In the simile, the place seems clearly Carthaginian. The relationship of the lion to the hunters, particularly to the one (*latronis*) who wounded him, suggests the relationship of Dido and Aeneas at Carthage: though wounded by him, she viewed him with furious contempt. Verbal echoes are unmistakable; line 5 echoes the opening lines of Book IV, while *latronis* recalls Dido's epithets (e.g., *perfide,* IV.305) and indicts the hunter as an outsider. Other details from Book IV are suggested: the figure of the wounded doe (69 f.), the nightmares of Dido in which the hunter Aeneas runs her down (465 f.).

Like Dido, Turnus cooperates in bringing about his own downfall. But in both cases the *vis superum* is responsible for that downfall. Turnus is, in fact, caught by the same fierce divinities who destroyed Dido—Juno as friend, Venus / Jupiter as enemy.

Friend to Turnus as she was to Dido, Juno plays a major though indirect role in Book XII. She operates through Juturna, the sister of Turnus. I would like to turn here to Juturna and examine her curious role in the development of the tragedy of Turnus. Juturna is the fourth semidivine being whom Juno commissions at an important juncture in the poem. The first was Aeolus, keeper of the winds; the second was Iris, rainbow goddess; the third was Allecto, fury from hell; the fourth, Juturna, is a river nymph, Turnus's sister, endowed by magnanimous Jupiter with a mixed blessing.

Unlike the earlier assignments, Juno's commission to Juturna lacks particularity. But in other respects there are interesting similarities. As in the commission to Allecto, there is no clear purpose; Juno is moving to postpone the inevitable, to spread fury, to abort the enterprise

—even though she knows this last is impossible. Too, as in the speech to Aeolus, Juno's words to Juturna combine cajolery and compassion.

But her words are awkward (as was Venus's appeal to her husband Vulcan on behalf of her bastard son). She addresses Juturna as one of those many nymphs (*cunctis*) who slept with Jupiter: "quaecumque Latinae/ magnanimi Iovis ingratum ascendere cubile" (144). The meaning of *magnanimi* is embittered by the twin-edged scorn of *ingratum*.[4] She indulges in false hope—"forsan miseros meliora sequentur" (153)—but when Juturna rather weeps in despair, Juno becomes imperious (*Saturnia*) and commands her: "auctor ego audendi" (159).

The figure of Juturna, endowed with nymphhood and immortality as reward for ravished maidenhood (*erepta pro virginitate,* 141), is symbolically fitting. Like Cassandra's or Troy's, her reward is bitter; her status and presence at the ceremonies anticipate the fall of Laurentum and of Turnus. Her presence at the covenant scene is felt before we are made fully aware of it—reflected perhaps in Turnus's pallor as he approaches the altar, "demisso lumine ... / tabentesque genae et iuvenali in corpore pallor" ("his eyes cast down, his cheeks wasted, a pallor over his youthful body," 220 f.). His demeanor reflects Juturna's despair and the whole Latin situation. The emphasis on Turnus's youthful body suggests his lack of maturity and stability.

Aeneas on the other hand is firm, marked by clarity and strength of purpose. This is no effeminate plunderer, no rapist in the tradition of Phrygian Paris, but rather a divinely chosen chief of state, majestic in his certainty. In the covenant with Latinus, Aeneas takes full moral command of the situation. There is no sign here of the warrior who gave full play to his bloodlust in the carnage of X or who sabotaged his own peace overtures in the surprise march of XI. Hoping the end of the war is in sight—*oblato gaudens componi foedere bellum* (109)—he lays down terms that are markedly fair, avoiding completely the wild excesses in which Ascanius indulged in Book IX. He is rightfully called *pater Aeneas* (166) and *pius Aeneas* (175); even when the truce is broken, he remains *pius Aeneas* (311). The epithet is again appropriate. At the altar, he solemnly invokes the gods and places himself fully at the disposal of his destiny; he solemnly com-

mits his people to depart if he should lose, and to an honorable coop-
erative union if he should win.

Though the terms are generous beyond expectation and the Latins
are ready to accept them, Turnus's followers are plagued by guilt.
Turnus's appearance at the altar emphasizes the reaction of the Rutulians to what they see, indicating nothing of Turnus's own feelings.
Thus, when Juturna assumes the guise of the great warrior Camers
and reproaches the Rutulians, her words strike just the right note:

> 'non pudet, o Rutuli, pro cunctis talibus unam
> obiectare animam?'   (XII.229–30)

"Rutulians, are you not ashamed to expose one man's life in place of all of
these men?"

The words are revealing, as is the whole speech. While *obiectare* does
not specifically mean sacrificing Turnus, the context implies that
meaning. At the same time, her reproach makes no more sense than
did Aeneas's resolve to fight and die at fallen Troy; it is a war cry, ir-
rationally playing upon fears and emotions. Yet so contagious is the
sense of guilt that the Latins also respond (240 f.).

Juturna's success with her reproach and with the omen she sends is
far-reaching. But it must be kept in context. She cannot save Turnus;
her unwilling participation in these events can only exacerbate her
anguish in the end. There is harsh irony here. Juno herself made it
clear that Jupiter's friendship brings only misery to those he befriends,
even while she was herself sending Juturna on a mission of misery.

Furthermore, Juturna's words highlight the tragedy of Turnus's
death. She herself cannot die; Jove's gift has made her immortal. But
she remains human enough to taste the bitterness of that ultimate
violence. Flaying the Rutulians for letting Turnus be a scapegoat, she
insists also on the glory of his heroism. The dual emphasis will haunt
her in the end; here it evokes the larger framework of death in the
whole poem. In a sense, every book of the *Aeneid* (with the possible
exception of VIII) is sealed and, as it were, consecrated by death.

Death is of course expected in an epic of journey and war. But the
cumulative effect of death in the *Aeneid* is quite unlike what one expects in heroic song. Vergil has shaped this common material into

complex symbolic rhythms—the deaths of fathers and leaders, and of sons; the deaths of quasi-sacrificial victims, like Orontes and Palinurus, each on the way to Sicily, each marked as one dying for the many. Cajeta's death severed the last tie of Aeneas to the old world; Book VII also has the first fruits of war in Italy, the old man and the young singled out as the *primitiae.* The deaths of Mezentius and Camilla prelude the death of Turnus. Mezentius was a stand-in for Turnus during his absence; as for Camilla, the last great hope in the war, her protesting spirit flees with a moan to the world of the shades: "vitaque cum gemitu fugit indignata sub umbras" (XI.831), anticipating the last line of the poem (XII.952).

What Juturna leads to, by her speech, reminds us disquietingly of the misguided defense of Troy in Book II. This is one of many details which link Book XII to the rest of the poem. Subsuming much that has gone before—by allusion in image or word or action—Book XII affords a new and fuller perspective on the whole poem. A full analysis of XII would further illuminate Vergil's complex artistry and structural design. Here, space permits only a few remarks. The simile comparing Turnus to the war-god Mars (XII.331–36) is similar in structure to those comparing Dido to the goddess Diana (I.498 f.) and Aeneas to the god Apollo (IV.143 f.). These three similes are unique in the detailed comparison of hero or heroine to god or goddess. Forming a kind of triad, they suggest some complex interrelationships between the three characters.

In larger terms, the middle section of Book XII—lines 257–649, from the renewal of the fighting to Turnus's return to Laurentum—reenacts in some measure major episodes of Books VIII–XI. In this section there is another example of Venus assisting Aeneas in a particular and significant way (see VIII); Aeneas again absent from the war and Turnus's carnage during that absence (IX); Juturna leading Turnus away from Aeneas (see Juno, in X); Turnus and Aeneas alternately destroying the enemy (IX and X). Too, the attack on Laurentum recalls the abortive attack on the city at the end of XI, a siege which had its beginnings with the breaking of the truce in mid-XI. In Book XI, it was during the fight at the city gates that Aeneas and Turnus came closest to a duel, but that meeting was quite accidental; in XII, Aeneas attacks Laurentum by design.

In this enlarged context, the omen that Juturna sends takes on some grim meaning. Just before it, the *murmur* caused by Juturna *serpit ... per agmina* (239)—the serpentine image recalls Book II particularly. In its own way, the omen of the eagle and the swans is quite as misleading as were the omen of the serpents and the death of Laocoon. Misinterpreted, as it was intended to be, the omen confirms and encourages the wrongheaded fury of Rutulians and Latins. Recalling Book II as if it were an archetype, this omen is followed by sacrilege (283 f.) and foreshadows the fall of the city of Laurentum.[5]

Whether or not Juturna shoots the arrow that wounds Aeneas (318–23) is of small moment. Juno later hints that it was she (813–15), but, as Maguinness remarks, Juno is a confirmed liar. In any event, when Aeneas finally returns to the battle, Juturna desperately tries to save Turnus by taking the place and the form of his charioteer, Metiscus. She knows the doom of Turnus. She has recognized both Aeneas and what he must do (*agnovit,* 449; see XI.910). Aeneas comes now, like a tempest destroying the fields and the crops—suggesting, perhaps the destruction of Laurentum, but in a larger way imaging the dualism suggested throughout VII and running beneath the currents of subsequent episodes. He comes for Turnus, wishing to fight none but Turnus:

> solum densa in caligine Turnum
> vestigat lustrans, solum in certamina poscit.   (XII.466–67)

In the dense gloom, he hunts Turnus alone, searching for him, challenging him alone to battle.

In Juturna's action, as in Aeneas's grim determination, portentousness is emphasized. The simile of the swallow (473 f.) foreshadows the birdlike *Dira* attendant on Turnus's death (862 f.); the maze Juturna leads him through, recalling the labyrinth, adumbrates the terrifying sleepwalking passage (908 f.). The resemblance of her action here to Juno's in Book X emphasizes her immediate function—to render a final service to Turnus. And like Juno's, this is itself a large disservice. The difference between the two—in X, Juno led Turnus away by providing a phantom-Aeneas, while here Juturna merely takes him to the opposite end of the battlefield—only deepens the ominousness. For as Juturna goes round and round, urging that this is the path to victory ("qua prima viam victoria pandit," 626), Turnus feels himself wildly confused. He fights well, but his actions become almost mechanical and mindless. Claiming he knew her presence ("*a-gnovi*," 631), he maintains his conviction of heroism (646 f.). Receiving word that the city is falling, he shakes himself out of his confused state and addresses Juturna with renewed heroism. The words are strong if fatalistic; he accepts fate, the gods, harsh fortune, and proclaims the absolute necessity of his encounter with death, even while recognizing that he has allowed Juturna to lead him away:

> 'iam iam fata, soror, superant, absiste morari;
> quo deus et quo dura vocat Fortuna sequamur.
> stat conferre manum Aeneae, stat, quidquid acerbi est,
> morte pati, neque me indecorem, germana, videbis
> amplius. hunc, oro, sine me furere ante furorem.'   (XII.676–80)

"At this very moment Fate is prevailing over us. Think not to cause delay. Let us follow where God and our own hard fortune call. I am resolved to meet Aeneas hand to hand, and bear whatever bitterness death may hold for me. Sister, never again shall you see me forget my honour. But first, I entreat you, let me do this one mad deed before I die." (Tr. Knight)

It has been necessary to move far ahead in Book XII, to suggest something of Vergil's achievement in the superb depiction of Juturna. The presence of Juturna at her brother's side in these agonized scenes lends a special depth to his tragedy. And Turnus himself understands her particular misery:

> 'sed quis Olympo
> demissam tantos voluit te ferre labores?
> an fratris miseri letum ut crudele videres?'   (XII.634–36)

"But who sent you from Olympus and made you endure such a heavy burden? Was it so that you might witness your poor brother's death agony?"

As we shall see, Juturna is not permitted even this. Her condition as Jove's onetime bride will not allow it.

We turn now to Aeneas. His firmness and certainty stand out in the covenant scene and the madness that follows it. Unarmed, he tries to stop the renewed battle. Wounded by the mysterious arrow, he maintains his dignity. His short lecture to Ascanius, on true valor, is noble and unpretentious. When he returns to the battle, he seeks only Turnus, his rage controlled by the real hope that he might put an end to the carnage. It is at this point that Juturna takes the reins of Turnus's chariot and wheels him away. A javelin hurled by Messapus shears off the top of Aeneas's helmet. Now, unable to pursue Turnus, he is forced to fight lesser, inappropriate foes:

> tum vero adsurgunt irae ...
>   . . . .
> terribilis saevam nullo discrimine caedem
> suscitat, irarumque omnis effundit habenas.   (XII.494, 498–99)

As his wrath swells, the slaughter he unleashes is both terrible and indiscriminate.

At this point, the poet utters his final invocation, startling in its barely disguised bitterness and in the echo of the first invocation ("tantaene animis caelestibus irae?" I.11):

> Quis mihi nunc tot acerba deus, quis carmine caedes
>   . . . .
> expediat? tanton placuit concurrere motu,
> Iuppiter, aeterna gentis in pace futuras?   (XII.500, 503–4)

What god can now unfold such horrors, sing of such slaughter . . . ? Was it your will, O Jupiter, that nations destined for eternal peace should clash so bitterly?

The following passage portrays the alternating butchery of Aeneas and Turnus. The whole is epitomized in one line of the invocation:

> inque vicem nunc Turnus agit, nunc Troius heros   (502)

—a line which is almost prosaic and flat ("now Turnus, now the Trojan hero takes his turn" at slaughter) and most effective for just that reason. Aeneas and Turnus are rhetorically juxtaposed, commin-

gled, almost identified with each other. Vergil invites attention to the
obviously balanced structure: 505 *Aeneas,* 509 *Turnus,* 513 *ille*
(Aeneas), 516 *hic* (Turnus), 529 *hic* (Aeneas), 535 *ille* (Turnus). The
alternating movement gathers a stark inevitability; the two heroes
pursue their work of butchery quite methodically, almost keeping
time with each other. Gradually, the view changes, marked by syntac-
tic shift, to the victims, and the two heroes become anonymous agents
of death as our attention is drawn to the recurring figure of the victim dying on alien ground. Finally, the action broadens into large
slaughter: *omnesque Latini,/omnes Dardanidae.*

At the center of this passage is a striking double simile with symbolic exegesis by the poet:

> ac velut immissi diversis partibus ignes
> arentem in silvam et virgulta sonantia lauro,
> aut ubi decursu rapido de montibus altis
> dant sonitum spumosi amnes et in aequora currunt
> quisque suum populatus iter: non segnius ambo
> Aeneas Turnusque ruunt per proelia; nunc, nunc,
> fluctuat ira intus, rumpuntur nescia vinci
> pectora, nunc totis in vulnera viribus itur.   (xII.521–28)

Like fires released from different directions upon a parched forest, where
thickets of bay-trees crackle, or like foaming rivers roaring in violent descent from mountain-heights, and each devastating its own track in its
haste to reach the plains, were Aeneas and Turnus, as, swift and eager,
they tore through the battle. Then, if never before, the rage within them
grew tempestuous. Their unconquerable hearts swelled to bursting, and all
their might was behind their every blow. (Tr. Knight)

The simile distinctly recalls one from Book II (304 f.). There, Aeneas,
roused out of sleep after the vision of Hector, *heard* the sounds of battle and destruction. He was *inscius pastor;* the noise came like that of
a fire raging through a cornfield, or a mountain torrent destroying the
crops.

In the later simile, the *flamma* becomes *ignes,* the *torrens* becomes
spumosi amnes: the plurals exacerbate the ferocity. The final word of
the simile is notable: *iter.* Each of the fires, each of the rivers has cut
its own destructive path. Syntactically, the clause *quisque suum popu-*

latus iter refers to *amnes,* but 'the connection with *ignes* is inescapable. This effect, overleaping syntax, is heightened by the poet's explanation. The actions described in the simile are divided thus: *fluctuat ira* suggests the *ignes; rumpuntur pectora* suggests the *amnes; itur* reflects *iter.* But however one sees these lines, the symbolism of the journey becomes part of the rhythm in this dance of death *à deux.* The impersonality of *itur* enlarges the poetic context.

In a specific way, images of the journey are central to Book XII. Turnus's journey is confused and uncertain, a function both of Juturna's futile impulse and of his own furious valor. The direction of his journey seems, at times, frightfully clear:

> 'vos o mihi, Manes,
> este bonis, quoniam superis aversa voluntas.
> sancta ad vos anima atque istius inscia culpae
> descendam magnorum haud umquam indignus avorum.'   (XII.646–49)

"O you Spirits below, be good to me, since the High Powers above have withdrawn their favor. I shall come down to you a guiltless soul with never a taint of the coward's sin, for never will I bring disgrace on my exalted forefathers." (Tr. Knight)

At all times his action, not reducible (as some critics would have it) to mere, naked *violentia,* is driven by a mixture of heroism and fury and love: "et furiis agitatus amor et conscia virtus" (XII.668). Early in the battle, he makes his way vigorously and victoriously through the enemy lines—"sic Turno, quacumque viam secat, agmina cedunt" (368). In the end, "quacumque viam virtute petivit / successum dea dira negat" (913 f.): Jove's *Dira* frustrates him whichever way he turns. The metaphor is telling, as it defines the preceding few lines, the reduction of Turnus's journey to the mockery of somnambulism (908 f.).

For Aeneas, on the other hand, the *iter* of the simile echoes his own words (XI.17, "nunc iter ad ... muros Latinos") and preludes the attack on Laurentum ("iret ut ad muros," XII.555). He is quite different now from the *pastor inscius* figure of II; that difference was pointed up by the moving simile of the *pastor* and the *apes* (XII.587 f.) which richly compresses the memorable images of the bees (I.430 f., VI.707 f.) with those of the *pastor* Aeneas (II.304 f., IV.70 f.: also *nescius* there), amid a symbolic movement climaxing in the recurrent image of *vacuas it fumus ad auras* (592).

Aeneas's impulse to make the *city* the direct object of his destructive journey comes from his *genetrix pulcherrima* (554—the epithet is ironic). What she adumbrates here is *pugnae ... maioris imago* (560): this "greater battle" recalls that other occasion, when she unveiled the profound mystery of Troy burning under the interdiction of Jupiter. But here, as Aeneas himself says, Jupiter is on the Trojan side: *"Iuppiter hac stat"* (565). Aeneas cryptically indicts the city of Laurentum as *"causam belli"* while identifying his Trojans as its citizens: *"cives"* (572). His imagery is garnered from memories of fallen Troy (e.g., *"fumantia culmina,"* 569) and its fate; thus he speaks to Latinus as if he were another Laomedon (582).

Aeneas's attack on the city, initiated by bloodlustful Venus, does not have a clear strategic purpose; it suggests angry destruction.[6] It does bring about the duel finally, but that is not its function. The attack reflects his frustration, his lingering fury and his capacity for such fury, his bitter memories of Troy, and most of all his wrath at Latinus, the chief of state, who can no longer hide behind pious protestations. If it is strange that Aeneas has *not* attacked the city before (and he wonders at himself on this score), his act now insists on the large guilt of Latinus and sets in relief his own stature as a chief of state.

Surprisingly, the attack itself is not described; after the rich simile of the *pastor* and the *apes* (587 f.), the fall of the city is embodied in the suicide of Amata, an action which shatters Laurentum: *totam ... concussit funditus urbem* (594); the city is central to the act. The foundering of Laurentum in the figure of Amata parallels the symbolic fall of Carthage in the suicide of Dido (see *concussam urbem:* IV.666).

This reenactment may be no less moving than Dido's death; however, it is repulsive. The short passage (21 lines, including the questioned 612–13) would richly reward close analysis; only a few details can be noted here. The counterpoint of *fortuna* and *fatum* informs the whole passage, each force linked to the "ruin" of the city. Amata's name is never mentioned (though Turnus, Latinus, and Lavi-

nia are all named); but her link with Turnus is emphasized. Her symbolic connection with the city is expressed in the verbal texture: *urbs*
(594, 608, 610), *tecta* (595, 596), *muri* (596), and *aedes* (607); she
is *regina* and *infelix,* incorporating the destruction and death of the
city. She calls herself the *causam ... crimenque caputque malorum*
(600), as if accepting Aeneas's own indictment of the city:

'urbem hodie, causam belli ...'   (567)

'hoc caput, ... haec belli summa nefandi'   (572).

Her words provide a startling gloss on her speech to Turnus at the
beginning of Book XII (56 f.).

Immediate to Amata's madness is the fear that Turnus is dead: as
Servius suggested, she did not think Turnus would allow the city to
be besieged if he were still alive. Her fate is bound up with Turnus: if
he is dead, she too must die—*moritura* in 602, echoing 55, emphasizes this. In the attack on the city, she sees the final crumbling of the
old order, the final result of its instability and code of passion. The
image of her death—"nodum informis leti trabe nectit ab alta"
(603)—recalling Jocasta's, suggests fully enough what the outcome
would have been had she lived and Turnus lived. But the incestuous
overtones are less important than what they symbolize—the inevitable doom of the old order, rendered here painfully explicit. As in
Dido's primitive madness the power of individual passion was discredited, so here the force of antique heroism is also discredited. Both
succumb to the divinely wrought strength of the new chief of state, as
he continues his relentless journey.

The death of Amata and the flames rising from the city galvanize
the narrative; the last 300 lines rush headlong to the finale—and
the finale will be abrupt, stark, bewildering. The last episodes are
noisy, violent, dark, charged with power and destiny, verging at times
on the demonic. After a brief pause, Turnus hurtles ahead, his fury in-
creasing, until another pause, poignant and moving, and then he settles into death; Aeneas's fury counterpoints Turnus's and the whole
movement on the fields of Latium is attended by harsh sound and surrealistic imagery—circles tightening around Turnus, mysterious
shrieks of arrows real and imagined, Jove's frightening bird, the terror

of the gods. The scene in heaven gives only the *illusion* of ordering all this.

Before leaving his sister, Turnus stops, *amens subsistit* (622), and in his speech contemplates both the downfall of his comrades and his own death (632–49). Then Saces bursts into the scene (*volat, vectus, ruit*), breaking the momentary stasis, almost a tableau, with news of the city. The disruption is reflected in Turnus's own confusion:

> obstipuit varia confusus imagine rerum
> Turnus et obtutu tacito stetit; aestuat ingens
> uno in corde pudor mixtoque insania luctu
> et furiis agitatus amor et conscia virtus.   (XII.665–68)

Confused by this multiple picture of disaster, Turnus was struck silent, and stood there, speechless, his eyes fixed. In his heart surged both great shame and madness mingled with grief, and love hounded by fury and certainty of his own valor.

The brief image of the burning city glows in the fire of his eyes (*ardentis*, 670), and he takes leave of his sister in an agitated speech, ending with the disturbing rhythm of: " 'hunc, oro, sine me furere ante furorem' " (XII.680). And then suddenly comes the outburst of energy, of decisive motion (681–83: *saltum dedit, ruit, rumpit*), defined by the noisy energetic simile that follows (684–89) and the repeated *ruit* (682, 685, 690).

In counterpoint with Turnus is *pater Aeneas:*

> At pater Aeneas audito nomine Turni
> deserit et muros et summas deserit arces
> praecipitatque moras omnis, opera omnia rumpit
> laetitia exsultans horrendumque intonat armis.   (XII.697–700)

Then the leader Aeneas, hearing the name of Turnus, abandoned the walls and abandoned the lofty fortress, and breaking off all delay and putting aside all other tasks, he rejoiced and exulted and thundered terribly in his armor.

The parallels are too pointed to miss: Turnus "sororem/ deserit" (682 f.), "rumpit" (683), and "magno simul incipit ore" (692). In a noisy and energetic simile Turnus is compared to a boulder crashing down headlong, dragging trees and beasts and men in its fall; Aeneas, on the other hand, towers like a great mountain, Athos or Eryx or "old Father Appenine himself, with his rustle of shimmering holm-oak trees, joyously lifting his snowcovered head to the sky" (701 f.: tr. Knight). Around the two heroes, Trojans and Latins form a ring. The heroes themselves are described only indirectly. As Aeneas and Turnus clash, the earth groans—the confident, majestic mountain and the hurtling boulder have been subsumed in this phrase: *dat gemitum tellus* (713). The next line is noteworthy:

> congeminant. fors et virtus miscentur in unum.   (XII.714)

The opening word belongs syntactically to the preceding line, but position and rhythm link it significantly to *miscentur,* and its very sound echoes and anticipates the groans and bellows of preceding and following lines (*gemitum,* 713; *gemitu,* 722). If the words suggest *arma* and *vir,* they cannot be distinguished in the two heroes themselves; the pattern Vergil suggested earlier (504 ff.), in the businesslike rhythms of alternating butchery, is being fulfilled here. The noise of the earth's groan and of the following simile echoes the deaths of Amata and Dido and the shrieks of *furor* when Amata and Laurentum were both falling. *Fors* and *virtus* belong to both Aeneas and Turnus; there is travail on earth—the travail of a world dying while a world is being born. That travail is reflected in the simile of the two great bulls: "illi inter sese multa vi vulnera miscent" (720). As they fight, "gemitu nemus omne remugit" (722).

Gradually we realize how uncharacteristically noisy the poem has become. In the final episodes, sounds and silences have grim implications, particularly the strident sound of the arrow when describing the descent of Jove's *Dira* to earth (856 f.) and the ominous emptiness when Turnus hurls his stone—Turnus moving like a sleepwalker, in that state when powerlessness to cry out is equivalent to total impotence: "non lingua valet, non corpore notae / sufficiunt vires nec vox aut verba sequuntur" (911–12). The description of Aeneas's spear, *hasta ... stridens* which *volat atri turbinis instar* (923 f.), echoes

the sounds linked to the *Dira* (*celeri ... turbine ... sagitta ... stridens,*
855 f.). The Rutulians' outcry—

> consurgunt gemitu Rutuli totusque remugit
> mons circum et vocem late nemora alta remittunt.   (XII.928–29)

—echoed in the hills and the high forests, has its final echo in the
groan of Turnus as he dies, *cum gemitu* (952).[7] At the least, all the
noise symbolizes the final stages of disorder, the necessary frenzy of
violence in this great encounter, the total clash of *vir* and *arma*.

Amid all the noise, the interlude on Olympus (791–842) is almost shockingly calm. The poem modulates from the battlefield to
the heavens in a remarkable passage (766 f.). Here the narrative
slows down as Aeneas and Turnus are stymied by preternatural forces.
Both are weaponless. Turnus's sword (actually that of Metiscus) shattered on Aeneas's armor; Aeneas's spear is fixed in the stump of the
wild olive tree sacred to Faunus. Both receive help from their divinities. Juturna brings Turnus his own sword; Venus springs Aeneas's
spear loose. Rearmed, the heroes stand facing each other, breathless
but ready to battle once more. The myth of Faunus provides subtle
context: "we feel . . . the land's resistance to the invader." [8] But
the land can resist only a short time: for the gods have much at
stake here, and Faunus and the land count little among them.

In the interlude in heaven, Jupiter reproves Juno without conquering; Juno wins more than she could ever have hoped. The rhythms
insinuate Juno's dominance (*Iunonem interea ...,* 791). Jupiter may reproach her sternly, but the sharpness of his words and the clarity of
his utterance are belied when he yields before her. The emphasis is on
Saturnian Juno (807, 830); her ancient hatred remains—and Jove
bows to it: "es germana Iovis Saturnique altera proles" (830).

Juno's victory is larger than it seems. Aeneas's quest was for a
homeland, a true city; he had called his followers *Aeneadae* (III.18).
The identity he sought is ultimately denied him. There is a hint of
this in the word Jupiter uses early in his speech: "indigetem Aenean
scis ipsa ..." (XII.794). The primary meaning of *indiges* is the title
—national demigod or patron saint—which Aeneas will, accord-

ing to legend, receive after his disappearance from earth. But the word also carries the clear suggestion of *indigena,* "native," and this land is, after all, the land originally of Dardanus. Yet it is precisely the *indigenous* identity that Juno wishes denied, wiped out; the Trojan name and race is to be subsumed in the Latin, and the Latins are to retain the identity of *indigenas* (823). Jupiter grants this: "do quod vis" (832). Almost in passing, and with a smile, Saturnian Jove wipes out the Trojan race as a race and removes the last shred of Aeneas's personal identity. It seems quite clear that this doesn't really matter to Jove at all.

Juno's attitude toward *her* favorite is not much different. She seems grudging as she bows before superior Fate—"(esto)" (821)—the word is parenthetical, as if to say, "All right, all right." The attitude is the same as that she showed another favorite, Dido; in either case the misery caused is quite irrelevant to her. Perhaps from the very beginning of the poem, there has been no reason to think these deities might regard the human heroes as anything more than pawns for their cosmic chess game; but the chasm between the interests of the gods and those of men has been largely ignored by the commentators. Jupiter may speak of men's *pietas* (839), but he himself is the god of power. At this point, he and Juno have reached their goals—they have all they really want. The groans of earth reflect not so much divine displeasure as the impact of divine will on human history.

We are reminded of this in the following passage, which describes a small corner of Jove's resources of power: the *Dirae* and all their function. He dispatches one as *omen Iuturnae* (854) and it comes, like a whirlwind, *celeri ... turbine,* or like an arrow screaming through the air, *stridens et celeris incognita transilit umbras* (859)—and the noise of the world's travail is renewed. Juturna knows at once: "Dirae stridorem agnovit" (869). Her words suggest the ominous meaning:

> 'alarum verbera nosco
> letalemque sonum, nec fallunt iussa superba
> magnanimi Iovis. haec pro virginitate reponit?
> quo vitam dedit aeteram? cur mortis adempta est
> condicio? possem tantos finire dolores
> nunc certe, et misero fratri comes ire per umbras!'   (XII.876–81)

"I know that deadly sound, the beating of those wings, and am not deceived as to the imperious commands of magnanimous Jove. Is this the return he makes for my virginity? Why did he give me immortality, why did he steal from me the right to die? Oh if only I could now end such agony and accompany my poor brother through the shadows!"

Juturna is illuminated in ghastly brillance by this Fury, for she is one of those mortals who crossed the line between divine and human and was embraced by an immortal. "Magnanimous Jove" took her virginity but gave in return neither joy nor the possibility of ending her sorrow by death. Juturna's condition expresses a complex motif recurrent in the poem: the price mortals pay for divine blessings. We recall Cassandra and Anchises as obvious examples, but the fuller meaning of this motif is felt in Dido, Turnus, and Aeneas himself. Each, to greater or lesser extent, is victim of the *vis superum.*

The *Dira* is sent to officiate at the death of Turnus; Juturna's fate is symbolic foreshadowing of that. She knows now the final horror; she has been cut off from her brother, as from all mortality:

> caput glauco contexit amictu
> multa gemens et se fluvio dea condidit alto.   (XII.885–86)

Sobbing and groaning, the nymph covered her head with a gray mantle and concealed herself in the depths of the river.

The words are carefully chosen—even to the echoing *gemens.* Juturna has *not* the freedom to die; the earth cannot swallow her; she cannot descend to the shades. Rather, she can only cover herself—unprotectively, only symbolically—and plunge into the water, hide herself there, feebly enacting the truer and nobler death coming to Turnus.

The *Dira* remains. In her awesome presence, Turnus seems a man mad:

> ac velut in somnis, oculos ubi languida pressit
> nocte quies, nequiquam avidos extendere cursus
> velle videmur et in mediis conatibus aegri
> succidimus—non lingua valet, non corpore notae
> sufficiunt vires nec vox aut verba sequuntur:

sic Turno, quacumque viam virtute petivit
successum dea dira negat.   (xii.908–14)

As sometimes at night when, in our dreams, a languid quiet lies heavy on
our eyes, we seem to strive desperately—but in vain—to run ever
onwards, and as we make our greatest effort we sink down helpless: the
tongue can do nothing, the body's normal powers do not respond, and
neither voice nor words will come—so it was with Turnus, for no matter what way he tried by valor, that dread goddess denied him progress.

We should note how the poet has involved us in this superbly
wrought simile; Turnus's experience belongs to the experience of
men; he is, in Conrad's words, "one of us." The final *negat* is harsh
and inexorable.

Reality has been closing in on Turnus. From the beginning of the
duel, the movement of enclosure has been felt in language, rhythm,
incident, simile, and metaphor. Unconsciously echoing Juturna's action (*contexit ... condidit*), Aeneas challenges Turnus: "clausumve
cava te condere terra" (893). Everything in the real world has begun
to fail him; the emphasis on his *virtus* (913) simply underscores this.
The sleepwalking imagery and the simile are labyrinthine in their implications. Turnus is trying to break out, to escape the ever-constrict-
ing circle.

One of the central passages for the imagery of enclosure is the simile of the trapped stag earlier in the duel (749 f.). Turnus and Aeneas
were fighting like two great bulls, we recall, when—in an
aside—the poet tells us that Jupiter hung out the scales, sign of im-
mutable Fate (725 f.). Turnus's sword breaks; weaponless, he can only
flee in aimless circles, for the Trojans enclose him all around, as do
the deep marsh and the high walls:

et nunc huc, inde huc incertos implicat orbis;
undique enim densa Teucri inclusere corona
atque hinc vasta palus, hinc ardua moenia cingunt.   (xii.743–45)

Now this way, now that, he entwined aimless circles, for all about the
Trojans enclosed him, in a crowded ring, while on one side a broad
swamp and on the other the steep battlements encircled him.

The texture is rich in circle metaphors: men, nature, even the artifacts
of civilization encompass Turnus. Aeneas presses hard on the fleeing
Turnus; action and feeling are expressed vividly in the simile:

> inclusum veluti si quando flumine nactus,
> cervum aut puniceae saeptum formidine pennae
> venator cursu canis et latratibus instat;
> ille autem insidiis et ripa territus alta
> mille fugit refugitque vias, at vividus Vmber
> haeret hians, iam iamque tenet similisque tenenti
> increpuit malis morsuque elusus inani est:
> tum vero exoritur clamor ripaeque lacusque
> responsant circa et caelum tonat omne tumultu.   (XII.749–57)

He [Aeneas] was like a hunting dog when, knowing that he has a stag
closed in by a river or hedged about by the terror of the red-feather
scares, he presses him close, running and barking; the stag, in fear of the
snares and of the river's high bank, runs back and forth a thousand ways;
but the tireless Umbrian hound hangs on to him, his jaws wide open, and
now he has him, or seems to, snapping his jaws, still eluded, but biting
nothing. And now the noise becomes a roar; the riverbanks and pools
around reecho, and all heaven thunders with the tumult.

The elements—the hunting dog, the stag, the tightening movement, the noise and echoes of it—make this a notable expanding
simile. The connections to the duel episode, and especially the motifs
of noise and enclosure, appear clear enough. (The simile also evokes
sections of Book IV—Dido's dreams, her flight from Aeneas, her
growing isolation.) But it is interesting that the hound does not quite
get his prey: the encirclement tightens but does not fully close. The
first word—*inclusum*—is the most crucial. The stag's attempts to
break out are a paradigm of Turnus's whole condition. But his assail-
ant presses on him: *instat* (751). After this passage, the chase around
the city walls ("quinque orbis explent cursu totidemque retexunt / huc
illuc," 763 f.) has its own labyrinthine implications.[9]

Turnus is enclosed by the old world and the new. As with the deer
in the simile, Turnus's shouts are echoed by lake and riverbank and
heavens, and they come back in upon him. He is enclosed by the gods
and their power, the *vis superum*. So, Venus's act of ripping Aeneas's
sword out of the sacred olive tree—"telum ... alta ab radice re-

vellit" (787)—demonstrates her superiority to hapless Juturna; so, Jupiter looks on it all as over (see 799, especially the striking "victis"): "ventum ad supremum est" (803); and Juno speaks offhandedly, "Turnum ... reliqui" (809) and "conubiis pacem felicibus (esto)/component" (821 f.); while Aeneas is referred to by Jupiter as one of theirs (797). The surrealistic *Dira* is perhaps the most powerful expression of the supernal pressure on Turnus (865 f.). His horror is, significantly, expressed in the same terms used for Aeneas when Mercury came to him at Carthage: "arrectaeque horrore comae et vox faucibus haesit" (868; see IV.280). The echo underlines both the connection between the events and the difference.

All of these details energize Turnus's response to Aeneas's taunts: "non me tua ferrida terrent/ dicta, ferox; di me terrent et Iuppiter hostis" (894–95). The ambivalence about the Scales is now resolved, at least in part; though Turnus has his own gods, they are no match for the power of the Olympians. Thus reality does not respond to him: that is the meaning of his unnatural strength as he lifts the great boulder so great that twelve men could not hoist it ("vix illud lecti bis sex cervice subirent," 899). One must assume some sort of divine aid, coming from Turnus's own gods. The incident is not an imitation of Homer but a transformation of him: read rightly, it induces terror and leads directly into the somnambulistic passage which follows. Throwing the huge thing, Turnus is called *heros,* poignantly (902):

> sed neque currentem se nec cognoscit euntem
> tollentemve manus saxumve immane moventem: (XII.903–4)

But he was not aware that he was running or even moving, or that he was lifting his hands or hurling the mighty rock.

Finally, in this nightmare of frustration, impotence, and defeat, he realizes how totally and absolutely isolated he is. The *Dira* frustrates his every movement (913 f.); Turnus looks to Rutulians and to city and to imminent death:

> letumque instare tremescit,
> nec quo se eripiat, nec qua vi tendat in hostem,
> nec currus usquam videt aurigamve sororem.   (XII. 916–18)

He shuddered at the imminent death hovering over him, but could find nowhere to escape, no strength to use against his foe; nor could he see anywhere his chariot or his sister the charioteer.

Ultimately, he has been isolated, self-enclosed by his own code, the code which included the brutal slaying of Pallas. All these other things lead directly to his defeat; the code by which he lived and claimed his heroic stature, and by which he donned and exhibited his victim's *balteus,* has destroyed his physical life.

Unable to accept the new world or even fully to recognize it, Turnus wished to remake it in his own heroic image. Others accepted that world—Latinus in his weakness, Drances in his intrigue. But Turnus refused it, kept trying to build it in his own heroic image, until too late. Mezentius and Camilla, and Dido long before them, tried to prolong the dead world; so did Juturna and Amata in their diverse ways, but both finally had to yield, and Amata, unable to accept the bitter reality she had to recognize, plunged to frenzied death. Though she blamed herself for Turnus's imagined death, her suicide was a result of the nature of her world, a nature seen in episode after episode: the outbreak of the war; the violent passion of Venus and Vulcan; the collapse of strategies on both sides in Book IX; the destinies of Pallas and Lausus in Book X; the mistakes of the council, the march, the ambush, the doomed strategy of Book XI.

Turnus's history in the last books suggests, though it does not quite achieve, a pattern of understanding. When, in Book XI, he accepted single combat and recognized his duty to the common good ("si ... tantumque bonis communibus obsto," XI.435), he was devoting himself ("animam ... devovi," in solemn ritual terms) to an isolation whose full measure he could not comprehend. At the covenant in Book XII, he approaches the altar, "demisso lumine .../ tabentesque genae et iuvenali in corpore pallor" (220 f.). The stark isolation is what Juturna points up as she harangues the Rutulians:

> 'non pudet, o Rutuli, pro cunctis talibus unam
> obiectare animam?'   (XII.229–30)

"Are you not ashamed, Rutulians, to expose one man's life to destruction for the safety of all of you?"

By deferring the single combat so long, while building up pressure for it, the poet allows complexities to accrue. Turnus embodies a desperate but heroic nobility, doomed but unforgettable; the foregone conclusion deepens the resonance here. For Turnus becomes both hero and victim as he goes down to a defeat that is more ritual than real. The final scene climaxes the pattern of his isolation. Accepting his defeat, he gives up Lavinia and asks only that his body—alive or dead, it hardly matters—be returned to his aged father.

The final gesture of Turnus is a familiar one in the poem: *dextramque precantem/ protendens* (930–31). It is a gesture of simple humanity. The emphasis on appeal (*supplex, precantem, oro*) does not argue a man afraid to die; his plea puts little emphasis on his own life. He gives Aeneas a choice—either let me live out of pity for my father or, at least, return my dead body to him. In either case, Turnus's concern is specifically for his father, so that, however one qualifies this action by reference to the heroic-death rituals, one cannot ignore the fundamental *pietas* which Turnus shows. Granted this, his last words may be read as indicating a genuine concern for humaneness: *"ulterius ne tende odiis"* (938).

In this episode, the gesture of the right hand outstretched in supplication identifies Turnus as the human figure, Aeneas as the agent or instrument of destiny. The gesture climaxes a highly significant pattern in the *Aeneid*, a pattern that is worth brief notice. The gesture of the hand or hands signifies human connection (or attempt at connection) of various kinds. One kind is that which Aeneas sees on the gates of the temple at Carthage, in the figure of Priam beseeching his conqueror: "tendentemque manus Priamum conspexit inermis" (I. 487). Achaemenides, the luckless follower of Ulysses, runs desperately toward the Trojan strangers—"supplexque manus ... tendit" (III.592)—and is willing to accept death at their human hands: "si pereo, hominum manibus periisse iuvabit" (III.606). But it is not necessary: "ipse pater dextram Anchises .../ dat iuveni" (610 f.). In Italy, Latinus complains at Aeneas's absence from the Trojan embassy and lays down a condition: "pars mihi pacis erit dextram tetigisse tyranni" (VII.266).[10] There is an interesting echo of this later when the Latin ambassadors boast of having touched Diomedes' hand, which destroyed Troy: "contigimusque

manum qua concidit Ilia tellus" (xi.245); there is a different kind of
echo in Evander's recollection of his youth and his admiration for Anchises:

> 'mihi mens iuvenali ardebat amore
> compellare virum et dextrae conjungere dextram,'   (viii.163–64)

"I burned with youthful ardor to go up to him and clasp his right hand in
mine."

When the Trojans arrive in Arcadia, Pallas greets them warmly: "ex-
cepitque manu dextramque amplexus inhaesit" ("He took [Aeneas]
by the hand and held him in a warm clasp," viii.124)—almost as
warmly as Evander embraces Pallas on his departure: "tum pater
Euandrus dextram complexus euntis/ haeret ..." (viii.558).

In prayer, the outstretched hands are commonplace—as Sinon
shows, by desecrating the ritual action (ii.153: "sustulit ... ad sidera
palmas"). Often enough, the ritual is formal, as in Aeneas's prayer
after the vision of the Penates (iii.177) or Turnus's to Iris (ix.16) or
Latinus's at the covenant (xii.196). At other times, the prayer itself is
spontaneous, the overflow of powerful feeling—Aeneas's prayer
during the storm (i.93) or at Sicily, as the ships burn:

> tum pius Aeneas umeris abscindere vestem
> auxilioque vocare deos et tendere palmas.   (v.685 f.)

Then the pious Aeneas tore the garments off his shoulders and called on
the gods for help, stretching forth his palms.

The gestures of prayer are, of course, gestures of supplication qualified at times as desperate hope. So are many gestures on the battlefield. The supplication takes varied forms. Thus Liger begs Aeneas for
his life—"tendebat inertis/ infelix palmas ..." (x.595 f.); thus
Magus embraces Aeneas's knees (x.523 f.); and, in an inversion,
Aeneas extends his hand to the dying Lausus (x.823: "ingemuit
miserans graviter dextramque tetendit").[11]

But the motif finds its richest expression in the attempts of Aeneas
at human connection with those who should be closest to him. On

the beach at Carthage, he complains to his mother Venus, "cur dex-
trae iungere dextram non datur ...?" (I.480 f.). In his last moments at Troy, he reaches out to his wife Creusa—now a shade—
and tries, three times, to embrace her (II.792 f.). At Carthage, when
he has been forced to give up his human connection with Dido, she
reminds him of the gesture that symbolized it and unwittingly describes its disastrous effect:

> 'nec te noster amor nec te data dextera quondam
> nec moritura tenet crudeli funere Dido?'　　　　　　　　(IV.307–8)

"And can nothing hold you, not our love, nor our once plighted hands,
nor even the cruel death that must await your Dido?" (Tr. Knight) [12]

In Hades, it is true, Anchises stretches out both hands toward his approaching son—"alacris palmas utrasque tetendit" (VI.685)—but
there can be no connection between them. We are not told that father and son touched; we must, indeed, infer that they did not, could
not, for Aeneas cries out, "da iungere dextram,/ da, genitor, teque
amplexu ne subtrahe nostro" (697 f.), a plea and a gesture that are
futile in the event: "ter conatus ...,/ ter frustra comprensa
manus effugit imago" (VI.700 f.). The incident recalls the plea Aeneas
made to the apparition of Anchises' shade at Sicily: "quis te nostris
complexibus arcet?" (V.742). [13]

That the gesture is ultimately futile for Aeneas is defined, only too
clearly, in the encounter with Palinurus in Hades. Palinurus entreats
him, by his father and by his son—"per genitorem oro, per spes
surgentis Iuli,/ eripe me his, invicte, malis:"—and the supplication ends, "da dextram misero et tecum me tolle per undas," ("Give
your poor friend your hand, and take me with you through the
waves"). But the Sibyl intervenes and severely enunciates the unalterable law:

> 'unde haec, o Palinure, tibi tam dira cupido?
>
> . . . .
> desine fata deum flecti sperare precando.'　　　　　　　(VI.373, 376)

"Whence comes, Palinurus, this mad desire? . . . Give up your hope that
divine decrees can be changed by prayers."

This scene may well be regarded as a rehearsal for the final scene of the poem, and the Sibyl's example a paradigm for Aeneas. When Turnus stretches out his hand in supplication, Aeneas hesitates and struggles with himself:

> stetit acer in armis
> Aeneas volvens oculos dextramque repressit;   (XII.938–39)

Fierce in his armor Aeneas stood, his eyes restless, and he held back his right arm.

But Aeneas's destiny has left no room for human connections. He must be the executor of the *fata deum*. He must reject the appeal to *pietas,* to his own fatherhood, to his very humanity, and slay the last individualist in the poem. He must watch the thread of human feeling snap without profound agitation; the frail life of humanity can no longer be his prime concern. He must act in a kind of vacuum, responsive mainly to the exigencies of history and the *vis superum.* His reaction to the *balteus* is not the reaction of revenge. His furious words are merely the heroic convention, as he executes an act of policy. What feeling he has may well reflect his sense of the fundamental anomaly of his position. He is the high priest carrying out the ordained rite, sacrificing one man for the good of all. But he might, himself, prefer something quite different. Aeneas as chief of state, performing the necessary action, is far from the Aeneas we saw first in the poem, the Aeneas who lamented lost Troy, *pius* in his solicitude for his followers, uncertain of his destiny and not terribly distressed by that uncertainty. There has been a twofold change in him—the renunciation of the old heroism and the renunciation of his old self, the loss of identity.

The final lines end the poem abruptly, but with a resonance that is haunting:

> hoc dicens ferrum adverso sub pectore condit
> fervidus. ast illi solvuntur frigore membra
> vitaque cum gemitu fugit indignata sub umbras.   (XII.950–52)

Saying this and boiling with rage Aeneas buried his blade full in Turnus's breast. His limbs relaxed and chilled; and the life fled, moaning, resentful, to the Shades. (Tr. Knight)

There are many echoes here, including that in the verb *condit*—
the verb used in the fifth line of the poem for the act of founding a
city ("dum conderet urbem"). But the poet may also expect us to remember here that the isolation of Turnus, in death, is like the isolation Aeneas himself felt at the beginning. On the ship, during the
storm at sea, the same kind of chill terror assailed Aeneas and melted
his limbs: "extemplo Aeneae solvuntur frigore membra" (1.92). The
connection is unmistakable. The difference is that for Aeneas this was
the beginning. There, he railed at the world and the gods and the
reality all about him, and grasped for a world that was lost and could
never be his again:

> 'o terque quaterque beati,
> quis ante ora patrum Troiae sub moenibus altis
> contigit oppetere! o Danaum fortissime gentis
> Tydide! mene Iliacis occumbere campis
> non potuisse....'   (1.94–98)

"Oh, three and four times blessed were you who had the good fortune to
fall before your father's eyes beneath the lofty walls of Troy! O Diomedes,
the bravest of the Greeks, why could I not have fallen on the battlefields
of Ilium. . . ."

In the years ahead, on the quest, he had slowly to rid himself of all
the vestiges of that world, and particularly of the desire for it. This
was accomplished, slowly, vexatiously, by way of the story of Troy
and the reliving of his nightmare; by the achievement of perspective
(of a sort) on the miniature Troys he makes and leaves behind; by
the loss of wife, father, mistress, old nurse; by the erosion of his cher-
ished beliefs and hopes—until only Destiny and Power are left to
him. The old self is gradually but fully eradicated—the old self of
Troy, of Carthage, of the inattentive figure in the underworld, even
the self that escaped for a brutal hour of carnage in Book x.

There is a striking consistency in the figure of Aeneas through the
last thousand lines of the poem. His march on the city, his swearing
to the covenant, the terms he lays down, his speech to Ascanius, and
finally his victory over Turnus—all these have the assurance and
certainty which was lacking earlier. It is true that he wavers a moment at Turnus's plea. But through his trials, he has been hardened to

an abstract kind of justice and executive activity, has indeed become detached from human frailty. Thus, seeing the *exuvias*—the *remnants* of Turnus's old world—he can carry out the necessary act of killing Turnus, not as the distorted kind of double *pietas* which Servius impossibly argued, but as the act appropriate to the Chief of State. This is the corporate Aeneas, sharply contrasted to the individualist hero. This is the Aeneas who spoke to Ascanius, *fata docens* (XII.111)—for Ascanius is now a prince learning the trade of sovereignty—and who lectured him soberly and cogently on civic morality and the ethos of selfless responsibility (XII.435 f.). The speech is a remarkable one, a speech Aeneas could not have made at any earlier point in the poem. It rings true, it expresses a coherent person, managing somehow to hold his own despite the power beyond him and despite the interventions of Venus.

In a sense it may be said that, having achieved the necessary detachment and selflessness demanded of him, Aeneas the man establishing the city has also achieved the status of that figure in the first simile of the poem, who, imposing in his *pietas* and his achievements, controls the unruly mob: "pietate gravem ac meritis ... virum ...; / ille regit dictis animos et pectora mulcet" (I.148 f.). But the poem has reshaped our perspective on that figure; it has laid bare the cost of that *pietas* and those *merita,* the weight of them. It is paradoxical, of course, that Aeneas has achieved such stature when, enraged, he kills Turnus. Servius was on the verge of being right in his curious view, but he had to conform to a simplistic scheme of *pietas* and to an assumption of insight into auctorial intention. The death of Turnus was necessary. Spiritually an adolescent, Turnus represents the old order; embodying all the half-conscious follies of Latinus (who fails in the end), he stands for the aged and the past rather than the young and the "future"; the future belongs to Ascanius.

Aeneas has come to terms with the necessities and meanings of this new world; he has learned, he has grown. We may feel somewhat uneasy about him—we ought to—but we cannot deny him either admiration or sympathy. Turnus, though attractive and tragic, was possessed of a *violentia* too extreme to survive the development of civilization. The logic of the poem and of the world demands his death. But we must recognize that although Turnus lost Lavinia and his he-

roic supremacy in Italy and his very life, these losses are not as painful to him as the loss of Troy, of Dido, and of identity was to Aeneas.
In the end, Turnus feels the terror of his isolation and of the inexora-
bility of history, symbolized particularly in hostile Jupiter—"di me
terrent et Iuppiter hostis"—and goes down to the shades; Aeneas
has the resources to come to terms (humanly unsatisfactory though
this may be) with the world he has had a hand in making.

In strictly heroic terms, Aeneas achieves only a dimmed glory.
Inevitably, the reader is deeply troubled by the end of the poem. The
death of Turnus and the victory of Aeneas provide only a partial reso-
lution to the whole work. Aeneas acts not in his own name but in
that of Pallas, and of Pallas's father, and of *Iuppiter hostis,* and even
(unwittingly) of Juno to whom Jupiter promised, "nec gens ulla tuos
aeque celebrabit honores" (XII.840). His consort will be Lavinia,
that figure deliberately made shadowy and unreal, to preserve the
contrast between her and the passionate Dido or the warm gentle
Creusa.

Aeneas has grown throughout the poem by harrowing sacrifice; at
the end, he has achieved a kind of cosmic grandeur. Readers have
been tempted to use the Christian terms: "Whoever shall seek to save
his life shall lose it; and whosoever shall lose his life shall preserve it"
(Luke 17:33). But the poet's vision does not include the hope of salvation, any more than it is illuminated by the spread of the Roman
legions' standards. The poem ends in an uneasy truce, between power
and justice, between history and humanity, between *arma* and *pietas.*

Killing Turnus, Aeneas acted with towering wrath at the sight of
the *balteus.* His *pietas* could not stand alone; to be the proper instrument of history and destiny, he needed also the brutality of *vis.* It is
Aeneas's glory and his tragedy that he is remarkable for both: *pietate
insignis et armis.* The epic does not rail against the one or bemoan
the assaults on the other. It sees the two balanced in an equilibrium
that is necessarily perilous, and thus defines the human condition.

NOTES

CHAPTER ONE
CARTHAGE: SEARCH FOR THE CITY

1. Thomas Greene comments perceptively on Aeneas: "He is preserved to create another context, another social fabric elsewhere—which he individually is never to enjoy, having created it. He will scarcely have time to descend from his Mount Pisgah. That is his real loss. Troy falls to rise elsewhere, but in him, in his life, it remains fallen. That is why he is so weary, so reluctant, hesitant, and erring, why he lacks the marvelous, Homeric vital energy. He has no place." *The Descent from Heaven* (New Haven, 1963), p. 90. In this chapter, as throughout thie book, I have consulted John Conington and Henry Nettleship, *The Works of Vergil with a Commentary* (Hildesheim reprint, 1963). The best guide available is R. G. Austin's recent *Aeneidos Liber Primus* (Oxford, 1970); unfortunately, it appeared after this chapter was finished. On Book IV, the older commentaries of A. S. Pease (Cambridge, Mass., 1935) and Corso Buscaroli (Milan, 1932) remain massively important in their meticulous scholarship, but here too R. G. Austin's penetrating recent commentary (Oxford, 1955) is, for my purposes, the most relevant kind of guide to the poem. The most interesting recent studies dealing substantively with the opening of the poem and the Dido story are Brooks Otis, *Virgil: A Study in Civilized Poetry* (Oxford, 1963), especially chapter 2 and pp. 238–40, 264–71, and Viktor Pöschl, *Die Dichtkunst Virgils* (Innsbruck, 1950), translated by Gerda Seligson as *The Art of Vergil* (Ann Arbor, 1962), especially pp. 13–24 and 60–91. See also Lilian Feder's thoughtful essay, "Vergil's Tragic Theme," *CJ*, 49 (1953–54), 197–209; R. D. Williams on the ecphrasis, "The Pictures on Dido's Temple," *CQ*, 10 (1960), 145–51, and F. L. Newton, "Recurrent Imagery in *Aeneid* IV," *TAPA*, 88 (1957), 31–43.

2. Pöschl (tr. Seligson), pp. 18–20.

3. Austin (*ad* 1.466 f.), noting the first three pairs, sees line 488 as a "single line . . . , Aeneas . . . fighting among the Greeks," followed by "two scenes from post-Homeric myth (Memnon and Penthesilea, both killed by

Achilles). It is hardly accidental that the last figure in the series is a woman, a brave equal of men."

4. On *virgo* (340), Servius says that the Carthaginians gave Elissa the name Dido, the Punic word for *virago,* because she killed herself rather than agree to marry an African king. (See Austin and Pease.) Note that Penthesilea is defined as *bellatrix . . . virgo* (493) and note the recurrence of *virgo* in the preceding scene (315 twice, 327, 336). Aeneas wonders aloud, "An Phoebi soror?" 329—quite appropriately, for Apollo's sister was Diana (or Artemis, also known as Hecate).

5. Pöschl, p. 64, also remarks the connection. On the simile itself, Austin's remarks are highly perceptive. He implies, incidentally, that, as compared to the Homeric simile in *Odyssey* VI.102 ff., Vergil's simile plays down the huntress image.

6. Note that Venus "vera incessu patuit dea," 405; Juno imagined herself, "ego, quae divum incedo regina," 46. Shortly, Aeneas himself has the appearance of a god: lines 588–89. Such interrelationships in texture abound in Vergil: Aeneas bursts out of the protective cloud because, as Achates says, "omnia tuta vides" (583)—a phrase echoed in the later description of Dido (IV.298), "omnia tuta timens."

7. Venus's thoughts are dominated by fire: [Cupid] "incendat reginam atque ossibus implicet ignem" (660); "tela Typhoëa," the thunderbolts with which Jupiter killed Typhoeus, 665; "cingere flamma," 673; "flammis . . . Troiae," 679; and the final line, perhaps uniting fire and serpent, "occultum inspires ignem fallasque veneno," 688. The siege image is carried mainly by the verbs—*capere, cingere,* 673; *teneatur,* 675.

8. *At regina:* see IV.296, *At regina dolos . . . ,* which begins the conflict with Aeneas, now ready to depart, and IV.504, *At regina pyra . . . ,* which begins the building of the funeral pyre. Austin points out that at the beginning of IV.133,

> reginam thalamo cunctantem ad limina primi
> Poenorum exspectant...,

reginam marks the day of her wedding; and at the beginning of IV.586,

> regina e speculis ut primam albescere lucem
> vidit...,

regina marks her realization that the Trojans have departed.

9. Immediately, the motif works in that the gods—Juno, Venus, Mercury—play chthonic roles in Book IV and establish the tone or atmosphere. Though almost every critic notes and comments on irrational elements in the Dido episode, I do not believe anyone has yet plumbed the

symbolic depths of this part of the epic. For some interesting forays: W. S. Anderson, " 'Pastor Aeneas': On Pastoral Themes in the *Aeneid*," *TAPA*, 99 (1968), 1–17, sees Aeneas as evolving from a pastoral purity to a political compromise of values; in this process, one step is his unconscious ("nescius," "inscius") alignment with the primitive *furor* which precipitates the tragedy of Dido. In an earlier essay, "Juno and Saturn in the *Aeneid*," *SPh*, 55 (1958), 519–32, Anderson pointed to the malevolence of *Saturnia Iuno* as an adherent of the old order; see also C. W. Amerasinghe, " 'Saturnia Iuno' —Its Significance in the *Aeneid*," *G&R*, 22 (1953), 61–69. Brooks Otis sees Dido and Aeneas as subject to a kind of fury, and Juno and Venus as engaged in an "unholy alliance." Juno he also sees as a "Carthaginian element of fury, of demonic opposition to Jupiter, of irrational wrath and violence, an element already given high symbolic expression by the great storm with which the epic began" (p. 79).

10. Austin, *ad* IV.24. Austin also points out (p. 41) the striking parallelism between Dido's sacrifice and that of Aeneas to the chthonic powers before his descent into the underworld (VI.243 f.).

11. *Curae* generally connotes the pangs associated with love or passion or internal agitation. See IV.1 and 5. The irony is heightened by Anna's echoing statement in lines 45–46:

dis equidem auspicibus reor et Iunone secunda
hunc cursum Iliacas vento tenuisse carinas.

12. *fatum:* see lines 14, 20 (twice), 30, 76. None of these, incidentally, is associated with Anna; she seems to remain outside the web of fate.

13. Austin, *ad* 80, recalls II.9; remarking that there Dido did not want to sleep, but now is not able to.

14. *ferali,* 462, and *ferus,* 466, might also be cited, though in the scansion of 466, *ferus* is deemphasized. The examples given in the text are supported by other reduplicated sounds throughout, sounds which clearly go beyond alliteration. See Norden, *ad* VI.110 and VI.426, 833. The first five lines of Book IV (see next note) are a striking example, but hardly unique.

15. The visitations in this passage also go far beyond the obsessions of the opening lines of Book IV, which they echo with poignant and bitter irony. Compare the sounds of 460–61 with those of 1–5, where the emphasis is on *vi-, ve-, vu-*.

hinc exaudiri voces et verba vocantis
visa viri, nox cum terras obscura teneret;   (IV.460–61)

At regina gravi iamdudum saucia cura
vulnus alit venis et caeco carpitur igni.

multa viri virtus animo multusque recursat
gentis honos, haerent infixi pectore vultus
verbaque nec placidam membris dat cura quietem.   (IV.1–5)

In 3–5, Vergil presents Dido's first waking dreams—the recurrent
viri virtus and *honos, vultus/verbaque;* sound is distinctly called into play,
with the interlocked pattern *vulnus—multa/virtus—multus/honos—
vultus.* In IV.3, *recursat* may have special meaning, linked to the presences
that obsess Dido.

16. As R. D. Williams points out, *imago* means apparition or vision sent
by Jupiter. *Aeneidos Liber Quintus* (Oxford, 1960), *ad* 722.

17. See Austin's penetrating comments on this passage and on related details, pp. 97, 141 f., 149 f.

18. Servius's comment on *omnipotens* (IV.693) seems acute—"aut pronuba, aut inferna." Iris: the figure of the rainbow; we note that later she is to
lead the fiery assault on the Trojan ships (Book V) and to work in tandem
with demonic Allecto (Book IX). Her link to the underworld and the
chthonic gods seems tolerably clear.

19. *Dardanus:* see also line 626, where Dido calls for an avenger against
the "Dardanios . . . colonos," and the final line of the Amata suicide:

multaque se incusat, qui non acceperit ante
Dardanium Aenean generumque asciverit ultro.   (XII.612–13)

(Mynors rejects the lines, as do many editors; they are substantively the same
as XI.471–72.) The possibility that *Dardanian* has thematically significant
meaning shaded off at times significantly from Trojan or Teucrian has been
pursued only by R. W. Cruttwell, *Virgil's Mind at Work* (Oxford, Blackwell's, 1947), pp. 41–54.

20. Note the striking parallel between line 666—

concussam bacchatur Fama per urbem

—and lines 300–1:

saevit inops animi totamque incensa per urbem
bacchatur, qualis commotis excita sacris.....

21. Austin's discussion of lines 331–61 is particularly detailed and sensitive: pp. 105–13.

22. Williams is surely right when he remarks that tone and metric are
used brilliantly in the beginning of Book V to bring the Dido story to a tem-
porary end that is not really an end but only seems like one: "Virgil leaves

at last a theme on which he could say no more but on which he could never feel that enough had been said. In order to resume his narrative without looking backwards any more, he had resources to familiar phrases which had come to him before." See *Aeneidos Liber Quintus,* pp. 33, 35–36.

CHAPTER TWO
TROY: FALL OF THE CITY

1. See also *Inf.* v.121–26; Francesca says to the pilgrim Dante:

> "Nessun maggior dolore
> Che ricordarsi del tempo felice
> Ne la miseria; e cio sa 'l tuo dottre.
> Ma s'a conoscer la prima radice
> Del nostro amor tu hai cotanto affetto,
> Diro come colui che piange e dice."

> "There is no greater pain
> than to recall a happy time in misery
> and this your teacher knows;
> but if to learn the first root of our love
> you have such desire, I will answer
> like one who speaks and weeps."

La Divina Commedia, ed. C. H. Grandgent, rev. ed. (Boston, 1933). The translation is from H. R. Huse's straightforward translation in the Rinehart Editions (New York, 1954). Some of the best criticism of Vergil's second book can be found in the admirable commentary by R. G. Austin (Oxford, 1964) and in the incisive discussions by C. M. Bowra, *From Virgil to Milton* (New York, 1945); Michael Putnam, *The Poetry of the Aeneid* (Cambridge, Mass., 1965); and Bernard Knox's article, "The Serpent and the Flame: The Imagery of the Second Book of the *Aeneid," AJPh,* 71 (1950), 379–400.

2. James Joyce, *Ulysses* (New York, 1961), p. 34. The context insists on the Trojan relevance here; Mr. Deasy, the schoolmaster, says to Stephen, "A woman brought sin into the world. For a woman who was no better than she should be, Helen, the runaway wife of Menelaus, ten years the Greeks made war on Troy. A faithless wife first brought the strangers to our shore here, MacMurrough's wife . . ." (pp. 34 f.). Elsewhere in Joyce's second chapter: the "Pyrrhic victory . . . Pyrrhus . . . pier . . . disappointed bridge" chain (pp. 24 f.), the allusion to Cassandra (p. 33), and Mr. Deasy's pointed comparison of himself to Vergil's Priam, "I like to break a lance with you, old as

I am" (p. 35). These links might lead ingenious Joyceans to suspect that "bullockbefriending bard" (p. 36) momentarily makes Stephen a Vergil contemplating Laocoon's fate. Deasy's final thrust, while anti-Semitic in its reference, might well include the Wooden Horse: "Ireland . . . has the honor of being the only country which never persecuted the jews. . . . And do you know why? . . . Because she never let them in . . ." (p. 36).

3. See also *Myrmidonumque dolos*, 252; *ipse doli fabricator Epeos*, 264; *Danaumque patescunt / insidiae*, 309 f.; and see 390 and 421, where the Trojans have adapted these specific Greek traits. Too, Servius (*ad* II.79) reminds us that Sinon was first cousin to Ulysses, both of them descended from Autolycus.

4. *fortis* occurs 41 times in the poem, *virtus* 39 times; the few occurrences in II are not significantly below the statistical norm, but the reader would surely expect both of these words to occur much more often than the average in the tale of one of the great mythic battles, the last stand of Troy.

5. See also the simile, 355 f.: "inde, lupi ceu / raptores atra in nebula, quos improba ventris / exegit caecos rabies . . ." followed by "nox atra cava circumvolat umbra" (360). When the Trojans have disguised themselves, they fight many battles "per caecam . . . noctem" (397).

6. Cf. Austin, *ad* II.360, who argues that only night is meant, against Henry, who insists on symbolic darkness. It seems to me that the line includes both real night and symbolized death.

7. Note the remarkable juxtaposition—"Priamus? Troia . . ."—in 581:

'occiderit ferro Priamus? Troia arserit igni?'

8. Priam calls down divine wrath on Pyrrhus, "si qua est caelo pietas quae talia curet," II.536. In his note, Austin suggests that *pietas* means something like pity based on "an attitude of responsibility and care . . . in the relationship of the gods to man." But the contextual irony will not allow so generous an interpretation. Aeneas's prayer for Dido, I.603 f., was followed by the "blessings" of Venus and Juno; the altar here, as Austin himself points out (p. xx), does not protect Priam.

9. In 616, I read *nimbo*, following Knight and Mynors; Hirtzel has *limbo*.

10. This son Aeneas will later slay a son and a father, and other sons of fathers, in a scene that evokes this scene; see chapter 7, on Book X.

11. See Austin, p. xxi, for instance. Still, his instinct is absolutely right: "It is as if he [Vergil] had suddenly, blindingly, seen that human *pietas*— the linch-pin of the whole structure of the *Aeneid*—has no protection against the arbitrary ruthlessness of the gods, no necessary recognition from them: there is no appeal against *divum inclementia*."

12. Note how the diction expresses the return: *reddita,* 740; *respexi, reflexi,* 741; *repeto,*749; *renovare, reverti,* 750; *rursus,* 751; *repeto, retro,* 753; *refero,* 757; *reviso,* 760.

13. On this Conington comments that Vergil's "characteristic love of iteration leads him to employ three words to designate the spectre." But this is unlikely, as is the comment on line 781, "This definite prophecy of a home in Italy is inconsistent, as the editors remark, with what follows in the next book. . . ." Conington misses both the numinous and the human here by pursuing the quasi-scientific too rigidly. By contrast, see Austin's admirable comment on the scene.

CHAPTER THREE
THE WANDERER

1. There are numerous links between Achaemenides and Sinon; see R. D. Williams's commentary, *Aeneidos Liber Tertius* (Oxford, 1962), on III.602, 608, 610, 614. Note also in both episodes the importance of human sacrifice. On the Cyclops-snake link, note *arduus* (619), *ardua* (665), and the various verbal echoes of the serpents. Some of the similarities have also been noted by W. F. Jackson Knight, *Roman Vergil* (London, 1944), pp. 293 f., and by Richard Heinze, *Virgils Epische Technik,* 3d ed. (Stuttgart, 1957), pp. 112–13 (stressing Trojan *clementia*). Brooks Otis thinks the Achaemenides episode can "be understood only as a symbol of Anchises' death" (pp. 263–64).

2. Polydorus insists on flight, as Hector insisted in II.289–92; shortly, Apollo will tell Aeneas *where* to go (III.94–98), as if expanding what Hector suggested in II.293–95. Incidentally, Williams notes that the Polydorus story is relatively original with Vergil: see pp. 57–59.

3. One critic—Robert A. Brooks, *"Discolor Aura:* Reflections on the Golden Bough," *AJPh,* 74 (1953), 260–80—sees a causal relationship between Anchises' panic and the loss of Creusa. My view of Anchises elaborated here appears to be vigorously opposed to generally held views, which consider Anchises a source of inspiration and encouragement or as an interpreter of the divine will—e.g., Otis, pp. 245 f., 255, 261–68, 305–7; Austin (on II), p. 248; R. B. Lloyd, "The Character of Anchises in the *Aeneid,*" *TAPA,* 88 (1957), 44–55, as well as his articles on Book III, "*Aeneid* III, A New Approach," *AJPh,* 78 (1957), 133–41, and *"Aeneid* III and the Aeneas Legend," *AJPh,* 78 (1957), 382–400.

4. One might also see a further irony in that Aeneas, after what he had seen at the Fall of Troy, might well have believed and also have understood

Cassandra's words—had Anchises communicated them to him or consulted him about those well-remembered messages.

5. As Williams points out, *ad* 714, *meta* "means the turning-point at either end of a race-course . . . , and hence can mean the finish of the race as well as the turning-points during the race."

6. Used frequently earlier, for example, lines 78, 85, 145, 276, and 541.

7. My translation is based on Williams's careful discussion of the difficult phrase "exsortem ducere honores."

8. See *remigium alarum*, VI.19, for a striking sea-metaphor linked to labyrinth-building Daedalus. On the labyrinth, see Williams (*ad* 588 ff.) and the provocative researches and speculations by W. F. Jackson Knight in *Cumaean Gates* (Oxford, Blackwell's, 1936).

9. The *social* voice speaks again only at VII.601–3 (the Gates of War). Other passages that appear to be "editorial" belong, it seems to me, in the narrative or dramatic context and need not be read as editorial.

10. On the difficult phrase *recepti / nequiquam cineres* (80 f.), Servius says, "cineres pro ipso patre posuit, ac si diceret, salve pater de Troia liberate sine causa." See my discussion of VI.108 ff. in the next chapter.

11. The similarities between Palinurus and Orontes are noted by F. J. Worstbrock in his *Elemente einer Poetik der Aeneis* (Münster, 1963), p. 53; by Williams in the introduction to his commentary, p. xxvii; and by P. Jacob, "L'Episode de Palinure," *LEC,* 20 (1952), 163 ff., who goes very far indeed: "Il semble donc que, dans la pensée de Virgile au moment où il écrivit ces deux chants, le Palinure des Enfers et le pilote d'Oronte sont un seul et même personnage."

12. Williams gives "pervade" or "come over" for *pertemptant;* the meaning here must include the primary meaning, "to try," "to attack."

CHAPTER FOUR
HADES: JOURNEY THROUGH THE WOOD

1. *Remigium alarum* (VI.19) recalls the *inremeabilis error* of the labyrinth simile, V.591. For echoes of Book I, see particularly I.689 and I.663, 675, 710–16, and 749. Though the bibliography on Book VI is surely the richest that exists on almost any classical subject, this book remains the most elusive in the poem. Two recent essays are stimulating: Robert Brooks, *"Discolor Aura,"* cited above, and Charles Segal's two-part study, " 'Aeternum Per Saecula Nomen,' The Golden Bough and the Tragedy of History," *Arion,* IV (1965), 617–57, and V (1966), 34–72. The massive, magisterial commentary by Norden, *Aeneis Buch VI* (Leipzig, 1926), and the briefer

commentary by Fletcher (Oxford, 1941) are useful in different ways. By and large, I have skirted many of the controversies about Book VI.

2. Who is *Iuno inferna?* Fletcher, while offering the conventional identification with Proserpina, points out the strangeness of the words and leaves open the possibility that it may well be Hecate. Cf. line 247 and see also Williams on III.75–76.

3. In lines 194–96, addressing the "maternas ... avis," Aeneas thinks of the bough as shading the rich earth:

'este duces, o, si qua via est, cursumque per auras
dirigite in lucos ubi pinguem dives opacat
ramus humum.'

This surprisingly reverses the precise description which the Sibyl gave him.

4.   quam vellent aethere in alto
nunc et pauperiem et duros perferre labores!   (VI.436 f.)

Echoing lines of Achilles in *Odyssey* XI, this comment is not "editorial." (Fletcher says that these lines obviously show Vergil as opposed to the Stoic view of suicide. But that is hardly the point, is not demonstrable, and is irrelevant in any case.) The comment is part of context, just as the irony that Achilles himself has discovered in *Odyssey* XI illuminates the context there. One might even think of these lines as uttered by Aeneas or by the Sibyl, but that is not important; they provide the sense of the condition of life and setting for the next scene, the *lugentes campi.*

5. Line 460 virtually summarizes Aeneas's speech at the center of Book IV:

'invitus, regina, tuo de litore cessi.'

On other connections, see Austin *ad* IV.319.

6. On *monimenta,* compare the usage of the word in V.572 and VI.26. On *fatum,* see line 511, *fata mea,* as well as lines 515, 533, 538, 546, 547.

7. Musaeus recognizes the attempt to localize—"sed vos, si fert ita corde voluntas," 675—and without irony he suggests the distinction between *locus* and *voluntas* on the one hand and the free fields of Elysium on the other.

8. Other details strengthen the link between the simile and the Marcellus episode: *strepit,* 709, is echoed in *strepitus circa comitum,* 865; in both passages Aeneas cries out, moved deeply by what he sees, while there are no other such sudden expressions on Aeneas's part in this whole section of Book VI. Indeed, Anchises obliquely remarks on Aeneas's lack of reaction:

'et dubitamus adhuc virtutem extendere factis,
aut metus Ausonia prohibet consistere terra?'   (VI.806—7)

9. The emphasis on *pater* Anchises here is in pointed contrast to Aeneas's feeling toward Anchises expressed in 695, "tua me, genitor, tua tristis imago," and in the appeal for human, father-son contact, "da iungere dextram,/ da, genitor, teque amplexu ne subtrahe nostro," 697 f. Vergil subtly insinuated the contrast in the opening line of the passage—"At pater Anchises...," 679; Anchises remains *pater* throughout this episode (see 719, 854, 863, 867) as he speaks with authoritative voice of Roman history and Roman grandeur.

10. Here commentators face the temptation to evoke the notorious "fact" of the "incomplete" state of the poem. It is, indeed, easy to assume (once one has divined the Vergilian "intention") that many a crux would have been solved had Vergil completed the revisions. But that assumption must be patently fallacious. Certainty about what in the poem remained incomplete is elusive at best; there appears to be as little firm agreement about the details of incompleteness as there used to be, in the Homeric Question, about interpolations in Homer. In any event, one must deal with the *Aeneid* as it is, not as one guesses it might (or should) have been.

11. In 852, I read *pacique,* with Knight and Mynors, rather than *pacisque* (Hirtzel).

12. In 882, I follow the punctuation suggested by Page and Fletcher. Mynors has not adopted it in his revision of Hirtzel.

CHAPTER FIVE
ITALY

1. For Circe, see VII.10 f., 189 f., 280 f. On Juno, it is worth recalling that the might-makes-right principle enables her to employ Allecto just as Zeus employed Kratos and Bia in *Prometheus Bound.*—We have no commmentaries on individual books in this latter half of the poem comparable to the Oxford commentaries on Books I through VI. Two interesting essays on the second half are W. H. Alexander, " 'Maius Opus' (*Aeneid* 7–12)," *U. of Cal. Publ. in Class. Phil.,* 14 (1951), 193–214, and W. S. Anderson, "Vergil's Second *Iliad,*" *TAPA,* 88 (1957), 17–30. On Book VII itself, W. Warde Fowler has a humane, perceptive, sympathetic discussion in *Virgil's Gathering of the Clans* (Oxford, Blackwell's, 1916). Various points of view are defined in recent criticism: see especially Pöschl, pp. 24–33, on the Allecto scenes and their symbolism, and 91 ff., the important revaluation of Turnus; E. Fraenkel, "Some Aspects of the Structure of *Aeneid* VII," *JRS,* 35

(1945), 1–14; K. J. Reckford, "Latent Tragedy in *Aeneid* VII, 1–285," *AJPh*, 82 (1961), 252–69; S. G. P. Small, "The Arms of Turnus: *Aeneid* 7:783–92," *TAPA*, 90 (1959), 243–52; and R. D. Williams, "The Function and Structure of Virgil's Catalogue in *Aeneid* VII," *CQ*, 11 (1961), 146–53.

2. *Sanguineam aciem*, 399, recalls IV.643, *sanguineam volvens aciem*. For the various contexts of *sanguis* in Book VII, see, for example, 271, 318, 423, 534, 541, 547, 554, 595.

3. Cf. the objection of Macrobius, *Saturnalia*, V.17. But the complaints are naïve; history has shown us, as it had shown Vergil, how precarious the human situation can become.

4. See Isaiah 2:4: "And he shall judge among the nations, and shall rebuke many people; and they shall beat their swords into ploughshares, and their spears into pruninghooks: nation shall not lift up sword against nation, neither shall they learn war any more." See also the conclusion of *Georgics* I, on the monstrous nature of civil wars:

> tot bella per orbem,
> tam multae scelerum facies, non ullus aratro
> dignus honos, squalent abductis arva colonis,
> et curvae rigidum falces conflantur in ensem.   (505–8)

5. Cf. I.493, Penthesilea described as *bellatrix ... virgo*. The fame of the next four lines hardly justifies the noncriticism to which some highly qualified readers succumb. Fraenkel, for instance, simply abdicates when he writes about VII.808–17, "Rather than spoil a masterpiece in a vain attempt to paraphrase it we prefer to listen quietly to the poet's own words and, while we do so, enjoy the perfect diminuendo in which the martial rhapsody passes away and feel the intense sadness of so much grace and beauty doomed to death in battle" (p. 11). This kind of "appreciation" is inadequate as substitute for critical reflection; it blurs the poetry badly, so that Fraenkel can speak of the passage as "a most harmonious finale" to Book VII.

6. Reckford, p. 265; italics added. Reckford also calls attention to the "warning" involved in the gifts-motif and to the significance of Circe (pp. 267–68).

CHAPTER SIX
WAR IN ITALY

1. The prelude to Book VIII is largely paralleled by the prelude to IX, where Turnus is told of the Trojan gathering of allies. In IX.1–24, Vergil

has conflated elements like those in the second passage in VIII—Aeneas's fears and the apparition and advice of Tiber—in Iris's apparition to Turnus. The compression is effective in the context of the strenuous activity of Book IX. For discussions of Book VIII and its place in the poem, see J. R. Bacon, "Aeneas in Wonderland," CR, 53 (1939), 97–104; Putnam, The Poetry of the Aeneid, pp. 105–51; F. Bömer, "Studien zum VIII. Buche der Aeneis," RhM, 92 (1944), 319–69. W. Warde Fowler's comments are incisive and interesting as always: Aeneas at the Site of Rome (Oxford, Blackwell's, 1917).

2. Among recent critics, Kenneth Quinn is particularly troubled by Aeneas's rampage in Book X: Virgil's Aeneid: A Critical Description (Ann Arbor, 1968), pp. 17 f., 223 f. Few others find the episodes quite so distressing; most critics continue to justify the rampage in terms of Aeneas's quasi-paternal "devotion" to Pallas. See, for example, Henry W. Prescott, The Development of Virgil's Art (Chicago, 1927), pp. 453 f.; Fowler, The Death of Turnus (Oxford, 1919), p. 156; W. S. Anderson, The Art of the Aeneid (Englewood Cliffs, N.J., 1970), pp. 83, 99; Pöschl, p. 106; W. A. Camps, An Introduction to Virgil's Aeneid (Oxford, 1969), pp. 13, 24 f., 28 f. Brooks Otis reflects the conventional wisdom in many places (pp. 316, 340 f., 351 f., 357), and then excoriates Vergil for not being convincing and for unsuccessfully attempting to evoke a situation from Homeric epic (361).

3. Hirtzel and Mynors, along with Mackail, Sabbadini, and Knight, all paragraph after line 369, but Day Lewis and Conington paragraph at line 369. For my purposes, either is acceptable; the line is transitional.

4. Viribus: the heavy sexual atmosphere is developed by diction in the passage. Note, besides coeant and acuant in 385–86, also cura, 396, 401; almost all of 403; infusus gremio, 405; mollibus, 415; most of 417.

5. George E. Duckworth, Structural Patterns in the Aeneid (Ann Arbor, 1962), pp. 8 f. Duckworth's major interest in the book and in several articles, particularly "The Significance of Nisus and Euryalus for Aeneid IX–XII," AJPh, 88 (1967), 129–50, is in elaborate structural analysis, which often appears quantitative or predetermined or both. Camps, pp. 132, 135, considers the slaughter which Nisus and Euryalus inflict on their enemies and "the style and scale of the rewards promised" to be "out of accord with the Virgilian context" and, thus, to be "imperfections of execution and design in the poem." Mlle A.-M. Guillemin, on the other hand, refers to the Nisus-Euryalus story as "bel épisode, si populaire"—which amounts to dismissal: Virgile: Poète, Artiste et Penseur (Paris, 1951), p. 297. Jacques Perret, Virgile: L'homme et l'oeuvre (Paris, 1952), p. 119, sees the episode as highlighting the difference between "cette même vertù guerriere" and "la naïve brutalité italienne"; see also p. 124. See also Prescott, pp. 440 f., 192 f., 203 f.; Conington, III, 158 f.; Putnam, The Poetry of the Aeneid, pp. 60 f.

But cf. Quinn, pp. 13, 198 ff., and Anderson, *The Art of the Aeneid,* pp. 78–80—a very acute reading. Brooks Otis sees a clear structure in Book IX, by way of its relationship primarily to Book V, secondarily to Book XI, and by way of the absent-Aeneas theme (pp. 342 ff.); Otis misleadingly emphasizes the poet's "overt editorializing" and the assimilation of the Nisus-Euryalus episode into "the ideology of Roman patriotism" (pp. 388 f.).

6. Roger A. Hornsby, *Patterns of Action in the Aeneid* (Iowa City, 1970), says that the Trojans were enjoined *from leaving the camp,* but the text emphasizes the prohibition against engaging the Latins in combat. Overreading here, Hornsby is right, however, in describing the Nisus-Euryalus episode as a "fascinating exploration of moral ambiguity" and in comparing the rage of Turnus with "the rage of Nisus and Euryalus—a rage for glory and destruction, a rage of maddened beasts thirsting for blood" (pp. 65 f., 68 f., 85 f.).

7. The irony of Neptune's destroying Troy was pointed up earlier in the poem, in phrases like "fumat Neptunia Troia" (III.3). See also Austin's commentary on *Aeneid* II (Oxford, 1964), p. xx and *ad* 610.

8. See Putnam, *The Poetry of the Aeneid,* pp. 50 ff., and Hornsby, pp. 10–13. Clear echoes of Book II help to enlarge this context, especially echoes of II.252 f. and 265 f.: compare IX.164 f., 189, 236, 242, 316 f., 336 f.

9. Hornsby, who mistakenly applies the simile to Euryalus (pp. 10, 65, 71, 120) as does Putnam (*The Poetry of the Aeneid,* p. 52), sees in this simile Vergil's "moral indictment on the two youths" (p. 66).

10. They are betrayed by the moonlight reflected off Euryalus's helmet (373 f.), just as, later, Camilla is fatally betrayed by her heroic passion for shining armor (XI.768 ff., 801 f.).

11. Lines 708 f. and 752 f., combined with the simile of 679–82, evoke Book II.626–31, where the fall of Troy is compared to the crash of a giant tree. See also Hornsby, p. 82.

CHAPTER SEVEN
PIUS AENEAS AND THE WAGES OF WAR

1. See lines 27 f. and 58 f. Interestingly, in X.4, Jove looks on the "castra Dardanidum," but Venus's speech and Juno's are marked by "Teucri, Troes, Troia, Pergama"; Juno uses "Dardanius" just once (92), in a scornful reference to Paris which implies that Paris is the model for Aeneas's present course.

2. The emphasis in the council on Troy may serve a further purpose—to prepare the way for later scenes in Book X which depend for impact on evocation of Book II. This may also be the function of at least part of lines 215–59.

3. The first of these similes was also used in VII.586 f., and seems derived from *Iliad* XV.618 f. and XVII.747 f. The second, according to Conington, has three Homeric sources: *Iliad* XI.414 f., XIII.471 f., XVII.61 f. For the third (see *Aeneid* IX.339), *Iliad* XII.299 f., III.23 f., and again XVII.61 f. The last simile in this passage, without specific Homeric antecedent, compares Mezentius to great Orion: *Aeneid* X.763–67.

4. The intention to immolate the eight youths, says Conington, is a "barbarity which was regarded with horror" in Vergil's own time. Thus, no explicit reproach on the part of the poet is necessary. See Quinn, p. 225*n*. See above, note 2, in chapter 6, on Aeneas's rampage and the critics.

5. Appropriately, the Trojan Serestus "arma.../ lecta refert umeris tibi, rex Gradive, tropaeum" (541–42). The shock of the contrast between the priesthood of Apollo-Hecate and his fate as trophy to Mars is achieved by the expert design in the six-line passage (537–42) in which elements of light and dark, consecration and immolation, are set off against each other, within the frame of priesthood and trophy.

6. F. A. Sullivan, "Virgil's Mezentius," in *Classical Essays Presented to James A. Kleist, S. J.,* ed. R. E. Arnold, S. J. (St. Louis, 1946), p. 112. See also Alexander, "Maius Opus," p. 208; Otis, p. 360; cf. Quinn, p. 232.

7. Pyrrhus was slain, "patrias ad oras," by Orestes, the filial avenger of Agamemnon: III.332. See Conington and Williams, *ad locum;* Vergil's compression and scholarly doubts about the exact referent are noteworthy.

CHAPTER EIGHT
AENEAS AND TURNUS

1. Brooks Otis, pp. 366–68, sees Turnus as utterly wrong and motivated by fear. But Otis's conclusions here depend on conjecture and speculation, not on persuasive interpretation of the plain text. For example, one cannot agree with his reading of Juno's plucking Turnus off the battlefield in Book X; Turnus's reaction is properly heroic.

2. See the Polydorus episode in Book III; "Threissa.../ Harpalyce" (I.316 f.) and Austin's detailed note; and *Georgics* IV.462, "Rhesi Mavortia tellus" (a connection suggested to me by Austin in a letter).

3. Despite the commentaries by W. Warde Fowler, *The Death of Turnus* (Oxford, Blackwell's, 1919), and W. S. Maguiness (London, 1953), one must still rely, even for Book XII, on the older commentaries on the whole poem. Putnam has a challenging, often acutely perceptive, chapter (*The Poetry of the Aeneid,* pp. 151–201); Pöschl's analysis of the character of Turnus (pp. 91–138) remains important.

4. The tone is, indeed, so complex that Henry thought Juno must be lying in XII.145.

5. Line 282 curiously echoes leitmotifs from Book II:

sic omnis amor unus habet decernere ferro.

6. Putnam, *The Poetry of the Aeneid,* pp. 174 f., attributes the episode to "Aeneas' madness."

7. Note also, for instance, the noise of lines 921–23:

murali concita numquam
tormento sic saxa fremunt nec fulmine tanti
dissultant crepitus. volat atri turbinis instar....

8. Steele Commager, ed., *Virgil: A Collection of Critical Essays* (Englewood Cliffs, N.J., 1966), introduction, p. 10.

9. Pöschl overlooked this important simile (as well as the one at 715–22) when he asserted that Vergil compared Aeneas to a "beast of prey only once," that is, in II.355 f., while "Turnus' fury in battle is repeatedly illustrated by reference to wild animals" (pp. 98 f.). In connection with the enclosure imagery, one should note also the deliberate evocation shortly of Achilles and Hector going round the walls of Troy (*Iliad* XXII) and the contrasts presented in the Vergilian scene—the heavy movement of Aeneas, the narrowing circle around Turnus. The verb *instat* (751) is used strikingly in lines 762, 783, 887, and 916. Other imagery related to the labyrinthine may be noted in lines 831, 841, 848, 855, 858, 889 f., 915, 922, 928 f., and 939.

10. Latinus seems petulant here; at the end, Aeneas is furiously indignant as he stands before Latinus's city walls and stretches out an accusing hand, indicting Latinus for his role in the war:

ipse inter primos dextram sub moenia tendit
Aeneas, magnaque incusat voce Latinum
testaturque deos iterum se ad proelia cogi....   (XII.579–81)

11. In related phrases, unarmed Aeneas on the one hand tries to stop the renewed fighting—"At pius Aeneas dextram tendebat inermem," 311—and Turnus, on the other, finds himself weaponless after his sword has shattered: "dextramque aspexit inermem" (734).

12. See also IV.314, 316: "per dextramque tuam.../ per conubia nostra, per inceptos hymenaeos." Note the emphasis on *dextram,* as the external symbol of *conubia.*

13. Venus does finally respond to Aeneas's early plea for contact; in VIII.615, we read, "et amplexus nati Cytherea petivit." The detail is notable. When Vulcan hesitated (presumably because the request for arms was made on behalf of the bastard son), she won him by her contact: "cunctantem amplexu molli fovet" (388; discussed in chapter 6). The embrace is associated with the violence-sex theme of that episode. Earlier, in Book I, Aeneas merely wanted human contact; she can give it now, not in the role of mother so much as the role of arms-bringer, and thus in the name of the dynasty promised her by Jupiter.

BIBLIOGRAPHY

This list includes works consulted more than merely in passing, whether or not cited in introduction and notes. Despite some idiosyncrasies, the list would provide a substantive education for the serious student of Vergil.

TEXTS AND TRANSLATIONS

The texts primarily used were the *Opera* edited by Frederick Hirtzel (1900) and recently by R. A. B. Mynors (1969) in the Oxford Classical Texts series. I have also consulted other texts, such as those by Remigio Sabbadini (Rome, 1930), J. W. Mackail (Oxford, 1930), and H. R. Fairclough (Cambridge, Mass., 1934).

There are so many translations of the *Aeneid* that the interested reader should examine several. Bishop Gavin Douglas's lively rendering "in to Scottish Metir" (1513) remains one of the most attractive. John Dryden's neoclassic version is often interesting, sometimes surprising (1697; numerous modern editions, including one with introduction by poet Robert Fitzgerald, New York, 1965).

Modern prose translations include those by J. W. Mackail (New York, 1908; available in the Modern Library); H. R. Fairclough (Cambridge, Mass., 1934–35; Loeb Classical Library, bilingual); W. F. Jackson Knight (Baltimore, 1955; Penguin Books). The more interesting modern verse translations are those by C. Day Lewis (London, 1952, and Doubleday Anchor Books); L. R. Lind (Bloomington, 1963; F. O. Copley (Indianapolis, 1965); and Allen Mandelbaum (Berkeley, 1971).

COMMENTARIES

Conington, John, and Henry Nettleship. *P. Vergili Maronis Opera. The Works of Vergil with a Commentary.* Vol. II, 4th ed., London, 1884; Vol. III, 3d ed., London, 1883. Reprinted, Hildesheim, 1963.
Henry, James. *Aeneidea, or Critical Exegetical, and Aesthetical Remarks*

on the Aeneid. 4 vols. London, 1873–92. Reprinted, Hildesheim, 1969.

Heyne, Christian G., and G. P. E. Wagner. *P. Vergilius Maro, varietate lectionis et perpetua adnotatione illustratus....* 4th ed. 5 vols. Leipzig and London, 1830–41.

Mackail, John W. *The Aeneid, with Introduction and Commentary.* Oxford, 1930.

Page, Thomas E. *The Aeneid of Virgil.* 2 vols. London, 1900.

Rand, E. K., *et al. Servianorum ... commentariorum editionis Harvardianae.* Vol. II, Lancaster, 1945; Vol. III, Oxford, 1965.

Thilo, Georg, and Hermann Hagen. *Servii Grammatici qui feruntur in Vergilii carmina commentarii.* 3 vols. 1881–87. Reprinted, Hildesheim, 1961.

P. Vergili Maronis Opera cum commentario Christophori Landini. Florence, 1487.

—— *Cum Servii commentariis ... Ad hos ... Landini & A. Mancinelli commentarii.* Venice, 1507.

—— *Opera Virgiliana cum decem commentis docte et familiariter expositis....* Lyons, 1529.

—— *Opera omnia ... cum commentariis A. Mancinelli, B. Ascensii ... et M. Vegii Landensis libro....* Venice, 1544.

Commentaries on individual books:

Book I, ed. R. G. Austin. Oxford, 1970.

Book II, ed. R. G. Austin. Oxford, 1964.

—— ed. V. Ussani. Rome, 1952.

Book III, ed. R. D. Williams. Oxford, 1962.

Book IV, ed. A. S. Pease. Cambridge, Mass., 1935.

—— ed. E. Paratore. Rome, 1947.

—— ed. R. G. Austin. Oxford, 1955.

Il libro di Didone, ed. Corso Buscaroli. Milan, 1932.

Book V, ed. R. D. Williams. Oxford, 1960.

Book VI, ed. Sir Frank Fletcher. Oxford, 1941.

Aeneis Buch VI, ed. Eduard Norden. Leipzig, 1926.

W. Warde Fowler, *Virgil's Gathering of the Clans.* Oxford, Blackwell's, 1916.

—— *Aeneas at the Site of Rome.* Oxford, Blackwell's, 1917.

—— *The Death of Turnus.* Oxford, Blackwell's, 1919.

Book XII, ed. W. S. Maguiness. London, 1953.

SECONDARY WORKS

Alexander, W. H. "'Maius Opus' (*Aeneid* 7–12)," *U. of Cal. Publ. in Class. Phil.,* 14 (1951), 193–214.

Amerasinghe, C. W. " 'Saturnia Iuno'—Its Significance in the *Aeneid*," *G&R*, 22 (1953), 61–69.

Anderson, William S. *The Art of the Aeneid*. Englewood Cliffs, N.J., 1970.

—— "Juno and Saturn in the *Aeneid*," *SPh*, 55 (1958), 519–32.

—— " 'Pastor Aeneas': On Pastoral Themes in the *Aeneid*," *TAPA*, 99 (1968), 1–17.

—— "Vergil's Second *Iliad*," *TAPA*, 88 (1957), 17–30.

Bacon, J. R. "Aeneas in Wonderland: A Study of *Aeneid* VIII," *CR*, 53 (1939), 97–104.

Bailey, Cyril. *Religion in Virgil*. Oxford, 1935.

Benario, H. W. "The Tenth Book of the *Aeneid*," *TAPA*, 98 (1967), 23–36.

Berger, H. "Archaism, Vision, and Revision: Studies in Virgil, Plato, and Milton," *The Centennial Review*, 11.1 (Winter, 1967), 24–52.

Bömer, Franz. "Studien zum VIII. Buche der *Aeneis*," *RhM*, 92 (1944), 319–69.

Bowra, Cecil Maurice. *From Virgil to Milton*. New York, 1945.

Brooks, Robert A. *"Discolor Aura:* Reflections on the Golden Bough," *AJPh*, 74 (1953), 260–80.

Büchner, Karl. *P. Vergilius Maro: Der Dichter der Römer*. Pauly-Wissowa Realencyclopädie. Stuttgart, 1958.

Camps, W. A. *An Introduction to Virgil's Aeneid*. Oxford, 1969.

Cartault, A. *L'art de Virgile dans l'Eneide*. 2 vols. Paris, 1926.

Commager, Steele, ed. *Virgil: A Collection of Critical Essays*. Englewood Cliffs, N.J., 1966.

Comparetti, Domenico. *Virgilio nel medio evo*. New ed. by Giorgio Pasquali. 2 vols. Florence, 1937–41.

Cook, Albert S. *The Classic Line: A Study in Epic Poetry*. Bloomington, 1966.

Cruttwell, Robert W. *Virgil's Mind at Work: An Analysis of the Symbolism of the Aeneid*. Oxford, Blackwell's, 1947.

Decembrio, Angelo. *De politia literaria libri septem*. Basel, 1562.

Di Cesare, Mario A. *A Critical Study Guide to Vergil's Aeneid*. Totowa, N.J., Littlefield, Adams, 1968.

—— *Vida's Christiad and Vergilian Epic*. New York, 1964.

Duckworth, George E. "The *Aeneid* as a Trilogy," *TAPA*, 88 (1957), 17–30.

—— "The Architecture of the *Aeneid*," *AJPh*, 75 (1954), 1–15.

—— *Recent Work on Vergil (1957–1963)*. Reprinted from *CW*, 57 (1964), by the Vergilian Society, Exeter, N.H.

—— *Recent Work on Vergil: A Bibliographical Survey, 1940–56*. Reprinted from *CW*, 51 (1958), by the Vergilian Society, Exeter, N.H.

—— "The Significance of Nisus and Euryalus for *Aeneid* IX–XII," *AJPh*, 88 (1967), 129–50.

Duckworth, George E. *Structural Patterns in the Aeneid.* Ann Arbor, 1962.

Eliot, T. S. *On Poetry and Poets.* New York, 1957.

Feder, Lilian. "Vergil's Tragic Theme," *CJ*, 49 (1953–54), 197–209.

Fenik, B. "Parallelism of Theme and Imagery in *Aeneid* II and IV," *AJPh*, 80 (1959), 1–24.

Fraenkel, E. "Some Aspects of the Structure of *Aeneid* VII," *JRS*, 35 (1945), 1–14.

Galinsky, K. *"Aeneid* V and the *Aeneid," AJPh*, 89 (1968), 157–85.

—— "The Hercules-Cacus Episode in *Aeneid* VIII," *AJPh*, 87 (1966), 18–51.

Graves, Robert, "The Virgil Cult," *Virginia Quarterly Review*, 38 (1962), 13–25.

Greene, Thomas M. *The Descent from Heaven: A Study in Epic Continuity.* New Haven, 1963.

Grimm, R. E. "Aeneas and Andromache in *Aeneid* III," *AJPh*, 88 (1967), 151–62.

Gullemin, A.-M. *Virgile: Poète, Artiste et Penseur.* Paris, 1951.

Harding, Davis P. *The Club of Hercules: Studies in the Classical Background of Paradise Lost.* Illinois Studies in Language and Literature, 50. Urbana, 1962.

Heinze, Richard. *Virgils Epische Technik.* Reprint of 3d ed. Stuttgart, 1957.

Highbarger, Ernest Leslie. *The Gates of Dreams: An Archeological Examination of Vergil's Aeneid VI. 893–899.* Baltimore, 1940.

Highet, Gilbert. *The Classical Tradition.* Oxford, 1949.

Hornsby, Roger A. *Patterns of Action in the Aeneid: An Interpretation of Vergil's Epic Similes.* Iowa City, 1970.

Jacob, P. "L'Episode de Palinure," *LEC*, 20 (1952), 163–67.

Klingner, F. *Studien zur griechischen und römischen Literatur.* Zurich, 1964.

Knauer, Georg Nicolaus. *Die Aeneis und Homer.* Göttingen, 1964.

Knight, W. F. Jackson. *Accentual Symmetry in Vergil.* Oxford, Blackwell's, 1939.

—— *Cumaean Gates.* Oxford, Blackwell's, 1936.

—— *Roman Vergil.* London, 1944.

—— *Vergil's Troy: Essays on the Second Book of the Aeneid.* Oxford, Blackwell's, 1932.

Knox, Bernard M. W. "The Serpent and the Flame: The Imagery of the Second Book of the *Aeneid," AJPh*, 71 (1950), 379–400.

Landino, Christopher. *Camaldolensische Gespräche.* Translated from the Latin with introduction by Eugen Wolf. Jena, 1927.

—— *Christophori Landini Florentini Libri Quattuor ... de vita activa et contemplativa....* Strasbourg, 1508.

——*Disputationes Camaldulenses.* Basel, 1577.

Lloyd, R. B. *"Aeneid* III, A New Approach," *AJPh,* 78 (1957), 133–41.

—— *"Aeneid* III and the Aeneas Legend," *AJPh,* 78 (1957), 382–400.

—— "The Character of Anchises in the *Aeneid,"* *TAPA,* 88 (1957), 44–55.

Mambelli, Giuliano. *Gli annali delle edizioni virgiliane.* Florence, 1954.

—— *Gli studi virgiliani nel secolo XX: Contributo ad una bibliografia generale.* 2 vols. Florence, 1940.

Mendell, C. W. "The Influence of the Epyllion on the *Aeneid,"* *YCS,* 12 (1951), 205–26.

Newton, F. L. "Recurrent Imagery in *Aeneid* IV," *TAPA,* 88 (1957), 31–43.

Nolhac, Pierre de. *Petrarque et l'Humanisme.* Paris, 1892.

Otis, Brooks. *Virgil: A Study in Civilized Poetry.* Oxford, 1963.

Paratore, Ettore. *Virgilio.* Rome, 1945.

Patris, S. "Une Figure Feminine de l'Eneide: Amata, Reine des Latins," *LEC,* 13 (1945), 40–54.

Perret, Jacques. *Virgile: L'homme et l'oeuvre.* Paris, 1952.

Poliziano, Angelo. *Le Selve e la Strega, prolusioni ... 1482–1492.* Ed. Isidoro del Lungo. Florence, 1925.

Pöschl, Viktor. *Die Dichtkunst Virgils: Bild und Symbol in der Aeneis.* Innsbruck, 1950. Translated by Gerda Seligson, *The Art of Vergil.* Ann Arbor, 1962.

Prescott, Henry W. *The Development of Virgil's Art.* Chicago, 1927.

Putnam, Michael C. J. *"Aeneid* VII and the *Aeneid,"* *AJPh,* 91 (1970), 408–30.

—— *The Poetry of the Aeneid.* Cambridge, Mass., 1965.

Quinn, Kenneth. *Virgil's Aeneid: A Critical Description.* Ann Arbor, 1968.

Rand, Edward Kennan. *The Magical Art of Vergil.* Cambridge, Mass., 1931.

Reckford, K. J. "Latent Tragedy in *Aeneid* VII, 1–285," *AJPh,* 82 (1961), 252–69.

Rosenmeyer, T. G. "Vergil and Heroism: *Aeneid* XI," *CJ,* 55 (1960), 159–64.

Sabbadini, Remigio. *Le scoperte dei codici latini e greci nei secoli xiv e xv.* Florence, 1905.

Sainte-Beuve, C. A. *Étude sur Virgile.* Paris, 1857.

Salutati, Coluccio. *De laboribus Herculis.* Ed. B. L. Ullman. 2 vols. Zurich, 1951.

—— *Epistolario.* Ed. Francesco Novati. 4 vols. Rome, 1891–1911.

Segal, C. P. " 'Aeternum Per Saecula Nomen,' The Golden Bough and the Tragedy of History: Part I," *Arion,* IV (1965), 617–57.

—— ". . . Part II," *Arion,* V (1966), 34–72.

Sellar, W. Y. *The Roman Poets of the Augustan Age: Virgil.* Oxford, 1877.

Sforza, F. "The Problem of Virgil," *CR,* 49 (1935), 97–108.

Small, S. G. P. "The Arms of Turnus: *Aeneid* 7:783–92," *TAPA*, 90 (1959), 243–52.

Sullivan, F. A. "Virgil's Mezentius," in *Classical Essays Presented to James A. Kleist, S. J.*, ed. R. E. Arnold, S. J. St. Louis, 1946.

Syme, Ronald. *The Roman Revolution*. London, 1960.

Taylor, M. E. "Primitivism in Virgil," *AJPh*, 76 (1955), 261–78.

Tillyard, E. M. W. *The English Epic and Its Background*. London, 1954.

Turolla, E. "La 'seconda Eneide' e una determinazione di maniere diverse nell'opera virgiliana," *GIF*, 7 (1954), 97–112.

Vida, Marco Girolamo. *Poemata omnia....* 2 vols. Padua, 1731.

Voigt, Georg. *Die Wiederbelebung des klassischen Alterthums....* 3d ed. Ed. Max Lehnerdt. 2 vols. Berlin, 1893.

Wetmore, Munroe Nichols. *Index Verborum Vergilianus*. New Haven, 1911.

Williams, R. D. "The Function and Structure of Virgil's Catalogue in *Aeneid* VII," *CQ*, 11 (1961), 146–53.

—— "The Pictures on Dido's Temple (*Aeneid* I, 450–93)," *CQ*, 10 (1960), 145–51.

—— *Virgil*. Greece & Rome, New Surveys in the Classics, No. 1. Oxford, 1967.

Worstbrock, Franz Josef. *Elemente einer Poetik der Aeneis*. Münster, 1963.

Zabughin, Vladimir. *Virgilio nel Rinascimento Italiano: Da Dante a Torquato Tasso*. 2 vols. Bologna, 1921–23.

INDEX OF PASSAGES FROM AENEID

BOOK I		598-99	7
1-11	2-3	603-10	7-8
2	1	617-18	16, 27
11	219	648-53	15
27	12	660	242n7
29-32	4	685	137
32	62, 101	688	14, 242n7
33	2	691-94	17
68	11	691	18
92	237	713-14	15
94-101	5	718	137
94-98	237	749-53	13
148-53	8-9		
148 f.	238	BOOK II	
159-61	77	1	18
168-69	77	10	17
198	5	45-49	41
203-6	5-6	153	234
237	10	195-96	39
253	10	202	42
278-79	11	206-11	42
283-85	118	220-24	43
408-9	7	228-32	43
437	2	234-42	44
460-61	12	238	57
464-65	13	255-56	43
480 f.	235	289-95	46
487	233	291	158
498-502	14-15	304-8	47
573	29	354	48
597	16	355 f.	246n5

360	49, 150, 246n5	772-73	57
367-68	40	775	58
369	49	776	102
390	40	777	58
391	49	780-84	58
402	52	788	58
426-27	51	789	58
429-30	45	792-94	59
470-75	51	803	59
495	49	804	59
497	49		
503-4	49		
508	50	BOOK III	
509-10	50	1-12	61
536	246n8	12	155
540-41	50	78-79	76
547-48	200	85-89	63
548-50	50	85 f.	76
550-53	50	94-98	63
551-53	190	102	73
557-58	51, 92	132	66
560	100, 192, 194	136-37	66
573	52	163-67	67
581	246n7	187-88	73
602	52	276-77	76
608-18	52	349-51	67
610	62	374-76	70
622-23	53	379-80	70
625	62	383	70
642-44	54	395	70
655	54-55	433-40	69
662-63	54	493-97	67-68
668	54-55	511	77
670	54-55	592	233
693-98	55	606	233
708-10	56	610 f.	233
728-29	56	709-11	74
735-36	57	710-11	30
738	57	710 f.	77
745-46	56	711	86
749-51	57	714-15	75
755	57	716	30
763-67	57	718	30

BOOK IV

1-5	243-44n15
1-2	13
5	18, 30
45-46	243n11
65-67	183-84
65-66	21
66-69	14
78-79	21
83	21
88-89	21
100-1	20
133-34	242n8
165-66	20
169-72	20-21
259-64	31
265-67	32
300-3	25-26
300-1	244n20
307-8	235
314	255n12
316	255n12
337-39	33
340-44	33
350	76
351-55	75
351	25
351 f.	34
353	25
360-61	34
366-67	24
384-87	24
393-96	35
427	25
441-46	35
460-61	243n15
461-62	137
465-68	23
469-73	23
552	25
586	242n8
601-2	26
610	26
620	26
640	28
646 f.	28
655	29
657 f.	28
661-62	27
665-71	29
666	244n20
682-83	29

BOOK V

1-7	36
17-18	89
49-50	79
80-83	86
80 f.	248n10
83	100
227-31	80
389	81
430	81
431 f.	80
439	80
453-57	81
474-76	81-82
483-84	82
533-34	83
572	96
576	83
588-91	83
604	84
617	77
624-25	85
631-34	85
658	85
685-86	234
687-92	85
701-3	86
704-5	78
709-10	78
717-18	78
719-20	86
724-25	87
731-35	87

741-42	87-88	370	105
742	235	373	105, 235
756	88	376	105, 235
785-88	88	390-91	105
810-11	89	403-4	105
814-15	89	406 f.	105
827-28	92	436-37	249n4
833-34	90	450-54	106
838-41	90	458-60	34
843-46	90	458	107
848-49	91	460	249n5
854-56	91	461 f.	137
859-60	91	463	107
870-71	92	465-66	107
		466	34
BOOK VI		472-74	107
7-8	94	475-76	108
9-13	94-95	477	108
24-26	96	478	108
27	96	486-87	108
61-65	97	492-93	109
68-69	97	552-54	109
74-76	97	580	110
85 f.	98	625-27	110
88-91	98	638-39	110
93-94	98	646	111
95-97	99	648-50	110
102-5	99	673-75	111
108-14	100	675	249n7
112	101	681-83	111
123	101	684 f.	112
126-29	101	685	235
128	103	690	112
133	101-2	695	250n9
135	101-2	697-98	112, 235, 250n9
136-39	102-3	700-2	112
146-47	103	700 f.	235
194-96	249n3	707-9	113
268-69	104	713-15	114
270-72	104	716-18	114
282-84	121	716	112
292 f.	122	717	111
313-14	104	719-21	114

720	112	345	127
721	105	363-64	139
749-51	116	365-66	129
781-87	116	398-99	130
792-95	117	444	130
806-7	118, 250n8	454-55	130
823	117	460-62	48, 130
832-35	117	534	131
837	118	536	132
838-40	118	581	136
847-53	119	582-84	132
848	112	600	132
855-58	120	635-36	132
861 f.	120	643-44	132
865-66	120	649-50	133
878-80	120	786-88	133
882-83	121	808-11	134
883	113	814-17	134-35
885 f.	121		
893-96	121	BOOK VIII	
899	122	6-8	140
		17	140
BOOK VII		63-64	146
4	194	91-93	146
5	123	96	146
8 f.	124	124	234
44-45	126	163-64	234
54-57	127-28	311	147
58	128	312	147
120-23	124	314-15	147
157-59	124	319-20	146
239-40	137	324-27	147-48
244	139	340-41	147
266	127, 233	351-52	148
270-73	127	356	147
271-72	128	364-68	148
281-83	138	369	149
293-94	125	370	150
297-98	125	376 f.	151
308-12	125	382-83	151
317-22	138-39	387-92	152
318-19	128	388	150, 256n13
338-40	128-29	393	152

394	152
403	153
405-6	150
407-14	153
441	151
455-56	148
502-3	142
508	142
511-13	143
524-29	143
537-40	144
557	144
558	234
583-84	144-45
598-99	149
609-10	149
615	256n13
620-22	155
630 f.	154
678-81	154-55
700-3	155
710 f.	112
729-31	156
730	112

BOOK IX

3-4	170
44	157
96-97	158
126-27	158
133	158
135	158
136-39	159
136-37	180
140-41	159
144-45	159
150-55	161
184-87	161
187	164
194-95	161
205-6	161-62
266	162
272-73	162

310-13	162
315-16	163
320	163
339-41	163
342-43	163
354	163
364	165
373-74	164
384-85	165
391-93	165
444-45	164
446-49	164
450	166
599	159
602	160
607-8	160
614-16	160
617	159
656	166
688-90	167
728-30	167
742	167
756-61	168
778-80	169
815-18	169

BOOK X

1-2	174
11-14	174
18-19	174
29	176
62 f.	175
65 f.	175
97-99	177
100	177
108	176
111-13	176
113	175, 207
159-60	199
270-75	178
278	181
280-82	182
284	182

356-61	177	755-61	187
375-76	178	762	186
429-30	179	768	186
433-36	179	781-90	191-92
436-38	179	791-93	192
442-43	182, 200	810-12	193
443	189	821-30	193-94
467-72	180	823	234
487-89	181	830	196
492-94	182	851	194
497-99	182	878-79	194
500-5	183	898-908	195
508-9	181		
519-20	188	BOOK XI	
523-25	189	1-4	198
534	189	17	201, 221
535-36	189-90	96-97	201
537	190	98-99	201
541-42	254n5	111	202
554-58	190	113	207
566-67	189	122-23	202
569-70	189	128-29	202
581-83	190-91	130-31	202
591	192	134-35	201
595-96	234	165-66	200
597-98	191	177-81	200
600	191	182-83	201
613-14	184	217	202
636	185	223	203
642	185	224	203
652	185	245	204, 233-34
663-64	185	255-59	204
685-86	185	280	205
688	185	312-13	203
689-90	185	352-56	203
691-92	186	376	206
694-96	186	415	205
712-13	186	425-27	205
714	186	435	232
716	187	440-42	205-6
729	186	445	206
742	186	453-54	206
743-44	187	476	207

Passage	Page
646-49	207
652	208
659-63	208
690-91	208
736	208-9
778-79	209
782	209
801-2	209
831	216
881-82	209
908-11	209-10
913-14	199

BOOK XII

Passage	Page
4-9	212
11	211
17	210
49	212
55	211
59	211
61-62	211
74	211
80	210
101-2	212
109	214
141	214
144-45	214
159	214
220-21	214, 232
229-30	215, 232
239	217
282	255n5
311	255n11
368	221
466-67	217
494	219
498-99	219
500	219
502	145, 219
503-4	219
521-28	220
521 f.	145
553	145
555	221
565	222
567	223
572	223
579-81	255n10
592	222
594	222
600	223
603	223
612-13	244n19
626	218
634-36	218
646-49	221
665-68	224
668	221
676-80	218
680	224
697-700	224
701 f.	225
713	225
714	225
720	225
722	225
734	255n11
743-45	229
749-57	230
763-64	230
787	230-31
794	226
803	231
821 f.	231
830	226
840	239
859	227
868	231
876-81	227-28
885-86	228
893	229
894-95	181, 231
899	231
903-4	231
908-14	228-29

913-14	221	930-31	233
916-18	231-32	937	210
921-23	255*n*7	938	233
923 f.	225	938-39	236
928-29	226	950-52	236

GENERAL INDEX

Abas, 179

Acestes, 77-78, 83, 88

Achaemenides, 65-66, 139, 233, 247*n*1; compared with Sinon, 65-66, 247*n*1

Achilles, 4, 167, 170, 189, 249*n*4

Actium, 155, 156

Adrastus, 108

Aegaeon, 189

Aegyptus, 183

Aemilius Paullus, 118

Aeneas: barbarism of, 144, 145, 188-92, 193, 196-97, 252*n*2; compared with Dido, 16; compared with Turnus, 145, 188, 199, 219-22; as hero, 5, 48, 102, 239; humanity of, 4-8, 11, 55-56, 87, 100, 112-13, 233-36, 237-39; knowledge of, 6, 60, 66, 78, 156; as leader, 59-60, 74, 79, 81, 201, 214, 219-22, 225, 237-239; *pietas* of, 5, 11, 32, 35, 74, 100, 102, 106, 123, 192-94; relationship with Anchises, 30-31, 34, 54, 55, 59-60, 71-77, 86-88; relationship with Pallas, 143-45, 179; Shield of, 149, 154-56

Aeolia, 4

Aeolus, 4, 125, 175, 213, 214

Aeschylus, *Agamemnon,* 126, 176, 204

Aletes, 162

Allecto, 109, 125, 127-31, 139, 141, 155, 207, 213

Almo, 131

Amata, 127-30, 135, 136, 138, 139, 203, 211-12, 222-23, 225, 232

Amor (Cupid), 14, 17, 21, 137, 175

Anchises, 16, 30, 53-56, 63, 66-67, 87, 111-21, 159, 173, 194, 228, 235, 247*n*3, 249*n*8, 250*n*9; and dynasty, 111-19; relationship with Aeneas, 30-31, 34, 56, 71-76, 100, 156

Androgeos, 96

Andromache, 67, 68

Anna, 19, 22, 29, 35, 243*n*11

Antenor, 10

Antigone, 6

Antony, 154

Antores, 188, 191-92

Anxur, 189

Aphrodite, 14, 152

Apollo, 16, 21, 23, 63, 66, 70, 72-73, 95, 96, 166, 190, 208, 216

Apollonius of Rhodes, 37

Arcadia, 145-49, 157, 201, 234

Ares, 152

Arruns, 209

Artemis, 14

Ascanius, 10, 20, 26, 34, 76, 129, 131, 154, 160, 162-63, 166-67, 196, 237, 238

Assarchus, 118
Atlas, 19
Augustus Caesar, 116, 118, 149, 154, 156, 172
Austin, R. G., 27, 29, 57, 241*nn;* quoted, 19, 22, 24, 31, 33, 60, 76, 246*nn*

Bacchus, 21
Bellona, 155
Berecyntia, 160
Beroe (Iris), 85
Bitias, 157, 166-68, 170, 208
Bowra, C. M., 39
Brutus, 117
Butes, 166, 208

Cacus, 146
Caeculus, 189
Caere, 149, 150
Caesar, Julius, 117
Cajeta, 123, 216
Calypso, 65
Camers, 215
Camilla, 133-35, 142, 206, 207-10, 216, 232; heroism of, 208, 210
Camps, W. A., quoted, 252*n*5
Carmenta, 147
Carthage, 1-37 *passim,* 65, 77, 78, 107-8, 213, 222, 235, 237; as symbol, 29-30, 65, 222
Cassandra, 45, 49, 67, 73, 214, 228, 245*n*2
Catalogue of Latins, 132-35
Cerberus, 104
Ceres, 21
Charon, 104, 105
Charybdis, 74
Chekhov, Anton, 114
Chloreus, 209
Circe, 126, 127, 138
Circle (image), 44, 57, 101, 150, 165, 223, 225, 229-31

Cisseus, 188
City (symbolic), 1-2, 8, 11, 28, 29-30, 31-32, 37, 65-68, 77, 80-81, 88, 93, 100, 138-39, 141, 213, 214, 222-23, 224, 225, 226, 236-39
Cleopatra, 154, 155
Clonus, 183
Conington, John, 134, 208, 241*n*1; quoted, 6, 58, 149, 247*n*13, 254*n*4
Conrad, Joseph, quoted, 229
Coroebus, 40, 49
Crete, 66, 68
Creusa, 16, 56-59, 87, 102, 113, 235, 239
Cumae, 71, 94, 96, 103, 139
Cupid (Amor), 14, 17, 21, 137, 175
Cybele, 66, 113, 158, 209
Cyclops, 66, 151, 153, 247*n*1

Daedalus, 95, 106
Dante, 6; *Inferno* XXXIII.4-6, 38; *Inferno* v.*121-26,* 245*n*1
Dardanus, 27-28, 30, 36, 37, 110, 116, 142, 227, 244*n*19
Dares, 80-82
Day Lewis, C., translation quoted, 134, 164, 200
Death, 25, 27, 89, 92-93, 180-81, 200-1, 211, 215-16, 222-23, 232, 237
Dedalus, Stephen, 38
Deiphobus, 106, 108-9
Demodocus, 13
Diana, 11, 16, 95, 208, 216
Dido, 2, 7, 8, 11-37 *passim,* 65, 106-7, 129, 135, 136, 137, 176, 183-84, 208, 213, 216, 222, 225, 227, 228, 232, 239; compared with Aeneas, 16; compared with Fall of Troy, 28, 223; compared with Latinus, 126, 135-36; name of, 242*n*4; primitivism motif, 19-26
Diomedes, 99, 139, 140, 141, 203, 204-5, 207, 233-34

Dira, 109, 217, 221, 225-26, 227-31
Dolon, 170
Drances, 202-6, 232
Duckworth, George E., 157, 252*n*5

Ecphrasis, at Carthage, 11-13; at Cumae, 95-96; Shield of Aeneas, 149, 154-56
Elissa (name of Dido), 242*n*4
Elysium, 103, 104, 105, 110-11, 114, 116, 123, 173
Entellus, 80-82
Epirus, 67-68, 71
Eryx, 82
Euripides, *Hippolytus,* 14
Euryalus, 157, 161-66, 170, 173, 209, 252*n*5, 253*nn*
Evander, 99, 127, 140, 141-45, 148, 200, 234

Fate(s), 1, 3, 10, 16, 34, 35, 41-44, 70, 84, 98, 102, 107, 158, 180, 207, 227, 236
Faunus, 226
Fire, flame, 17, 36, 46, 47-48, 55, 59, 71-72, 126, 145, 152, 153-54, 213, 220-21, 242*n*7
Fraenkel, E., quoted, 251*n*5
Freud, Sigmund, 125
Furies, 23, 26, 176

Galaesus, 131
Games, 79-84; Game of Troy, 82-83, 84, 96
Genitor/pater, 30, 74, 75-76, 79, 81, 100, 124, 144, 192, 194, 214, 224, 250*n*9
Gifts (motif), 15, 28, 41, 137-38, 139
Gods, 28, 51, 55, 174, 187-88, 239; chthonic, 20, 23, 126, 176, 242*n*9, 243*n*10, 244*n*18; justice of, 174-77, 226-27, 229; power of, 3, 55, 88-89, 174-77, 228, 231, 246*n*11; victims of, 45, 54, 70, 133, 214-15,

218, 228, 233; wrath of, 3, 51, 53, 77-78, 174, 187-88
Greene, Thomas, quoted, 241*n*1
Guillemin, Mlle A.-M., quoted, 252*n*5
Gyas, 79, 188

Hades, 65, 96-104 *passim,* 109, 114, 121-22, 123, 155, 189, 235
Haemon, 109
Hand outstretched, gesture of, 59, 105, 112-13, 191, 233-36, 255*nn,* 256*n*
Hecate, 14, 26, 95, 96, 104
Hector, 5, 16, 45-48, 158, 170, 205, 220
Helen, 52, 109, 139, 159, 245*n*2
Helenus, 68-71, 97
Henry, James, 14; quoted, 187
Hephaistos, 150, 152, 154
Hera, 150, 152
Hercules, 144, 146, 149, 180, 188
Heroism, 13, 40, 46-48, 50, 55, 60, 79-82, 108-9, 110, 161, 166-71, 178-83, 194, 200, 221, 223, 236-39. *See also* Aeneas; Camilla; Lausus; Mezentius; Pallas; Turnus
Hippolytus (Euripides), 14
Homer, 50, 80, 150, 154, 176, 207, 231; *Iliad,* 50, 150, 152, 180, 189; *Odyssey,* 152, 249*n*4; and Vergil, 30, 64-65, 252*n*2
Hunt (motif), 14-15, 16, 20, 23, 212-13, 229-30
Huse, H. R., 245*n*1

Iarbus, 2
Icarus, 96
Iliad, 50, 150, 152, 180, 189
Ilioneus, 126, 136-37
Images: Ajax, 4; Allecto, 131; altar, 43-44, 51, 144, 232, 246*n*8; Anchises on Aeneas's shoulders, 56, 72, 74, 100, 156; belt, balteus, 182-84; birth,

58, 170, 178, 225; blood, 128, 130, 138, 144, 156, 251n2; bosom, 137; Carthage, 29-30, 65, 222; cave, 154; circle, 44, 57, 101, 150, 165, 223, 225, 229-31; city, 1-2, 8, 11, 28, 29-30, 31-32, 37, 65-68, 77, 80-81, 88, 93, 100, 117, 138-39, 141, 213, 214, 217, 222-23, 224, 225, 226, 236-39; crane, 21-22; death, 25, 27, 89, 92-93, 180-81, 200-1, 211, 215-16, 222-23, 232, 237; elm tree, 121-22; enclosure, 229-31, 255n9; Fama, 22; fire, flame, 17, 36, 46, 47-48, 55, 59, 71-72, 126, 145, 152, 153-54, 213, 220-21, 242n7; Golden Bough, 103, 106, 110, 249n3; hand outstretched, gesture of, 59, 105, 112-13, 191, 233-36, 255nn, 256n; horses (Circe's), 127, 138; labyrinth, 83-84, 95-96, 217, 248nn, 255n9; light, 110; Mercury, 19, 31; mountain, 4, 225; night, 38, 49, 60, 150, 165, 198-99, 246nn; nightmare, 59, 185, 213; omens, 36-37, 55-56, 63, 66, 71-72, 77, 82-83, 124, 136, 217; owl, 22-23; past, 13-14, 16, 37, 67, 103, 147-49, 176, 237, 238; Priam, 1, 8, 12, 49-51, 92-93, 100; Rome, 1-2, 7, 8, 10-11, 117-18, 154-56, 173; Scales, Golden, 229; serpents, snakes, 17, 42-43, 45, 50-51, 53, 152, 217, 242n7, 247n1; sleepwalking, 217, 225, 228-29, 231; smoke, 62, 222; star, 55, 59, 71-72; Troy, 12, 16, 17-18, 29-30, 38, 51, 60, 62, 65-68, 70-71, 93, 98, 138, 161, 170, 176-77, 178, 190-91, 222, 236-37; victim (of gods), 45, 54, 70, 133, 214-15, 218, 228, 233; vision, 45, 55; water, 169-70; Wooden Horse, 28, 40-42, 43-45, 137. *See also* Motifs; Similes
Inferno XXXIII.4-6, 38; v.121-26, 245n1
Io, 133

Iris, 26, 82, 85, 157, 169, 213, 234, 244n18, 252n1
Isaiah 2:4, 251n4
Ithaca, 64

Jacob, P., quoted, 248n11
Janus, 149
Jocasta, 223
Journey (motif), 36, 62, 63-65, 84, 93, 95, 100-2, 108, 109, 111, 121-22, 220-21, 223
Joyce, James, *Ulysses* quoted, 38, 245n2
Juno, 3-5, 6, 19-20, 21, 26, 28, 53, 69, 84, 88, 124-26, 128, 131, 132, 135, 137, 138, 139, 146, 155, 174-77, 184-85, 207, 213-14, 215, 217-18, 226-27, 239, 243n9, 250n1
Jupiter, 9-11, 53, 158, 173-77, 180, 208, 213, 215, 222, 226-27, 229, 239
Juturna, 213-18, 221, 226, 227-29, 231, 232

Knight, W. F. J., 96; translation quoted, 4, 52, 108, 119, 128, 150, 180, 218, 220, 221, 225, 235, 236

Labyrinth, 83-84, 95-96, 217, 248nn, 255n9
Laocoon, 39-44, 45, 246n2
Laomedon, 71, 72, 159
Latinus, 124, 126-27, 131, 132, 135-38, 202-7, 210-12, 214, 222, 232, 233, 234, 238; compared with Dido, 126, 135-36
Latium, 124, 136, 141, 147, 172, 201, 204, 207, 223
Laurentum, 209, 214, 216, 217, 221-22, 225
Lausus, 133, 189, 191-94, 196-97, 200-1, 232, 234; heroism of, 178-81
Lavinia, 127, 128, 210-12, 238, 239

Lethe, 113, 116
Libya, 22
Liger, 189, 190-91, 194, 234
Lucagus, 189, 190-91, 192, 194
Lucretius, quoted, 152
Luke *17:33*, 239
Lycaon, 189
Lychas, 188

Mackail, John, 25; quoted, 31
Maguiness, W. S., 217
Magus, 189, 234
Marcellus, 96, 113, 115, 119-21, 150, 194, 249*n*8
Mars, 152, 154, 187, 208, 216
Memnon, 13
Menelaus, 245*n*2
Menoetes, 79
Mercury, 19, 31, 32, 34, 36, 37, 126; as symbol, 19, 31
Messapus, 141, 219
Metaphor. *See* Images; Motifs; Similes
Metempsychosis, 114-16
Metiscus, 217, 226
Mezentius, 133, 141, 142, 143, 178, 185-88, 191-92, 194-97, 210, 216, 232; heroism of, 186, 195
Milton, John, 6
Minotaur, 96
Mnestheus, 157
Motifs: fathers and sons, 54, 189-97, 246*n*10; gifts, 15, 28, 41, 137-38, 139; hunt, 14-15, 16, 20, 23, 212-13, 229-30; journey, 36, 62, 63-65, 84, 93, 95, 100-2, 108, 109, 111, 121-22, 220-21, 223; pastoralism, 145-49; primitivism, 19-26; sacrifice/ritual, 21, 26, 40, 42, 44, 80, 82, 88, 89-93, 96, 169, 198-99, 232, 236, 243*n*10. *See also* Images; Similes
Mummius, 118
Musaeus, 111, 113, 249*n*7
Mycenae, 118

Nautes, 77-78, 86, 87
Neptune, 8-9, 53, 88-89, 159
Nettleship, Henry, 241*n*1
Night (metaphoric), 38, 49, 60, 150, 165, 198-99, 246*nn*
Nisus, 79, 161-66, 170, 173, 252*n*5, 253*nn*
Norden, Eduard, 96

Odyssey, 152, 249*n*4
Odysseus, 13, 30, 64-65
Ogygia, 64
Olympus, 146
Omens, 36-37, 55-56, 63, 66, 71-72, 77, 82-83, 124, 136, 217
Orestes, 23, 139
Ornytus, 208
Orodes, 187
Orontes, 89, 105, 216, 248*n*11
Orsilochus, 208
Otis, Brooks, quoted, 183, 243*n*9, 247*n*1

Page, Thomas E., 36, 208
Palinurus, 89-93, 105, 113, 216, 235, 248*n*11
Pallas (son of Evander), 141, 143-45, 189, 200-1, 232, 234; belt of, 182-83, 184, 201, 232, 239; heroism of, 178-81, 182-83; relationship with Aeneas, 143-45, 179
Pallas Athena, 39-41, 44, 45, 53
Pandarus, 157, 166-68, 170, 208
Panthus, 45, 51, 190
Paris, 52, 109, 139, 214
Parthenopaeus, 108
Past (symbolic), 13-14, 16, 37, 67, 103, 176, 237, 238
Pastoralism in Arcadia, 145-49
Pater. See Genitor
Penates, 63, 66, 73
Penthesilea, 13, 14, 16, 208, 242*n*4
Pentheus, 23

Perret, Jacques, quoted, 252*n*5
Phaedra, 14
Phipeus, 51
Phorbas, 90
Phrygia, 16
Phthia, 118
Pietas, 121, 192-93, 196-97, 246*nn;* of Lausus, 192-93; of Mezentius, 194. *See also* Aeneas
Pilumnus, 170
Polites, 50-51, 194, 196
Polydorus, 66
Pompeii, 117
Pöschl, Viktor, 9
Priam, 26, 92-93, 190, 200, 233, 245*n*2; symbolic, 1, 8, 12, 49-51, 92-93, 100
Pygmalion, 16, 23
Pyrrhus, 50-51, 139, 167, 182, 190, 191, 194, 196, 200, 245*n*2

Reckford, Kenneth, quoted, 137
Remulus, 159-61, 190
Ritual. *See* Sacrifice
Rome, 1, 2, 8, 11, 26, 116-18, 147, 154, 164, 172, 250*n*9; symbolic, 1-2, 7, 8, 10-11, 117-18, 154-56, 173
Romulus, 11, 116, 117

Saces, 224
Sacrifice, 21, 26, 40, 42, 44, 80, 82, 88, 89-93, 96, 169, 198-99, 232, 236, 243*n*10
Salius, 79
Sarpedon, 5, 180
Saturn, 146, 147, 149, 156
Scheria, 64
Scylla, 74
Serestus, 157
Servius, 35, 59, 81, 211, 223, 238, 242*n*4, 246*n*3; quoted, 51, 55, 244*n*18, 248*n*10
Shield of Aeneas, 112, 149-56

Sibyl, 94-121 *passim,* 141, 235-36
Sicily, 65, 74, 96, 216, 234
Silvanus, 149
Similes, 23, 80, 117; Amazons, 208; ants, 35; Apollo, 208, 216; arrow, 227; Bacchante, 25-26; bees, 113, 221-22; boar, 185-86; boulder, crashing, 225; bull, wounded, 43; city, 29-30, 80-81; comets, 178; dance, 14-15; deer, 21, 131, 213; Diana, 208, 216; Dog Star, 178; fire, 47-48, 145, 220-21; housewife, 153-54; hunt, 16, 242*n*5; kettle, boiling, 131; labyrinth, 83-84; lion, hungry, 163, 186; lion, wounded, 212-13; Mars, 216; moon, 104, 106; mountain, 225; oak, 35-36; rainbow, 84; river, 49, 145, 220-21; rock, 186; sea, 131; serpent, snake, 50-51; shepherd, 21, 47-48, 220-22; sleepwalker, 228-29; stag, 229-30; statesman, 8-10, 238; swallow, 217; tiger, 167; top, spinning, 131; torrent, 47-48, 49, 145, 220-21; whirlwind, 227; windstorm, 177; wolves, 246*n*7. *See also* Images; Motifs
Sinon, 39-43, 234; and Achaemenides, 65-66, 247*n*1
Somnus, 90
Sophocles, 68
Strategy, 157-71
Structure, 12, 18-19, 39, 40, 80, 129, 135, 141-42, 173, 199-200, 216
Styx, 104
Sychaeus, 16, 22, 23, 25, 107
Symbol. *See* Images; Motifs; Similes

Tarchon, 141, 208
Tarquitus, 109-10, 189, 190
Tartarus, 125-26
Teucer, 16
Thebes, 23
Theron, 188
Thetis, 150, 154

Thyestes, 26
Thymoetes, 39
Tiber, 146, 170, 252*n*1
Tisiphone, 109, 187
Torquatus, 117
Troy, 2, 8, 37-60 *passim,* 62, 93, 100,
    138-39, 174-76, 190-91, 209, 216,
    222, 233, 236, 237, 239; symbolic,
    12, 16, 17-18, 29-30, 38, 51, 60, 62,
    65-68, 70-71, 93, 98, 138, 161, 170,
    176-77, 178, 190-91, 222, 236-37
Turnus, 48, 130, 131, 133, 135-37,
    143, 157-61, 172, 179-86, 200, 202-
    6, 210-13, 223-24, 226-33; armor of,
    133; heroism of, 48, 130, 158-59,
    166-71, 180, 184, 185, 202, 205-6,
    211-18, 232-33
Tydeus, 108

Ufens, 141
Ulysses, 40-41, 57, 65-66, 139, 233

Underworld. *See* Hades

Venus, 10, 17, 19-20, 21, 52-53, 88-
    89, 158, 174-77, 214, 222, 226, 232,
    238, 242*n*7; as mother of Aeneas, 6,
    7, 74, 150-51, 235, 256*n;* and Vul-
    can, 148-54
Vergil: *Georgics* I quoted, 251*n*4; and
    Homer, 30, 64-65, 252*n*2; in-
    completeness of poem, 250*n*10
Volcens, 163
Vulcan, 156, 214, 232; and Venus, 148-
    54

Williams, R. D., 80; quoted, 244*n*22,
    248*n*5
Wooden Horse, 39-44; as symbol, 28,
    40-42, 43-45, 137

Zeus, 150, 180